The Paper Revolutionaries

The Rise of the Underground Press

Laurence Leamer

Simon and Schuster   New York

Designed by Malcolm Frouman

The publishers wish to thank the following for permission to reprint material in this book. Any inadvertent omission will be corrected in future printings upon notification to the publishers.

Berkeley Tribe, for material from their issues of October 10–16, 1969, and December 5–11, 1969.
East Village Other, for material from several issues.
The Great Speckled Bird, for material from their issues of March 1968 and February 1970.
Liberation News Service, for material from their issues of September 1970 and December 1970.
Los Angeles Free Press, for material from their January 8, 1971, issue.
Newsweek, for the article "We'll Blow Up the World," from their October 12, 1970, issue. Copyright © 1970 by Newsweek, Inc.
Other Scenes, for material from their April 1967 issue.
The Rag, for material from their June 29, 1970, issue.
Rolling Stone, for the article by Gene Marine from their April 2, 1970, issue. Copyright © 1970 by Straight Arrow Publishers, Inc. All rights reserved.
San Diego Street Journal, for very short quotes from various issues.
Space City!, for material from their issues of July 4–17, 1970, August 1–21, 1970, and April 6, 1971.
The UPS-Free Ranger Tribe, for material from their March 16, 1970, issue.
The Village Voice, for the article by Howard Smith. Copyright © 1959 by The Village Voice.

Acknowledgements

I have always read acknowledgments with the same interest that I show to lists of Revolutionary War dead on monuments in small Vermont towns. I know better now. Many people in the underground press have been very generous with their time, their information, their food, their lodgings, and other things an American under thirty should never publicly mention. The collective at Liberation News Service let me work with them for several weeks, and all across the country underground-press people treated me with what I found to be an overwhelming openness and frankness. I have tried not to abuse that trust, and I have written a book that seeks to treat the underground press with the seriousness it deserves.

I would like to thank those who read all or part of the manuscript: Robert Watson, Danny Okrent, Mike Brown, Richard Levine, Chuck Pepper, Judi Jacobson, Leonard Robinson, Tom Forcade, Elie Abel, Art Kunkin, Kendall Vick, John Booth and Theodore Draper. The research on the book was supported by a grant from the Twentieth Century Fund, and there I would like to thank in particular Inderjit Badhwar, who shepherded this project through to completion. Mr. Badhwar may still have a damp shoulder.

If I understand correctly, it is part of the obligatory ritual of acknowledgments not only to thank those who have read and commented on the manu-

5

script but to say that they aren't at all responsible for the final project. This strikes me as a little foolish. If this book is any good these people deserve a good part of the credit; but if it is not, then at least one or two of them deserve at least some of the blame.

Another part of this ritual of acknowledgments is to say that without one's wife this book could not have been written. This is truer than anyone but Eliana and I could possibly know.

I must admit that I'm not much at home in the reporter's role. Life itself is just raw stuff to him to discard or use according to his personal values, theories or whims, all in the name of truth, sensation or professional craft. And I apologize here if I have taken anyone's life or truths and twisted them to my own ends, or have said what would better have been left unsaid, or left unsaid what simply had to be set down in print. Many other books could be written about the underground press—gay ones, scolding ones, personal ones, embittered ones, poetry, song, theory, memoir—and if the people in the underground press ever get the time and figure that it's worth their while, maybe we'll see them.

LAURENCE LEAMER

to
Steve "Pedro" Engle (1941–1968)
God knows why

Contents

"*The underground press is the loving product of the best minds of my generation, running screaming through the negro streets at dawn looking for an angry printing press.*"
— THOMAS KING FORCADE, *Orpheus*

"*The underground press in our country ... is essentially a fraud, from the name up ... This press is fake-tough, sterile and devoid of talent, a dunghill on which no flowers grow.*"
— EUGENE LYONS, in *Dateline*

Guard your health; preserve your powers;
Today is yours. But tomorrow is ours.
— EDNA ST. VINCENT MILLAY

APRIL, 1914   10 CENTS

The MASSES

Drawn by John Sloan   Shall We Have A State Constabulary In New York ?

1 Beginning Anew

Rock festivals. Be-ins. Revolutionary conventions. Street scenes. Demonstrations. Radical-youth culture lives a nomadic existence, sustaining itself on one short-lived gathering after another. As yet the "counter culture" has produced only one broad, unifying institution. It is not a political party or an organization at all, but a medium: the underground press. From Albuquerque's *Astral Projection* to Providence's *Extra,* from Charlotte's *Inquisition* to Denver's *Chinook,* from San Francisco's *Good Times* to Miami's *Daily Planet,* there is at least one underground paper in each of well over two hundred towns and cities.

This is an amorphous, variegated clan, whose only common link is allegiance to the heady pastiche of pot, peace, Panthers, rock, antiwar, anti-imperialism, anarchism and Marxism, that is the contemporary "Movement." The Movement's modern incarnation is as schizophrenic, contradictory and complicated as the society which it reluctantly inhabits. Some leftist theorists might talk about building a bridge between Marx and Freud, but no one could possibly devise a structure to encompass this Movement. It would have to be a grand geodesic dome fitted together from pieces of Marx, Freud, Zen, Artaud, Kesey, Lenin, Leary, Ginsberg, Che, Gandhi, Marcuse, Laing, Fidel and Lao Tzu, strung with the black banners of anarchy to which the sayings of Chairman Mao have been neatly embroidered, and with a 40-watt rock amplifier strapped to the top—a gaudy, mind-blowing spectacle and an impossible intellectual synthesis.

Only on the pages of the underground press, with its mélange of stories, articles, events, hunches, graphics, fantasies,. exposés and theories can one find the Movement. To do this the underground press has had to create a revolutionary medium that interweaves personal life, journalism and activism. In its early years the underground press took special inspiration from marijuana, LSD and other drugs, and to convey the radical reality of drug use, the papers created brilliant new graphic forms. Psychedelic drawings. Freaky cartoons. Collages. The underground press learned that the familiar forms of reportage were narrow and shallow, and the papers developed an intimate and personal prose that could convey their "reality." The underground press realized that their lives had to embody fully the ideals they set forth in their papers, and they developed editorial structures of unprecedented egalitarianism.

In the mid-1960's there were only a few of these tabloids put out by young men and women dropped out of the American dream. On little money and even less journalism background, they popularized New Left critiques and the hippie philosophy, rock music, and other hip cultural activities. Now all of that submerged anger, alienation and yearning has erupted into a mass radical-youth movement. By 1971 there were over a million teen-age runaways,[1] millions of adult dropouts, thousands and thousands who called themselves political radicals without fear or apology, countless sympathizers, hip areas in every major city in America, and communes from one coast to the other. Now the papers take a wealth of forms. There is a rich variety to the youth-oriented undergrounds; there are tens of undergrounds put out by GI's at great personal risk, hundreds of high-school undergrounds, women's-liberation papers, homosexual papers, commune papers, and college papers every bit as radical as the more militant undergrounds.

The underground press includes the largest-paid-circulation weekly in Georgia and one of the largest in California; the two biggest weeklies in Berkeley; and important papers in Chicago, Detroit, Philadelphia, Boston, and towns and cities across the United States. Some two hundred papers, publishing at any given time, are a part of the loose confederation known as the Underground Press Syndicate (UPS). The narrowest possible definition of the undeground press would be membership in UPS, and that alone adds up to a circulation over 1,500,000.* The formula employed by mass magazines (estimating six readers for each magazine) suggests a readership of over 9,000,000. And by including high-school undergrounds, reupholstered old-left papers, rock-culture papers, and other publications that identify with youth culture, it's possible to come up with a circulation figure of

---

* The Los Angeles Free Press is the only underground paper whose circulation figures are rated by the semiofficial Audit Bureau of Circulation (ABC). Other underground circulation figures are always somewhat suspect. Of course, it has always been good journalistic practice to exaggerate readership, and presumably underground editors are not above doing so. At the same time, though, many editors are so terribly unbusinesslike that they may, through ignorance, underestimate their circulation.

at least 3,000,000 papers, or 18,000,-000 readers, an even better indication of the enormous audience for a medium that is blatantly anti-Establishment. Thus even in terms of size, the most banal of yardsticks, this is a press to be reckoned with.

By themselves such circulation figures represent a striking criticism of Establishment journalism, a criticism that speaks the idiom of American publishing. Indeed, the entire history of the underground press can be viewed as a reaction against traditional newspapers and periodicals. During the 1960's, in which the proportion of public considering newspapers the most believable mass medium dropped from 32 to 21 percent,[2] the underground press was born and burgeoned. Here on the pages of the papers, dissident viewpoints are heard in full. Here are the voices and ideas that elsewhere receive only cursory or patronizing attention at best. Here is a vision of a different kind of world.

The Movement and its press are by no means new. Sixty years ago men and women were already identifying with the Movement, and even then they realized that *their* movement had roots deep in the American past. As John Dos Passos wrote during the 1930's, "The Movement [had begun as] that upsurge of revolt against the ruling businessmen of which Bryan was the first messiah in the West and which took in the I.W.W., the non-Partisan League, Progressivism, the huge growth of Eugene V. Debs's following, and the small-town revolt against convention, Sunday-school teachers, and the rusty corseting of conduct left over from the Victorian era. It's these waves of popular insurgency that have, from

the time of the Founding Fathers, left this country a democracy." [3] From its beginning, then, the Movement was free-form, neither sectarian nor narrowly political—though some have always tried to make it so.

These contemporary protest papers grow out of a venerable, if often barely tolerated, part of our journalistic traditions dating back to 1690 and America's first newspaper, Benjamin Harris's *Publick Occurrences.* This paper lasted only one issue, because Boston officials found it too critical. Thirty years later Benjamin Franklin's brother James found himself thrown into prison for satirizing the local government in his *New England Courant.* During the Revolutionary War there was a "fugitive press" and before the Civil War an "abolitionist press" that suffered severe harassment.

In the last years of the nineteenth century the protest and radical press grew immensely. The *National Economist,* the official organ of the populist Southern Farmers Alliance, in 1892 claimed that there were nearly nine hundred Populist papers.[4] By 1912–13 the Socialist press alone had a circulation that may well have exceeded two million.[5] From Girard, Kansas, came W.A. Wayland's *Appeal to Reason,* each week presenting his mixture of preachy, cracker-barrel socialism to over half a million readers. ("If you do not want to remain corporation slaves, why don't you quit voting for men or parties that believe in private ownership of monopolies? Either do that or quit striking against your masters.") [6] The *National Rip Saw* had about 150,000 subscribers, the *Jewish Daily Forward* 142,000, the *International Socialist Review,* 42,000, the *National*

Socialist 35,000, and the Halletsville *Texas Rebel* 26,000. In all, there were half a dozen daily socialist papers and well over a hundred weeklies in English and foreign languages. For the most part this was a vital, vivid press, mixing Marx and muckraking, and news of various radical labor and farmer movements with practical information and hints. The papers talked directly to workers and farmers, and only rarely indulged in stylized proletarian prose or sectarian propaganda. At the same time the papers made no bones about their radicalism. As the New York *Call* editorialized in its first issue in May 1908, "Being a workingman's paper, the *Call* is necessarily a So-

cialist paper. This latter fact follows as a logical sequence. No political movement other than Socialism is directed in the economic interest of the masses. Therefore this paper will frankly proclaim the Marxian propaganda and will strive to unite at the polls those who already are united along industrial lines that the scattered and impotent forces of Labor may be given a conquering cohesion." [7]

To find what one might consider the earliest precursor of the underground press, we must turn away from these journals of the working class to the *Masses*, the famous radical-literary magazine of the decade from 1910. The *Masses* was the first

Drawn by K. R. Chamberlain.

"Madam, this will make your Son more helpful and better mannered."

Socialist periodical to unite cultural and political radicalism, to burst out of that rusty corseting of conduct and try to embrace the broad movement. Here was a magazine that raged against the bourgeois restraints on conduct, against Sunday-school teachers and Victorian mores, as well as against the horrors of capitalistic society. Here was love poetry, marvelous caricatures, solid literary criticism, as well as political reportage (such as John Reed's accounts of the Mexican Revolution) and essays on Socialist theory. It was unprecedented. Never before had Socialist art and literature dared to be less than one-hundred-percent serious. A laugh, a touch of irony, a sentimental phrase, had always suggested that the writer might not care enough about the abuses of the capitalist system, that he might have some concerns that did not relate directly to the class struggle.

(The *Masses* was not terribly radical in layout and design. Wyndham Lewis's *Blast,* a short-lived London magazine, was the one periodical of the time that melded print and design in a manner at all suggestive of the contempory underground paper. In attacking bourgeois society not only did *Blast* print violent, shocking articles by Ezra Pound, Richard Aldington and others, but the magazine's ugly, jarring design was "typography's closest approximation to dynamite.") [8]

The *Masses* was very much a Greenwich Village magazine, and it fused the cultural radicalism of American Bohemianism with the political radicalism of Socialism. Max Eastman, the editor, thought that both were necessary. "I think there

is an Elizabethan gusto and candor in the strong taste for life which must be won back over the last relics of Puritanism," he told Norman Thomas. At the same time, Eastman absolutely despised *mere* Bohemianism, the "puny, artificial, sex-conscious, simmering in perpetual puberty of the gray-haired Bacchantes of Greenwich Village." [9] Despite all its fame and the extraordinary caliber of its contributors, the *Masses* had a circulation that according to Eastman reached no higher than 14,000. The magazine remained preeminently a middle-class journal at a time when Socialism was wedded in fact and theory to the working class, but not until the 1960's would this peculiarly American blend of political and cultural radicalism become at all popular.

The *Masses* was suppressed during World War I. By 1924, when the magazine was reincarnated in the form of the *New Masses,* the romantic individualism and Bohemian libertarianism were gone, lost somewhere between the garrets of the Village and the trenches of Europe. Of course, the radicals who founded the *New Masses* were not above shocking the bourgeois, but they were "serious" socialists. To them "Bohemian" was an epithet flung at literati and fallen bourgeois who through sloth or stupidity avoided the disciplines of the revolutionary struggle. These Communists and fellow travelers had seen the Bolshevik triumph and to them class struggle was more than a metaphor. They had no time for gaiety or dilettantish experimentation. They had become servants of the people—the working class. ("We artists of the people will not face Life and Eternity alone. We will face it from among the people . . . The Revolution, in its secular manifestations of strike, boycott, mass meeting, imprisonment, sacrifice, agitation, martyrdom, organization, is thereby worthy of the religious devotion of the artist.") [10] They had time, and scarcely time enough, for a journalism supercharged with a sense of "mass struggle," and with the 1929 crash they had every reason to believe that the millennium was at hand.

The gaiety and irreverence of the earlier years did not disappear, but became very much the property of the artistic avant-garde. Indeed, during the 1920's the cultural radicals waged a guerrilla warfare against the bourgeois, and their weaponry is found in the arsenal of the counter culture and the underground press today. The Dadaists who ran screaming out of bourgeois theaters or denounced religion from churchyards are spiritually aunts and uncles to the contemporary radicals who have thrown dollars down onto the floor of the New York Stock Exchange or taken advertisements and by changing words or adding a picture turned them into indictments of the Vietnam war. The shocking, scatological aspects of the contemporary undergrounds are attempts to purge the counter culture of any bourgeois prissiness and to expand reality—a more thoroughgoing if less literary approach to what many "little magazines" of the 1920's had attempted.

The 1930's are remembered with dread or nostalgia, as the "Red Decade," a time when the Left gained unprecedented power and support. In fact, the radical movement never regained the power it had at its peak in 1912–13. Despite the vicious economic realities of the Depression years, Socialism became more and more a radicalism of the head, the opium of the intellectuals. Granville Hicks, the critic and former Communist, remembers looking at his neighbors in Northampton during the 1930's—doctors, lawyers, bookkeepers, farmers, workers—and realizing that "the battle was between the intellectuals and everyone else." [11] Inevitably, those who wrestled with language and ideas to earn their living chose words as their weaponry. The mimeograph machine "played the same part in the American revolutionary movement that machine guns did in the Russian," Dwight MacDonald noted ironically years after the last ink of battle had dried. "The mimeographs were the instruments of production, which, as any schoolboy knows, are the base of power of every ruling class, and many a faction fight was decided by who seized control of them first." [12] Brilliant magazines such as Philip Rahv's *Partisan Review* or V.F. Calverton's *Modern Quarterly* were essentially by the intelligentsia, for the intelligentsia. Even the official historian of the *Daily Worker,* writing in 1944 to commemorate the twentieth anniversary of that Communist paper, had to admit sadly that so far the *Appeal to Reason* "has been the only Socialist paper really to reach the masses." [13]

This journey from 1910 to the 1930's, from the *Masses* to the *New Masses,* from *Appeal to Reason* to the *Daily Worker,* had taken modern leftist journalism from a broadly cultural, open-ended radicalism to a rigorously and narrowly political one. As will be suggested here, in the past half decade a good part of the under- ·

ground press has traveled much that same road, carrying along with it the intellectual baggage and *élan* of its own age. This contemporary radical press is, of course, not "underground" in the traditional sense. Californians don't risk their lives by reading the *Los Angeles Free Press* as Italians risked theirs perusing issues of the anti-Fascist *L'Italia Libera* during World War II. Neither is the staff of Milwaukee's *Kaleidoscope* about to be jailed for simply printing their paper as are those who dare mimeograph and distribute the clandestine papers of the Soviet Union. These contemporary American papers, then, are underground only in the sense that they are part of the radical-youth subculture and politics. There is nothing devious or crudely propagandistic about the use of the term "underground" though. No generation can freeze the meaning of a word, and to object to the use of the term "underground" to describe these papers is about as foolish as bringing a chafing dish to a pot party.

The history of the underground press is not a simple success story. "We blew it," says Captain Billy America in *Easy Rider,* and his remark could stand as an epitaph for each generation of underground papers. They blew it by accepting the hippie myth. They blew it by thinking that drugs could be a panacea. They blew it by jumping at the idea of a Marxist revolution. They fail, and they fail, and they fail again, and they move on, taking something from each experience, learning more about freedom and how to create an indigenous radicalism, and carrying with them a richer and more varied Movement.

This is a totally indigenous Movement crafted without recipe or mentor, and it has boldly danced up its share of dead ends. The underground press's success is evident in the creation of a mass youth movement, and our preoccupation here is as much with problems and failures as with accomplishments. Our preoccupation is a serious one, for by now the underground press and radical-youth culture seem to represent the beginnings of an undeniable potential for radical change. The forces of authority already recognize this, and underground papers have had their offices shot up, their printers scared off, and their staffs arrested on trumped-up charges. Perhaps it all could end, the dying of the last wave of popular insurgency, but it is far too early to tell.

To retrace the development of the underground press we will take detailed looks at a number of UPS papers as well as at the two service institutions that hold the underground press together. We will also look at some of the periodicals that have grown up out of the underground. Of course, the underground press does not stand still to be encapsulated in the pages of a book, all neatly embalmed for academic inspection. Indeed, it is almost impossible to write about the underground press without writing about youth culture and the Movement as a whole, and this narrative makes no attempt to do so. Instead, we will be viewing the underground press on its own native grounds, as an organic part of radical-youth culture, and we will be following that culture and movement as it developed in the last half of the 1960's and early 1970's.

the village Voice

5c

A WEEKLY NEWSPAPER DESIGNED TO BE READ

Vol. 1, No. 1 • Greenwich Village, New York • October 26, 1955

THE 'VOICE' NUMBER 1

With this issue, The Village Voice, a new weekly newspaper, makes its first appearance on the newsstands of New York. The Voice is the first regular newspaper to be launched in the Village since the establishment of the Villager in 1933. It will cost 5 cents a copy and it will be distributed on Wednesday mornings. The paper will serve not merely the Village proper but also the Cooper-Stuyvesant, Gramercy Park, Lower East Side, and Chelsea areas. Its editors expect it to have a wide circulation in uptown New York and elsewhere, since it is in part intended to provide thoroughgoing coverage of the special entertainment and other features of this unique neighborhood. They foresee a net paid circulation for the Voice of at least 10,000.

Publisher Edwin Fancher, 31, is a practicing psychologist with two degrees from the New School. His varied career has included research work for the Cornell Medical College and the Institute of World Affairs; a spell as a teacher of psychology at New Rochelle High School; and a period of enrollment at the Uni-

Continued on page 2 col. 1

NJ Youth, Ninth To Rob Store, Is Also Unluckiest

Eight times in the past eight years some kid after easy money has made a target of John Tintor's liquor store on West 12th Street. The eighth—but first robber this year—walked into the store Saturday night and achieved the dubious distinction of being the first one to get caught.

A radio car from one of the Manhattan dailies happened to be cruising in the area at the time that Thomas DeFabiis made his getaway, with the cash drawer containing $35 in a sedan car bearing New Jersey license plates. A call from the Mirror car's driver, Bob Wendlinger, brought reinforcements in the shape of three police cars and Voice reporter Howard Fertig.

Unaware that he was followed, DeFabiis, 18, of Jersey City, drove to a downtown Broadway address and was nabbed by police and taken to the Charles Street station.

Later white-haired John Tintor, 65, told the Voice: "These young punks come in all the time; this is the eighth since I took over this store in 1947. They always come around 9.30 at night and usually they have got away with it."

Furs make lasting gifts
Lewis & Lewis, 19 E. 9th St.—Adv.

—Joyce Wilson

Music-Makers Quit the Square (But Only for the Wintertime)

By John Wilcock

Roger Sprung, 25, runs a TV repair shop in Lake Mohegan, New York, but every week end during the summer he comes to the Village to play and sing folk music in Washington Square. He is one of more than 100 musicians, both amateur and professional, who could have been found in the Square almost any warm Sunday afternoon up to this month. Next Sunday, and for probably a few subsequent weekends, there'll still be occasional guitar players in the Square, but they'll be risking a brush with the law because previously they had a permit, now expired and not renewable until next spring.

A couple of Sundays ago, I wandered over to the fountain around which most of the Square's activity has always centered, to meet Roger and some of his friends. One of them, Al Myers, told me that he occasionally played the guitar but didn't consider himself sufficiently up to standard to join in when a really groovy session was under way.

"Roger's one of the top men in this group," he said. "He plays fiddle, guitar, banjo, mandolin, and sings as well. He's been playing for several years and has made some records, I believe. There's a lot of folk music about, you know, but it varies a great deal. Some of the best-selling stuff is just purely commercial—the kind of thing that maybe Gene Autry would sing—it sounds nice but when I hear it I never believe that the song writers ever meant what they were writing. Now you take a song like 'I'm Sad and I'm Lonely.' When the writer of that one says 'My

Continued on page 3 col. 1

No District 'Hopeless,' Republican State Head Tells Local GOP

President Dwight Eisenhower's statement—there is no such thing as "a hopeless district"—was quoted by the Republican State Chairman at a GOP meeting in the village last Thursday.

"The average party worker wants to change the world in a day, and it can't be done," L. Judson Morehouse told his audience at the First Assembly District Republican Club at 40 West 10th Street.

The speaker, elected to the post of State chairman last year, conferred with the President recently in Denver.

THE TIGER'S TIMBERS

The earliest traces of Dutch colonization in America—timbers found in the Village from Adrian Block's ship Tiger—have been placed on display at the Museum of the City of New York. The timbers, dating back to 1613, were discovered during excavations beneath the corner of Dey and Greenwich Streets, for the IRT, back in 1913.

If you don't know furs—know
Lewis & Lewis, 19 E. 9th St.—Adv.

VILLAGE TRUCKER SUES COLUMBIA

Seeks $50,000

A 36-year-old Village trucker, expelled from the New York School of Social Work of Columbia University in March, claims that his expulsion was improper and is suing the University for $50,000. Papers in the suit were served Monday.

Frederick Fleck of Christopher Street was expelled from the school on March 23rd of this year—the day after a signed editorial critical of the school's training methods appeared in a student publication of which he was editor. Fleck claims —and the school's spokesmen deny —that he was expelled because of his editorial criticism.

The editorial in the March issue of the student publication, The Process, criticized the school for teaching techniques applicable to only one type of community despite the fact that it solicited its students from many different parts of the world.

"The day the editorial appeared," Fleck told the Voice yesterday, "I was called to the office of Associate Dean Nathan Cohen and told that I would not get credit for the year's work, no matter what I did for the remainder of the semester. Three days later, in reply to my telegram asking a fuller discussion of the matter, Dean Cohen told me that the committee's decision was final and I was being asked to leave the school.

"Because of this I am clearly prohibited from advancing in my chosen profession. Under such circumstances no other school would accept my registration once I have been expelled from NYSSW. If I returned to social work I would be kept forever at the same level as when I left Arizona."

(Before being awarded a Fellowship from the School to study

there, Fleck had been working as a social worker among the Apache Indians in Arizona. That State's Public Welfare department granted him a year's leave and a monthly stipend to attend the school.)

Since his expulsion he has worked as a shop counsellor at a summer camp and as a trucker in the Village. In 1953 he received a master's degree in psychology from the New School, West 12th Street.

The school from which Fleck alleges he was improperly expelled had a different version of the story. Associate Dean Cohen told the Voice: "Fleck's story is 100 per cent wrong. He was before the committee on students almost from the time he came in; we have a larger file on him than on any student.

"In March we agreed to let him finish out the course but we indicated there was very little chance of his obtaining credits. He

—Joel Slocum

hadn't completed about three or four courses and didn't seem to be taking things as seriously as he might. There are many students dropped from this school: he is certainly not a single case.

"As for the article he wrote—his leaving the school was nothing to do with that. The publication is still running and still criticizing the school from time to time."

'Doodling' in Subway Wins Artist Prize

An oil painting of part of a subway station wall—complete with hearts and arrows, swear-words, and signs saying "Joe was here"— is one of the first prizewinners in a new show which opened Monday at the Village Art Center.

The picture, by Herb Young, is of the 86th street station—two blocks from his home.

Young and two other winners, Jean Hyson and Sally Mitchell, have only recently joined the Center and this is their first show. Remaining prizewinner Margaret Layton, has won prizes in at least five shows at the Center.

Current show is the 13th annual oil exhibition and runs through November 11.

Manuscript by Phil (aged 4) goes on show

Four-year-old Philip, one of the children attending the Greenwich House day school, has a manuscript—his first—on display this week at the East Side Savings Bank, 422 Sixth Avenue.

It is a short piece entitled simply "A joke by Philip," and it reads: "A horse can't say yes or say no—but a donkey can."

Furriers over half a century
Lewis & Lewis, 19 E. 9th St.—Adv.

2
The Precursors

... these have been the years of conformity and depression. A stench of fear has come out of every pore of American life, and we suffer from a collective failure of nerve. The only courage, with rare exceptions, that we have been witness to, has been the isolated courage of isolated people.

— NORMAN MAILER, *The White Negro*

When the *Village Voice* arrived in Greenwich Village in October 1955, that stench of fear still hung in the air. The first issue contained a banal mélange of community news, art features and movie reviews, but the paper did chance to have a cover story on folk singers in Washington Square. Folk singers were suspect. "The day the *Voice* hit the street everyone said, 'It's a Communist paper,'" says John Wilcock, the first news editor and later editor of several underground papers. "It was absurd, but because of the deep fears in American life after the McCarthy period, the *Voice* got the reputation for being a far-out, freaky paper. Almost despite itself the paper ended up the grandfather of the underground press."

The *Voice* never pretended to be a radical paper. Instead, the paper focused on what Ed Fancher, the publisher, called the "revolt of the urbs"—the struggle to preserve parks, playgrounds, the precious character of the Village, against city planners and real-estate interests.[1] There was a delicious melancholy in these futile fire fights against the steel-and-concrete monsters of modernity. Indeed, from early on nostalgia seemed to sink into the very paper on which the *Voice* was printed, a nostalgia symbolized by the Christopher Street office, a quaint wooden structure that might have been built for the archetypal crusading nineteenth-century newspaper.

The paper's founders had no inkling of the cultural and political upheaval that was shortly to engulf the United States. After all, in the mid-fifties the cultural and political Left were in disarray, garbed in sackcloth. C. Wright Mills stood largely ignored, an almost desperate figure. The few thousand Beats of the cultural Left appeared no less desperate and isolated; antipolitical, they did not traffic with the old Left. Gary Snyder—poet, Beat, hippie, Zen master—recalls the "sense of antagonism, hostility and paranoia which went through the fifties with an accompanying self-destructiveness, a tendency toward alcoholism or heroin addiction, suicide, and a kind of romantic mystery of self-destruction, so that it was tragically beautiful to see someone go down through drug addiction." [2] There were no exits. "Against the ruin of the world, there is only one defense, the creative act," [3] wrote Kenneth Rexroth.

The few politically radical publications of the time certainly did not inspire particular enthusiasm. The *National Guardian,* begun in 1948 as a spokesman for Henry Wallace's Presidential campaign, plugged along, supported largely by scattered Communists and fellow travelers. *Dissent,* started in 1956 by Social Democrats, addressed an aging, predominantly New York City audience. *I.F. Stone's Weekly* and A.J. Muste's *Liberation* were small and largely unnoticed.

Of course, no "serious" radical paid any attention to the scores of little magazines that about this time began appearing, disappearing, reappearing in Bohemian districts across America—*Beatitude* in San Francisco; *Combustion* in Toronto; *Big Table; Kulchur; Intercourse; C; My Own Magazine.*

The contributors to these magazines were "knights of the human spirit" who would wage "a sort of guerrilla warfare . . . against the organized forces of befuddlement," wrote *Beatitude.* "The brave commandos, Ginsberg Kerouac Rexroth & al versus the Hearse Press, the Loose Enterprises, and so forth, who have all but succeeded in stifling the human spirit." [4] Few in those Eisenhower years cared to join in such an irreverent, full-scale attack on American life. But by the early 1960's the whole tenor of the magazines was changing. The minuscule circulations still suggested that they were little more than the "ethnic" journals of a small Bohemian sect, but the writers and artists themselves could feel the first tremors of a broad political and cultural upheaval. Many of the magazines grew optimistic, even cocky. They began to deal openly with political issues. Ed Sanders' *Fuck You/A Magazine of the Arts,* declared itself dedicated to "pacifism, national defense through nonviolent resistance, unilateral disarmament, multilateral indiscriminate apertural conjugation, anarchism, world federalism, civil disobedience, obstructors and submarine boarders, peace eye, the gleaming crotch lake of the universe, the witness of the flaming ra-cock . . . mystical bands of peace-work stompers, total-assault guerrilla ejaculators, the Lower East Side *meshuganas,* vaginal zapping, the LSD communarium, God through cannabis, hashish forever, and all those groped by J. Edgar Hoover in the silent halls of Congress." [5]

The *Voice* could hardly ignore this fledgling movement, and slowly the paper turned away from such typical early articles as "What Men Think of the Greenwich Village Female" and "What Women Think of the Greenwich Village Male" toward accounts of off-Broadway theater, foreign and underground films, Jack Kerouac and the Beats, Allen Ginsberg, Lenny Bruce, new politics, dope, folk music—the first rumblings of a radical-youth culture.

The old forms and formulas of the newspaper craft could not begin to capture the subtlety and complexity of this new world in the making, and by the early 1960's the *Voice* had forged a new literary journalism, personal yet detached, concerned yet cynical, detailed yet selective—a style that has affected a generation of journalists and writers. Sometimes the style didn't rise above cocktail-party chitchat, treating politics as nothing more than an endless parade of personalities, and turning culture into narrow cult. At its best, though, a *Voice* article could capture the essence of an event in a few subtle images and descriptions. For instance, in the late 1950's, Howard Smith, now a *Voice* columnist, wrote about an evening when Jack Kerouac, the then newly famous author of *On the Road,* read his poetry in the Village Vanguard:

. . . He reads fast with his eyes theatrically glued to the little pad, rapidly, on and on as if he wants to get it over with. "I'll read a junky poem." He slurs over the beautiful passages as if not expecting the crowd to dig them, even if he went slower. "It's like kissing my kitten's belly . . ." He begins to loosen up and ad lib, and the audience is with him. A fast 15 minutes and he's done. The applause is like a thunderstorm on a hot July night. He smiles and goes to sit among the wheels and the agents, and pulls a relaxed drag on his cigarette. He is prince of the hips being accepted in the court of the rich kings, who, six months ago, would have nudged him closer to the bar, if he wandered in to watch the show. He must have hated himself in the morning—not for the drinks he had, but because he ate it all up the way he really never wanted to. As I was leaving, some guy in an old Army shirt, standing close to the bar, remarked: "Well, Kerouac came off the road in high gear. . . . I hope he has a good set of snow tires." [6]

The *Voice* had only just become a moderate success when, in 1958, twenty-six-year-old Paul Krassner began publishing the *Realist,* the other 1950's publication, whose style and content foreshadowed the underground press. The six hundred original subscribers thought they were getting a magazine of high-minded atheism and anticlericalism. But Krassner, who had been a minor comedian patterning his routines on the dark, ironic humor of Lenny Bruce and Mort Sahl, soon changed all that. Even the first (June–July) issue displayed the sense of irreverence, iconoclasm and (for that era) just plain bad taste, for which Krassner and the *Realist* would soon be notorious. Most of the articles were couched in the quasi-academic style that had long afflicted "magazines of thought." However, Krassner couldn't resist injecting satire into the headlines—"Sodomy in Kilts" over a serious piece on the liberalization of Scottish laws against homosexuality; "Is He a Good Guy or a Bad Guy? Or What Makes Wyatt Urp" above an article attacking Thomas Wyatt, a prominent faith healer. Even more significantly Krassner contributed a "Diabolical Dialogue" between John Foster Dulles and Bertrand Russell, the first of many imaginary discussions between famous people that would appear in the *Realist,* blurring the distinction

between fact and fiction:

DULLES: . . . and so in the interest of maintaining friendly Anglo-American relations, I've come to ask you to stop harping about H-bomb tests. You're only aiding the Communist cause.
RUSSELL: Nonsense. I'm opposed to all forms of totalitarianism.
DULLES: But suppose that the Communists come out in favor of deep breathing . . .

By the early 1960's Krassner had completely jettisoned the *Realist's* fundamentalist atheism and turned the magazine into a meld of often "unprintable," inevitably unpredictable articles and satire. Nowhere else could one read a piece by a seventeen-year-old boy on why he was a Nazi (or was it satire?); a fake letter from Billy Graham (it *did seem* real); satirical accounts of Luci Johnson's wedding night and John F. Kennedy's first wife (but there's a ring of truth to it). Krassner made no attempt to label what was "real" and what wasn't, and that uncertainty made the *Realist* even more outrageous and irritating.

"I wanted to blow peoples' minds," Krassner says, "and it's really a mind blower if you can't tell if something is real or not. Moreover, if a satire's possible it says something about the way things are. Several years ago, I had a serious article by a student at Berkeley about the violent peace movement. But people thought it was satire, and dangerous satire at that. Then we had a cartoon that showed a soldier with a bayonet saying to a pregnant Vietnamese woman, 'Is there a Viet Cong in there?' It was a prediction of the Song My massacre. Then, too, it was true. *She was hiding a Viet Cong in there!*

"Then I began to mix and play with satire and fact. When I described Tim Leary's psychedelic center at Millbrook, I described actuality. There was a psychedelic Burma Shave sign outside that said 'What is, is within.' Inside there was a copy of *Scientific American* on the table right next to the Bible. Upstairs I described how there was a bulletin board with a list of all the guides with stars pasted next to their names according to how far they had transcended their ego. Now that last bit about the stars I made up, but it was a way—a vehicle—to make an observation that those people were hung up on that. And because it was believed it said something."

Here in the early 1960's the high-school-civics-textbook image of American life was disintegrating before the very eyes of the young, and the tools of conventional journalism just were not calibrated closely enough to capture the subtlety, irony and pathos of that process. In 1946 George Orwell had already noted how politicians and political writers were debasing language to avoid dealing with the realities of the modern world:

In our time, political speech and writing are largely the defense of the indefensible. Things like the continuance of British rule in India, the Russian purges and deportations, the dropping of the atom bombs on Japan, can indeed be defended, but only by arguments which are too brutal for most people to face, and which do not square with the professed aims of political parties. Thus, political language has to consist largely of euphemism, question-begging and sheer cloudy vagueness. Defenseless villages are bombarded from the air, the inhabitants driven out into the countryside, the cattle machine-gunned, the huts set on fire with incendiary bullets; this is called *pacification*. Millions of peasants are robbed of their farms and sent trudging along the roads with no more than they can carry: this is called *transfer of population or rectification of frontiers*.[7]

Today the aboveground journalist is often merely a scribe. He copies verbatim the government's most dubious proclamations, and crops them down into neat, palatable news stories or one-minute TV spots. And he peddles this to the American public as "objective journalism." He is a willing dupe, too, for the forms of conventional journalism cannot begin to capture the "objective" realities of modern American life. After all, conventional journalism is the craft of accurately transmitting what frequently is only half understood or ultimately unintelligible. There is no room for irony, satire, black humor or sheer disbelief. There is no room for any of Krassner's crude, inelegant, irreverent, outrageous techniques—techniques that are a part of what would be needed in a journalism that could understand this new world.

The *Realist*, itself, represents no full vision of an alternative medium. Krassner—publisher, editor, top banana—*is* the *Realist*, and the magazine rests as much in the older tradition of one-man iconoclastic journalism (George Seldes' *In Fact;* Lyle Stuart's *The Independent*) as in the newer patterns of underground journalism. The *Realist* has remained limited by the borders of Krassner's mind—a wickedly original mind at that, zipping recklessly across the boundaries of the acceptable and the conventionally sane—but nevertheless the mind of one lone man. Krassner himself has become very much a part of the Movement, but by the last half of the 1960's, with the United States engaged in Indochina in what the left-liberal community considered a monstrous and immoral effort, and which, as the months and the excuses and the casualties mounted, appeared less a temporary aberration than a logical culmination, his satire in the *Realist* was having no more impact than a water pistol.

The *Village Voice,* for its part, never tried to bedeck itself with love beads and psychedelic drawings, or clenched fists and militant art, and has stayed very much an observer of the cultural and political revolt. The paper has stayed unashamedly a commercial enterprise as well, and an extremely lucrative one at that. It has no pretensions to being a part of the Movement and inhabits a no-man's land between the Establishment and radical media. Because of this the *Voice's* writers often sound estranged from the world they observe, writing with "intimate" detachment or else turning out highly personal, rambling essays that suggest that they and the universe are equals. Some of the paper's coverage—say, a Newfield piece on prisons or a Hentoff story on the meaning of the Chicago conspiracy trial—still has a vigor and energy found nowhere else in New York journalism, but the *Voice* as a whole has grown further and further removed from the hot and turbulent centers of the Movement.

Protestors Injured SEE BELOW

10ᶜ

TRAIN PROTESTS GREATEST SINCE 1916

Berkeley Barb

Vol. 1, No. 1 Friday Aug. 13 Berkeley, Calif.

JAIL TODAY
FOR FSM'ERS

SIX DEFENDANTS
CHOSE JAIL today rather than pay appeal bail. They were : Jack Weinberg, 120 days; David Goines, 60; Nicholas Zvegintsov, James Levenson, Anita Levine 25 day each, and Dunbar Aitken 15 days¦

by Marvin Garson

As of this writing, Friday the Thirteenth looks like the day of reckoning. It is then the: the Court will finally rule on our test motions, and after that no further stays seem possible.

Two weeks ago David Goines appeared before Judge Rupert Crittenden for sentencing. He had a toothbrush in his shirt pocket; since he could not raise his appeal bail, he was prepared to go to jail for the duration.

After he had been sentenced to sixty days (NOT suspended) and had filed notice of appeal, Judge Crittenden ordered him to post appeal bail of $550 or be taken into custody. Goines was taken away by the Sheriff's Department just as a rally was beginning in the park across the street.

There were a thousand people at the rally, many more than anyone expected, and as the afternoon session began they filled the courtroom. The sight of full galleries worked its magic on the judge and the district; attorney. After discussion in chambers they decided to grant to defendants the ten-day stay they had denied to Goines; and they released Goines himself after a few hours in jail.

The bail fight had begun.

Since then there have been several occasions when defendants unwilling to pay bail have been prepared for arrest; there have been legal maneuverings that strain the minds of lawyers and are utterly meaningless to laymen; there have been court sessions consisting of two with a few minutes in open court; and as of now, the situation is no clearer than it was at the start.

The basic facts are the same. The Free Speech defendants must raise a total of $400,000, or $40,000 in non-refundable premiums, if they want to stay out of jail during their appeal. It amounts to extortion.

See p 2

WHAT ABOUT THE CITIZEN?

GEORGE KAUFFMAN is a longtime Berkeleyan and fellow Co-oper. RYCHARD DENNER is a young, long-haired, mustachioed poet recently arrived from San Luis Obispo, whom we pressed into service. (See Editorial Comment, p.4).

by Rychard Denner

It is the second week of August. Berkeley. Where is THE CITIZEN? The only reader-owned paper in the United States to cover news of general interest has led to meet its projected "tar-

get date" of August 1, announced in its May newsletter.

In search of THE CITIZEN, I went to its new business office at 1476 University Avenue. No one there. I then went to the Co-op market. A grocery

See p 2

PEACE ACTION

GI'S CHEER; TRAINMEN JEER
by Bob Randolph

The recent events at the Santa Fe Stations in Berkeley and Oakland have been front page news. It is not often that American citizens attempt to stop troop trains with their cargo of GI's headed overseas, this time to South Vietnam. Not since 1916 has such opposition to U.S. war moves existed.

It was big news, yet the commercial press ignored the most revealing part of the story — the crudely lettered signs in the windows of one of the trains, put there by some of the troops on board. "I don't want to go," said one of them. Others said, "Lucky civilians," and "Keep up the good work, we're with you."

As the dingy old passenger cars passed the demonstrators at the Berkeley depot shouting "No! No! No!", dozens of GI's pressed their faces to the windows, some waving to the crowds outside, some quiet and reflective, some in groups in the dining cars, holding their rifles and looking out with looks of sarcasm and hostility.

The day before, the first of the three trains pushed through Berkeley without slackening speed and narrowly missed giving two young people under its wheels. As I heard of this, I thought back to the days in the early 1950's when I worked for this railroad, and I recalled that warm summer afternoon when a fireman on board one of the streamliners who risked his life on the engine's cowcatcher on the Martinez trestle in a vain attempt to scoop up a two-year-old child playing between the rails. He reached at the last instant and missed, and the child was cut to pieces. Yet he had tried. Now, in 1965, another trainman pursued his work under a different code, as did the conductor who leaned out of his vestibule and shouted invectives at the demonstrators in Berkeley as the attempted to do what they could to save more remote children caught in the path of another juggernaut in Vietnam.

The use of police in both Berkeley and Emeryville, advancing slowly along the tracks ahead of the trains, tearing down picket signs, roughly pushing the protesting demonstrators out of the path of the troop trains also marked a new symbolic aspect of the accelerating American juggernaut.

What is perhaps not new is the series of actions taken by the Berkeley City Council. On the main issue of the developing war in Vietnam, the City Council, in spite of its liberal majority, failed utterly to express itself. It confined its actions to the relatively petty complaint that the Santa Fe take its troop

AUGUST 12 --- BLACK DAY FOR BERKELEY

Thursday, August 12, 1965 ---- a day of brutality in Berkeley. Some of it was subtle and some was gross, but it all bespoke a growing ugliness in American life.

The Vietnam Day Committee told this reporte , that it notified the Santa Fe RR, the City of Berkeley, an d the Army of its intentions to demonstrate. It charges them with responsibility for today's injuries.

THIS IS WHAT HAPPENED:

1. A 20-car Santa Fe troop train forced its way into the ranks of demonstrators stretched along a mile and a half of track from Albany to the Berkeley station, scattering them indifferently like cattle.

2. The engineer loosed clouds of live steam from the locomotive to clear them from the track, but in fact the steam blinded them to the danger of his rapidly advancing engine.

3. Berkeley police clubbed and dragged protesting demonstrators f r o m the sides of the train. The civilians were clinging there in an effort to reach the troops caged inside. Three demonstrators were injured, two with suspected broken limbs. (They have been released from the hospital, and their present condition is unknown.)

4. A plainclothesman knocked a woman off the track, and in his pan-

ic left her lying stunned 8 inches from the rail. friend pulled her safety at the last instant.

5. Paralysis of Berkeley's City Council continued in the face of the real elements of the crisis. This is guild by inaction, a subtle form of brutality now central to American life.

6. The people of Berkeley and the rest of the country are generally and deeply ignorant concerning the issues in Vietnam which this is all about.

This is every day, not just this August 12th, and politically it is the American way of life. It is for this more than anything else that many foreign visitors are horrified

7. The quality of the American war in Vietnam rubbed off on Berkeley. The Vietnam War is beyond brutality. It is obscenity. It is the immediate and direct cause of the present events at the Santa Fe tracks in Berkeley.

WHAT ARE RAILWAY ENGINEERS? AUTOMATONS OR HUMAN BEINGS?

Two more troop trains are due in Berkeley next week. Suppose a thousand or more of the Berkeleyans who do have troubled feelings have a first hand look? Perhaps they will find some of their comfortable liberalism dislodged forever, to be replaced by feelings of outrage.

What would they say on hearing the GI on today's train who, in fact, shouted through the glass, "Stop the train! Stop the train!" What does the cry of this prisoner tell us? *— R.R*

See p 2

✱ FATE OF TOWNSMAN WHO NIXED $26,500 VIET WAR CONTRACTS **** See Inside pages for INTERVIEW

3
The Originators

Read the Barb, *it's a pleasure not a duty.*
— MAX SCHERR, of the *Berkeley Barb*

On May Day in 1964 Arthur Kunkin, a 37-year-old socialist intellectual and former die-maker, showed up at the gates to the Los Angeles Renaissance Faire, an annual event sponsored by radio station KPFK, and started passing out copies of the *Faire Free Press*. He wore not denims or patched corduroy but the green garb of Robin Hood and a feathered cap, and Los Angeles should have stood forewarned that Kunkin's thin and amateurish paper would not prove the typical left-wing publication. Indeed, rechristened the *Los Angeles Free Press,* it became not only the first, but eventually the biggest underground paper in America.

Kunkin was a man taken with an idea. "When I worked for socialist magazines like the *Militant* I had always felt that they weren't part of a real movement," Kunkin says. "I wanted the *Free Press* to build a local movement base." With what his more doctrinaire brethren of the Left considered crude expediency and what certain conservatives deemed a peculiar cunning, Kunkin patterned the *Free Press* after the *Village Voice* rather than such established left-wing political journals as the *Militant*. The *Freep,* as the paper is commonly known, foreshadowed the loose, wide-ranging content of the other underground papers. The *Free Press* copied the *Voice*'s layout and covered the cultural and political Left as its primary news beat, but unlike the Greenwich Village paper, the *Free Press* was unreservedly and unashamedly in favor of radical change. While at times strident, Kunkin's paper was not sectarian, and it could move from cause to cause and interest to interest without having to jettison a great deal of ideology.

The *Freep* did not set out to snare any set radical readership or to satisfy any particular constituency. Rather, to Kunkin the paper's community equaled whoever read that particular issue and as the crazy-quilt readership pattern developed it encompassed all those elements of the white middle class seeking to escape from the traditional patterns of American life. The readers were local burghers who liked to affect Bohemian style, radicals, homosexuals, youths, students, tourists, and closet Leftists. No leftist theorist had ever suggested that this audience was the human material out of which a revolution could be forged, but the overwhelming fact was that in the mid-1960's, in Los Angeles and across the country, this motley constituency represented the most radical element of white America.

Kunkin was simply astounded as he saw his paper mushroom. He knew perfectly well that, a decade before, editors of little magazines had lived off quarters and half dollars, drinking Chianti and cranking mimeographs through the long American night. Yet now, unattended by public-relations ballyhoo, the *Freep* was growing annually by the tens of thousands. Already by 1968 the *Free Press*'s impact was such that when the paper announced a free music festival, twenty-five thousand people showed up, and Kunkin decided that they wouldn't be able to have any more such gatherings. By 1971 the *Free Press* had a circulation rated at 90,000 by the sacrosanct Audit Bureau of Circulation, making it the second-largest paid circulation among weekly newspapers in the United States.

A half century earlier much of the *Free Press* audience would have been reading the *Masses*. The *Freep* did not come close to matching the artistic and literary achievements of the *Masses*, however, for the *Freep* was very much of a popularizer, a tabloid of the political and cultural Left. The hefty 40–64-page paper fit perfectly into the sprawling urban village that is Los Angeles. To get attention the *Freep* features headlines that would do credit to the *National Enquirer*—"Indians Fight Army: Jane Fonda How I invaded two U.S. forts simultaneously (at least that's what the establishment press implied) with 86 Braves on horseback."

"The paper is like a picture frame filling up each week with the activities of the community," says Kunkin. And what a picture frame it has been, filled with every cause, event and exposé that could be considered part of the cultural or political Left. The *Free Press* has covered everything from Gay Liberation Front threats to picket homosexual bars that prohibit customers in drag to macrobiotics, ecology, police repression, drugs, wife swapping, record pirating, Christian radicalism, rock, oppression in Mexico, and radical film makers. Andy Warhol, Bob Dylan, Sam Shephard, Frank Zappa, LeRoi Jones, and practically everyone even vaguely in the cultural avant-garde have received early, lengthy and perceptive hearings in the *Free Press*.

In its political coverage the *Free Press* generally uses the form and formulas of the mass media's "objective" journalism. Often there is that same posturing to a bland, moral neutrality. The whos, whats and whys are usually laid down in declining order of importance. The articles are devoid of literary style. But the *Free Press* takes those forms and formulas and flings them back into the face of the Establishment. Here are stories about police beating up Chicanos, hippies and radicals, instead of accounts of Attorney General Mitchell's "War on Crime." Here are articles on the use of a Vietnam defoliant in California instead of pieces on how industry is cleaning up pollution. Here are interviews with Black Panthers, Jane Fonda and Herbert Marcuse, instead of with Bob Hope, Dr. Rubin and Spiro Agnew. Here are stories about repression rather than about radical violence!

R. I. P. Denver Panthers

By Dennis Levitt

The fact that the Black Panther Party Office here in Denver had a very active program, and is now totally closed is "a reflection of the general attack on the Party and the unique situation in Denver." At least that is the opinion of Attorney Walter Gerash, who has been defending Black Panther Party members here. He went on to explain that the "unique situation" may lean heavily on the fact that only 7% or 8% of Denver's population is black, and the large oppressed minority would be counted as the Chicanos. Still, when the Black Panther Party (BPP) was active in Denver, they were operating three centers, were sustaining a comparably successful children's breakfast program, had begun liberation schools, etc. The support of the community seemed to be strong and was continuing to grow.

Two BPP members who are still in Denver have, through the counseling of Walter Gerash, been fighting extradition to Connecticut for seventeen months now. . . .[1]

The *Free Press* almost always assumes that the dissident, the accused, the rebel, and the militant version is correct. No matter if the teller be oppressed, kook or villain. Typically, Establishment reporters go to the police to learn the basic details of an event and then fit any other version into the structure provided by the authorities. The *Free Press* goes to the "victim" for his story and might not talk to police at all. (The Los Angeles Police Department still refuses to issue police cards to the *Free Press*, although the cards are issued routinely to other local media.) Whereas Establishment journals make the subtle assumption that the system is sound, the *Freep* assumes that it most certainly is not. Even those articles in the mass media critical of the system suggest that at most the Emperor has his pants undone and whispers gently that he should button up. The *Freep*, however, screams that the Emperor is indeed naked and an ugly specimen at that.

Other than current political events, the *Freep* is addicted to a kind of space-age muckraking that theorizes imaginatively on the basis of commonly available, minutely detailed facts. Mark Lane, the Kennedy assassination prober, is the master of the genre. His researches into the J.F.K. and R.F.K. murders have appeared prominently in the paper. So have front-page articles on Jim Garrison's investigations, on the possibility that there is more than one James Earl Ray, and on the thesis that the Vietnamese war is based primarily on United States needs for tungsten.

Taken together, then, the *Free Press* is a bulletin board of cultural and political movements, events, ideas and discussions. Eclectic to the point of occasionally heralding the most patent of absurdities, the *Freep* is no less or no more interesting than the events and ideas transpiring in the cultural and political Left.

The *Berkeley Barb*, the second-oldest underground paper, was founded by Max Scherr, a middle-aged radical with a full, silver-flecked beard, and a quaint, almost rigid sense of individuality. In the late 1950's after a life of various causes and careers, Scherr bought a dank, atmosphere-ridden bar, the Steppenwolf, a favorite haunt of Berkeley radicals. Here while tending bar Scherr would take part in discussions about the Free Speech Movement and the Vietnam Day Committee, the two movements that ushered in the era of mass student protests. "I not only listened, I was active in my own protests," Scherr remembers. "I organized picketing of the Atomic Energy Commission. Unfortunately, though, the community beyond the university gate could only find out about actions by going up on campus. Things only appeared in the papers afterward, and we all sensed a need for a real community paper." By the mid-1960's Berkeley already had the nucleus of a radical-youth ghetto based only loosely on the University of California, and it was toward this community that Scherr originally directed his paper.

Although the atrocious layout and graphics made the paper look like some half-conscious mimicking of a hand-set press of the 1820's, there was something gutsy and vital in the manner in which the *Barb* set out to cover the news.

The first weekly *Barb* came out on August 13, 1965, the day after Vietnam Day Committee demonstrators had tried to stop a twenty-car troop train outside the local Santa Fe station. The incident received national publicity. Liberal papers, which were just beginning to question our position in Vietnam, found it newsworthy, and in many of the local sheets the story made the front page. But despite all the coverage, only Bob Randolph of the *Berkeley Barb* cut to the heart of the matter.

His article, the lead story, not only described the fervor of the opposition but also recorded the striking fact that some of the GI's in the train had hung signs out of the windows supporting the demonstrators— signs reading: "I don't want to go" and "Lucky civilians" and "Keep up the good work, we're with you."

During the first year and a half of publication, Scherr tramped up and down Telegraph Avenue, the Champs-Elysées of youth culture, peddling the *Barb*. "I couldn't get anybody to sell them. I was a laughing stock. Each week to sell 1,200 copies, I had to speak to about 20,000 people. They'd take just one look at the masthead and flinch. 'What's that?' It was such an ugly-looking paper."

Scherr's progeny never lost its initial unattractiveness, and the *Barb* soon settled down into a predictable

Newspaper

LOS ANGELES
FREE
PRESS

15c 25 cents out of L.A. county

New Living Arts page 25

BLACK POLITICIANS IN WHITE SUBURBIA See Page 3

Vol. 6, #10 (Issue #242) $5.00 PER YEAR

In two parts: Part One
Copyright 1969
The Los Angeles Free Press, Inc.

WE-7-1970

March 7-14, 1969

"barrels of bullshit have been the quicksand these men have had to wade through only so that they could continue to be beautiful"
-- Stanley Crouch

B.M. JACKSON

Karenga & Co. found guilty

EARL OFARI

On Saturday, March 1st, over two hundred people gathered at a recreation center in the black community of Los Angeles where the "Black Alternative," a new black community group in L.A., held a black community tribunal against various black leaders of the Black Congress.

The "Black Alternative" is a loose coalition of various black militant groups in L.A. ranging from the Black Panther Party to SNCC. The "Black Alternative" was organized approximately two months ago under the leadership of Margaret Wright, a well-known leader in the black community.

The black community tribunal, called by the Black Alternative,

charged the leaders of the Black Congress (which is itself supposedly an umbrella organization composed of some fifth black "grass roots" organizations in L.A.) with the commission "of crimes against the interests of the black community." Specifically, the charges were that the leaders in question, Walt Bremond, Ron Karenga and Roygene Robinson, were: "derelict in their duty to the black community, showed cowardice in the face of the enemy, refused to be held accountable for the money which they received, and finally created turmoil and hysteria in the black community which led directly to the deaths of John Huggins and "Bunchy" Carter of the Black Panther Party."

Some thirty black community leaders were "subpoened" by the Tribunal to testify against Bremond, Karenga and Robinson. Various members of the five man tribunal board presented evidence themselves to show that Bremond, as director of the Black Congress, had, within a five month period, over $55,000 which was unaccounted for later. It was also intimated here that it was no accident that after this loss of money was uncovered, Bremond held a press conference and then resigned as director of the Balck Congress.

Tut Hayes, of the Afro-American Association detailed several other charges against Bremond
(Continued on Page 12)

Jim Garrison is not giving up despite Shaw's acquittal

Free Press Editor Art Kunkin came back from New Orleans on Tuesday with a severe cold and could not write a full wrap-up of the Clay Shaw trial for this issue. Next week his Free Press article will consider such questions as : Why the "Not Guilty" verdict? Is Clay Shaw really innocent? Is Garrison "unfit to hold public office"? Did the communications media report the trial fairly? Did the trial accomplsih anything? Do the trial results mean that the Warren Commission is vindicated?

ART KUNKIN

Last Saturday morning a New Orleans jury returned a verdict of "Not Guilty" in the six week trial of retired businessman Clay Shaw for alleged involvement in a conspiracy to kill former President John F. Kennedy.

This verdict was immediately followed by establishment editorials throughout the country that District Attorney Jim Garrison should resign for having conducted a judicial farce. In New Orleans itself, sentiment was expressed during television shows that Clay Shaw should be sent as United States Ambassador to the Paris peace talks or at least inherit the Maharishi's position as guru to American youth.

However, Clay Shaw's sudden personal popularity in New Orleans following his courtroom victory vanished when Jim Garrison, instead of acting crushed and defeated, continued to try to put Clay Shaw in jail.

On Monday, the District Attorney filed charges against Shaw for having committed perjury during the conspiracy trial by denying that he knew David W. Ferrie and Lee Harvey Oswald.

The first Free Press article from New Orleans on the trial, dated February 11, anticipated this latest development by saying then "The first five days of evidence seem to place Clay Shaw in close relationship with persons he has previously denied knowing, including 'Leon Oswald.'...If Shaw takes the stand and still denies having known Ferrie and/or Oswald, he may very well get a perjury conviction...But this week of testimony...does not seem to prove an overt conspiracy.")

Shaw did take the stand (during his trial) to deny that he knew Ferrie or Oswald and did not participate in a conspiracy with them. Although the jury said by their verdict that Garrison had not shown Shaw's involvement in a conspiracy beyond a reasonable doubt, Garrison is very confident that he will get a conviction in a trial where the relatively simple question of

lying about personal association is at issue.

(In its editorial of last Tuesday, March 4th, The Los Angeles Times inaccurately said of the New Orleans trial, "As weird a collection of witnesses as ever decorated a courtroom was brought in by the prosecution, only to destroy themselves by their own testimony." The Times may yet have to eat this hasty statement. Of the 49 witnesses brought forward by Garrison many were established and credible citizens who saw Shaw with Ferrie and/or Oswald. The testimony of any one of these, or others whom Garrison can bring forward in a trial which is also not concerned with the complicated question of the errors of the Warren Report, can, and probably will, send Shaw to prison for perjury.

I was with Garrison at the New Orleans Athletic Club last Monday as the city began to react to the filing of perjury charges against Shaw. He received a call from assistant District Attorney "Mumu" Sciambra informing him that a local TV station was demanding a press conference. Garrison turned to me and said with some indignation that the news media have for two years falsely charged him with flamboyance and that, from now on, there would be no more press conferences, only a daily filing of charges against guilty persons.

In line with what Garrison told me on Monday, on Tuesday his office charged a former Garrison investigator, Thomas Bethel, with having unlawfully stolen a memorandum from the District Attorney's office listing the name of each Garrison witness and the substance of the testimony they would give at the Clay Shaw trial.
(Continued on Page 2)

pattern of squat inky headlines, solid blocks of print, splotchy photos, shrill headlines, and highly pedestrian writing. No matter. The paper did not pretend to be a paradigm of the New Culture. Rather, the *Barb* set out to cover as news the New Left, drug culture, sexual freedom, occult, police brutality, macrobiotics and all the other schemes and dreams that lived together uncomfortably in the Movement. The *Barb* made clear that it was proselytizing for the Movement, and when outraged townspeople condemned the paper as "propaganda," they might just as well have criticized *Business Week* as a shill for capitalism or *Women's Wear Daily* as a creature of Seventh Avenue.

In the early years of the *Barb*'s existence, it was put out almost entirely by volunteer labor in Scherr's cluttered house. "The *Barb*'s editorial production days are regular weekly crises," wrote John Wilcock in 1967. "What seem to be dozens of contributors, editors, advertisers, troublemakers, well-wishers, etc., wheel in and out of the twenty-room mansion, tripping over kids, making themselves coffee, sleeping on sofas, bargaining for space and dropping astonishing rumors which a benign Max (as calm as his paper is angry) may or may not have the time to check out." [2] Eventually, Scherr acquired a store-front office furnished with a hodgepodge of vintage chairs, tables, desks, cardboard cases and a money box; a regular staff that was paid nominal "Movement" wages; and a policy that free-lance contributors would be paid a few dollars for their efforts.

"No Movement person will say we have been a Movement paper," Scherr admits. Rather the *Barb*'s relationship to the amorphous New Left radicalism, antiwar, antiracist actions that are the Movement has been similar to the role that Scherr played as bartender at Steppenwolf —within the circle, but not quite a part of it; ready with his services, but never quite sure that he would be accepted in another role. "We had a kind of symbiotic relationship. We gave the news to the community. The community saw itself reflected in the paper and went out to act in the way it was encouraged to act by seeing that it had done something of substance. That's what a newspaper does. It gives a person a chance to see what he has done, to see how it looks to other people. In this, we have been effective in an eclectic way. In fact, some guys tell me we've been a revolutionary paper, a paper that gave people a chance to open up their own minds to ideas that are revolutionary and maybe do revolutionary things."

During the historic Oakland draft-board demonstration of October 1965, Scherr ran backward along the line of march from Berkeley to Oakland, selling the *Barb* and shouting: "Read the *Barb*; it's a pleasure not a duty." That slogan encapsulated the formula that allowed the *Barb* to reach, by early 1969, a circulation of 90,000 with a forty-man staff and an army of up to five hundred street sellers. Learning about New Left politics by reading the *Barb* was no more tedious than learning about anthropology by looking at pictures in the *National Geographic*. The paper contained a wealth of information—legitimate exposés cheek by jowl with the most implausible allegations; lengthy statements from obscure political groups published without preface or comment; announcements about future actions and meetings masquerading as articles; accounts of the latest police brutality; advertisements for everything from avant-garde theater and organic foods to far-out rock groups and massage parlors.

In a typical twenty-eight-page issue (October 11–17, 1968), the reader's fifteen cents bought fifty articles and features jammed in among fifteen pages of ads. As always, the front page featured the *Barb* logo, a skeletal Don Quixote brandishing his spear from a skeletal horse. That week's cover was an old woodcut of Indians murdering a frontiersman and his family. The caption read: "Thanx [sic] for what, Paleface?" Articles included several pieces on Eldridge Cleaver's flight from imprisonment next to a cartoon of Cleaver brandishing a rifle before a picture of Che Guevara ("Eldridge Cleaver proved himself today to be a true revolutionary—a man true to his revolutionary word. He said he wouldn't turn himself in to the pigs —and he didn't"); a story on the Beatles next to a nude photo of John and Yoko Lennon; a lengthy statement by John Sinclair about the White Panther Party, the small Michigan-based organization of militant cultural radicals ("First I must say that this statement, like all statements is bullshit without an active program to back it up. . . . We are free mother country madmen in charge of our own lives and we are taking this freedom to the peoples of America in the streets, in ballrooms and teenclubs, in their front rooms watching TV, in their bedrooms reading *Fifth Estate* or the *Sun*

[underground papers] or jacking off or smoking secret dope, in their schools, where we come and talk to them or make our music in their weird gymnasiums—they love it—we represent the only contemporary lifestyle in America for its kids and it should be known that these kids are READY!")

There is a certain sanctity to print, and by printing stories and statements by the White Panthers, the Committee to Fight Exclusion of Homosexuals from the Armed Forces, the Sexual Freedom League, *et al.,* the *Barb* legitimized them as organizations and events worthy of journalistic attention. Scherr persuaded the youthful sons and daughters of the American middle class to make that leap of faith from the patriotism of the suburb to the New Left/New Bohemianism smorgasbord dished out in the *Barb.* "What I was trying to do was to create credibility," Scherr says. "The way I did it was by looking like a newspaper and printing mind-blowing facts down in straight columns. We had the first news of dope in the army—over three years ago—the first publication that the Johnson consensus was broken, so many firsts."

The two other earliest undergrounds, the *San Francisco Oracle* and the *East Village Other,* grew out of a different milieu. Not out of political radicalism—the intense and anxious world of pamphlet wars or protests or ideological discussions— but out of the cultural radicalism. In the mid-sixties young people began drifting into Haight-Ashbury, discovering that they were many, discovering drugs, discovering a camaraderie that few had known before, discovering what they thought to be freedom. In the fall of 1966 the *San Francisco Oracle* began. Dominated by such artists and writers as Gabe Katz, Steve Levine, Travis Rivers and Allen Cohen, the *Oracle* soon flowered into the finest of the psychedelic and hippie undergrounds. You could sell it to tourists and make some bread. You could learn from it—about Leary or Ginsberg or Allan Watts. You could groove on the layouts. You could feel so much a part of a revolution of the spirit.

The *Oracle* was the first paper to take full advantage of offset printing, a major technological innovation that brought the cost of printing down to where less than $200 usually was enough to bring out five thousand copies of a sixteen-page paper. Here was an innovation that on small papers would end the damnable conflict between editor and printer, the latter full of arcane, impenetrable reasons why *this* story can't run here; *that* picture has to go there; or *that* story has to end here. No longer would journalists have to be lepidopterists of the human species preserving human endeavor by pinning it down into narrow columns and rectangles of graphics. A paper could become whatever was written, typed, drawn, etched or photographed and pasted onto newspaper-size makeup pages. Thus "camera ready," the made-up pages were taken to the offset shop, where they were printed exactly as received. In the *Oracle,* print and graphics merged. An artist would draw his intricate, multicolored psychedelic patterns, and then the prose content would be neatly fitted into and around the art work. Centerfold paintings and full-page woodcuts seemed charged with

mystery. Soft colors bled into pages. "Its creators are using color the way Lautrec must once have experimented with lithography," wrote John Wilcock in a 1967 issue of his *Other Scenes,* "testing the resources of the medium to the utmost and producing what almost any experienced newspaperman would tell you was impossible." [2] The paper was a vision, a trip—more New Poetry than New Journalism. There was little hard news, and the print content depended on that conglomeration of Orientalia, acid, Indians and pacifism that during Haight-Ashbury's short summer of 1967 passed as the Way and the Truth.

The *Oracle* was the first underground paper to consciously try to integrate itself into the community it served. The *Oracle* people were neither journalists objectively reporting on community events nor gurus living apart from and talking down to the hippies, who made their daily bread selling the paper. They were as much involved with communes and drugs and mysticism as anyone in Haight-Ashbury. And the *Oracle* was only part of their lives and the utopia that they and others were trying to build there in that crumbling, star-crossed slum.

In late 1965 the *East Village Other,* the other paper that first defined the boundaries and interests of cultural radicalism, began publishing in New York City. In 1965 and 1966 the counter culture was not yet a full vision, a world on which a newspaper could focus its full attention, and *EVO* mixed old and new. Today those early issues appear as dated as daguerreotypes—the layout almost conventional; the cultural pursuits ranging from Beat poetry to Marcel

THE east village OTHER

VOL. I NO. 3   DECEMBER   15 CENTS

FBI ARRESTS CATHOLIC WORKER

FBI agents arrested lower east sider Murphy Dowouis in broad daylight last week on the corner of Delancy Street and the Bowery, charging him with draft evasion. Dowouis went limp when confronted by the FBI agents, and had to be dragged by the hair to a waiting auto.

According to the FBI, Dowouis had been evading the draft for over two years. In July, 1963, he had written his draft board that he would not voluntarily submit to classification or carry a draft card and would in fact return all correspondence the draft board sent him. He went so far as to invite the board to bring proceedings against him, which they finally did by calling for his arrest on October 5, 1965.

FBI men traced Dowouis to the lower east side where he was affiliated with the Catholic Worker Movement. They then contacted him, asking him where he wanted to be arrested, and arranged to arrest him in front of the offices of the Catholic Worker at 165 Christie Street at 10 o'clock in the morning of November 17.

Reporters and cameramen flocked in droves to the Worker office that morning to cover the arrest, apparently causing the FBI to have a change of heart.

Dowouis was therefore arrested while on his way to the Worker office, a half hour before the scheduled meeting.

He was jailed after failing to arrange $2,500 bail.

ILLICIT TATOO CLUBS

Tatooing, now illegal in most states is on the rise again, in the underground form of secret tatoo clubs, it was disclosed recently to the Other by an informant that did not wish

to be identified. "Advocates of tatooing as an art have formed clubs, like cults. Some right in this neighborhood," said our source, the leader of one such club.

"All the members are sorry that we had to go underground," he continued showing us an eagle tatooed in a very expressive manner in blue and bright reds. "The law just isn't right. They first said tatooing spread disease, but when it was demonstrated that health standards could be met, the Bench proclaimed tatooing "a barbaric survival" and dismissed appeal."

Tatooing has appeared, at one time or another, among all peoples. In Europe and America it has been most widely practiced among seamen who learned the art in the Orient. It was popular only a generation ago among the British and American upper classes who also formed clubs. The present core of tatoo enthusiasts on the Lower East Side seem to be those who sought the carnival for romance in their youth and feel its their right to tatoo their bodies.

The new generation of tatoo enthusiasts have taken to modern designs and mystical symbols by famous artists. The custom is spreading among the pepsi generation of the uptown hippies and the jet set. The most popular designs among women are shoulder embossed butterflies, white on dark skin or a

Cont'd on page 7

TWO MEN CLAIM PLANETS STARS

In the largest real estate claim in history, Hugo Koch and Frederick J. Pohlman of the Lower East Side have declared possession of all the unclaimed planets in the solar system and all celestial bodies beyond—with the exception of meteorites.

"We didn't claim the meteorites because we were concerned they might hit something, bringing damage suits," Pohlman said in an interview.

Koch and Pohlman claimed the stars and planets by placing an ad in the public notice column of a local paper for a full week. The notice, declaring their claim, is considered a perfectly legal way to claim previously unclaimed real estate. At least by Earthly standards.

Koch and Pohlman plan to sell off their holdings, but are undecided as to what prices to charge. Koch wants to sell each planet for $1,000, but Pohlman argues that this price is far too high; the world's money would run out leaving them with an overstock in planets and no market to sell them in. He prefers an offering price of 24 planets for a penny.

Numerous phone calls have resulted from the claim. A woman called to rent 25 acres

Cont'd on page 11

Marceau; the news coverage focusing on knife fights or heatless tenements or other events primarily on the Lower East Side.

Eventually *East Village Other* was able to set forth a full vision of what would become the "counter culture." The very name *East Village Other* helped to suggest what this radical culture would be, since by calling itself "East Village," then not a common term, the paper implied that it and eventually the "counter culture" would remain apart, above and oblivious to the older citizenry of the area—the Puerto Ricans, Ukrainians, Poles and others, who for generations had known the soot-streaked streets and fading tenements only as part of the Lower East Side. Instead, *EVO* chose as its desired readership and editorial concern the artists and Bohemians who in the mid-1960's were spilling out of high-priced Greenwich Village into the $65 one-bedroom flats and railroad apartments of the Lower East Side. "We hope to become the mirror of opinion of the new citizenry of the East Village," *EVO* declared in its first four-page issue, defining itself in a much narrower manner than the *Village Voice* ever had done. Having such an audience of artists and Bohemians gave *EVO* peculiar opportunities to affect cultural trends. There were certain risks too, for the paper—and the "new citizenry"—might prove just as provincial and self-contained as all the other ethnic groups that had ignored their neighbors when the Lower East Side had been their native grounds.

The early *East Village Other* paid obligatory obeisance to the remaining Beat poets and artists, yet it was clear that *EVO* was part of a new and unprecedented Bohemianism, an optimistic Bohemianism, American in psyche as well as location, looking sentimentally toward the future rather than toward the past. The third issue contained a "Proclamation" that declared: "The editors of this newspaper, who are all working artists, poets, playwrights, etc., have seen fit to expand the role of artist as Creator-Communicator into the sphere of journalism. For us it will be a journey into the possible; the *Canterbury Tales* of the newspaper trade in which we will try to influence and shape public opinion in relation to communal, political, social and economic problems of this world and others. It will be an overhaul of the personality to enable it to function a little bit better in a world made of both physical, mental and spiritual facts. Our only testament will be to Creation and Change; our only belief that to change is not to die but to be born again; our only reason, that in order for people to survive in the world at large it is not a necessity but Necessity itself." The Proclamation sounded as if it had been written with a heavy dose of *Medium Is the Message* hyperbole. However, as *EVO*'s Allen Katzman points out, "In those days we were doing what a year later McLuhan was only just talking about."

As "Creator-Communicators," *EVO* heralded the emergence of a youth religiosity in headlines ("YOUTH! The New Politics") and in editorials ("There is a new morality in America, and with it, a new hope for salvation. . . . A powerful burst of energy has been released onto the American soil: youth has found its voice"); lauded drugs by featuring quasi-academic pieces on marijuana, accounts of Ken Kesey's electric Kool-aid acid tests, Timothy Leary's lectures and starting in May 1966 a "Turn On/Tune In/Drop Out" column by the high priest of the drug culture himself ("To preserve your sanity and return to harmonious order you must quit your attachments to American society gracefully, lovingly, planfully"); and treated political affairs in a highly literate, irrepressible, even outrageous manner ("Ethel Kennedy soon arrived with a retinue of pale-cheeked Ivy League men and a couple of folk singers. She smiled the assured gilt-edged smile of one who vacations in the midwinter. She is a very knacky baby, considering she is 37 and the mother of nine . . .").

EVO mused intellectually about the little-publicized art happenings of Andy Warhol, the new theater of "Viet Rock" and La Mama, and the music of Bob Dylan ("What Dylan has done is to have found a loophole in Existence by using the "System" to project his ideas—which are the ideas of a poet linked up with the underground—and subliminally re-adjust the learning processes of housewives and teenagers across the nation which have too long been geared to a war mentality"). The paper lauded the first draft card burnings and mass protests against the Vietnam war and grew outraged at the ecological menace ("Those great shards of soot that settle on your window will come from the Consolidated Edison Plant on 14th Street, one of the architectural wonders of our age"). Graphics were something special as well—pictures of long-haired "Slum Goddesses," cheesecake for the Bohemian male; funky details from old books and

magazines; and weird comics.

The comics were the worst nightmare the censors at the Comic Code Authority ever could have imagined. "Fantom Fetus" (Beetle Bailey, who looks into a fetus inside a womb and says, "It sure looks like a virgin cunt but . . ." and other all-American comic characters messing with vaginas, naked women, and what have you); "Gothic Blimp Works" (the freakiest sexual fantasies); "No Salvation Comix" (bikers, brutality, chains, sado-masochism); "These Fabulous Freak Brothers" (the continuing saga of two potheads against the world). To young hips brought up on "Superman," "Captain Marvel," and "Wonder Woman," those comics were *real;* this was what comics had been all about underneath the pale gentility enforced by the censors. The underground comics meshed print and graphic art brilliantly. The comic could be read on several different levels, and sometimes they had to be to make any sense. Marshall McLuhan could have been talking about underground comics in particular when he wrote in *Understanding Media* that comics "provide very little data about any particular moment in time, or aspect in space, of an object. The viewer, or reader, is compelled to participate in completing and interpreting the few hints provided by the bounding lines. . . . Comics . . . are a highly participational form of expression. . . ."

EVO was on one of the earliest "media trips" living more in the never-never land of myth creation than in the perpetually grubby streets of the Lower East Side. This new universe of hip would be crafted out of the spirit, willed into existence by ignoring that familiar and tired

world of the old and the ugly. "There are literally thousands of young people . . . who have, in one form or another, dropped out of the system to the extent of just barely existing on its borders and who would benefit once and for all by seceding from the Union," wrote Allen Katzman in the summer of 1966. "Of course this movement would have to be combined with the formation of a loosely knit confederation of *people* rather than states."

The weird, unpredictable, far-out *EVO* of those early years turned a great many people onto the counter culture. "In 1967–68 *EVO* was really important to me," says Harry Jack-

son, a twenty-three-year-old writer for *Zygote,* a rock magazine. "It was into all these incredible things. For example, when they covered a demonstration, they would not have one picture. They would have an incredible collage of pictures. They reached what perhaps was the high point of American journalism—capturing fantasy as well as facts."

"*EVO* was the first thing that turned me on three years ago," says Bob Singer, a twenty-one year old high school dropout who now edits *Ace,* New York City's newest and most innovative underground newspaper. "I remember reading a Crumb comic and it blew my mind."

VOL. 4, NO. 1   DECEMBER 13, 1968   METROPOLITAN 15ᶜ

EVO's other importance lay in its guiding role as the founder of the first organization that would bring together what was to be called the underground press. In June 1966, John Wilcock, Walter Bowart and Allen Katzman of the *East Village Other,* sat in *EVO*'s scruffy office dreaming up a loose national organization to unify six obscure, struggling newspapers—*EVO;* the *Berkeley Barb;* the *Los Angeles Free Press;* the *San Francisco Oracle;* Lansing's *The Paper;* * and Detroit's *Fifth Estate.* It would serve as advertising agent and clearinghouse for the exchange of subscriptions and reprint privileges among members. All that was lacking was a name. "Underground," Wilcock suggested, and so the "underground press" and the "Underground Press Syndicate" were christened. In those days the word *underground* was appropriate enough. "I don't know what else it could have been called," says Wilcock. "It was underground, unknown, unnoticed, and a somewhat reviled piece of publishing."

The beauty of the term *underground* was that most of the editors could look at it and see something of themselves. To the political radicals it conjured up images of those dangerous and noble undergrounds that have always existed in repressive societies—so what if this all seemed as foreign as suttee; there were those who saw another America being born. *Underground* pleased those who like Wilcock thought of themselves as part of a cultural avant-garde. ("There's always an underground, always people whose ideas are unpopular and prophetic.") And then,

---

* The Paper *is no longer published.*

too, *underground* was a word with unquestioned *élan* and mystique. It could be used by those natural McLuhanites at *EVO* and elsewhere who considered change as manipulating myths and symbols ("For some," wrote Thorne Dreyer and Victoria Smith, "it [UPS] was intended as a 'pseudo event' to fool the commercial press. To create the illusion of a giant coordinated network of freaky papers, poised for the kill." [3] Thus *underground* was the broadest and most neutral moniker these radical-youth publications could hang on themselves. It emphasized their common ground and obscured such differences as the split between cultural and political radicals; it was a name that would come to cover a range and multitude of publications that far surpassed even the most extravagant prophecies and private dreams of most of these early editors.

seize the time!

LIBERATION NEWS SERVICE

No. 243

March 28, 1970

4
The Heads and the Fists

On New Year's Day, 1967, the *San Francisco Oracle* called together the historic Golden Gate Be-in, the first mass gathering of the youth nation. It would be, wrote the *Oracle,* a gathering at which "a union of love and activism previously separated by categorical dogma and label mongering will finally occur ecstatically when Berkeley's political activists and hip community and San Francisco's spiritual generation all over California meet for a gathering of tribes. . . ." There on that blessedly warm afternoon the hippies and pacifists and Marxists and Diggers and activists and Beats and resisters and freaks and Trots and gurus and poets would spontaneously unite into a revolutionary lava that would sweep down on a tired and uncomprehending America, burying it and creating a totally new world.

In those days the *Oracle* people were puffed up with the most extraordinary self-confidence. They and the other cultural radicals could call themselves "hippies" with neither affection nor self-consciousness. And why not? For dope, rock, communes, dropping out, and acid were so terribly new and pregnant with meaning that those who took part had reason to believe that they were part of a new mass elite, pied pipers who would lead the world out of its morass.

The political radicals weren't so sure. Jerry Rubin, then a fiery politico in the Berkeley Free Speech Movement, had come over from Berkeley, where just hours before he had been bailed out of jail after being charged with "defying a court order." He stood there on stage with ten thousand people before him in leather, feathers, denim, beads, cloaks, chains, sitting, smoking, doping, being, grooving. And he harangued them about Vietnam. There was little reaction, and a slightly bewildered Rubin sat down. Max Scherr of the *Barb* was infuriated. How could the Movement let such an opportunity go by without using it for radical purposes? "It was badly organized," Scherr told Oliver Johnson of the *East Village Other*. "There was great potential there for protest. If I could have gotten to a microphone I would have said what was in my heart. The organizers implied that they were against the war, but they didn't want to bother people about it on this occasion."

The arguments between the hippies and the Berkeley activists at that first Be-in were the earliest evidence of the tension in the Movement and the underground press between the cultural and the political radicals. The *Oracle* and the hippies argued that a person has to straighten out his own life if he wants to make a revolution. To do that he would have to drop out and live in an alternative society. Blocking trains, sitting-in, demonstrating just create more tensions and prolong the Vietnam war and evil. To this the *Barb* and Berkeley people countered by saying that the government wasn't about to let any mass alternative society develop. And even if it did, it wouldn't end the war, racism or poverty.

Three months later, when the first UPS convention opened on the first day of spring 1967 at a beach house north of San Francisco, the Berkeley people were a tiny minority, and some stoned wit dubbed the meeting the "hippies' Appalachin." The *Oracle*'s apocalyptic anarchy set the tone for the meeting. "Well, here we are, Uncle Sam on the verge of death," Ron Thelin, the managing editor of the *Oracle* began his welcoming letter. "A sleep-stupor symbol-addicted environment haunts our hearts, and what are we going to do about it?" [1] Not a great deal. The sweet anarchy of the cultural revolutionaries prevailed, and the two-day meeting created little but good vibes. One of the more memorable moments came when Rolling Thunder, a Hopi Indian, dressed in an old-fashioned black suit and a broad-brimmed black hat, informed the editors that the Indians were paying close attention to the underground press. An evil spirit could be contained, Rolling Thunder said, by circling it; perhaps, it might work with the Pentagon. Totally in the spirit the *Oracle* suggested that the Underground Press Syndicate should be renamed the Tribal Messenger Service.

When the *Barb*'s Max Scherr arrived in the midst of Rolling Thunder's talk, he was no more pleased than he had been three months before at the first Be-in. Scherr could do little, though, for a meeting near San Francisco in March 1967, complete with good dope and a living, breathing Indian, was not the place to bring up the war in Vietnam or police brutality. A different environment would probably not have been that much different since among the twenty-five UPS papers Scherr and the political radicals were patently a minority. Even most of those underground editors with impeccable Movement credentials, such as Thorne Dreyer and Dennis and Judy Fitzgerald of the Austin *Rag*, described themselves as having, "definite nonideological connection with the left-wing love, flower and freedom sect, anarchistic division of S.D.S.," that according to Dreyer previously "had freaked national S.D.S. out." [2]

The Underground Press Syndicate structure is very much a product of that loose, anarchistic cultural radicalism. At that first convention no one thought it necessary to set up a central office for UPS. All a paper had to do to join UPS was to agree to give the other UPS members free reprint privileges; to publish a list of UPS members occasionally; and to exchange free subscriptions. As the underground press grew, though, it became apparent that some sort of national coordinating office was necessary. There were national advertising revenues to worry about and new papers sprouting up so fast that it was hard to know just what was happening. And now new members have to pay a one-time twenty-five-dollar fee to a permanent UPS office in New York. This plus the sale of library subscriptions and a percentage of national advertising moneys is enough to provide subsistence for a small staff working out of a loft in lower Manhattan.

From those early days UPS retains a spaced-out style. It is full of openness and ease of the early cultural radicalism, and it values that over the common efficiency of the modern business office. Nevertheless, those exchange subscriptions do infuse the underground with a sense of common purpose. In a small town in the deep South or a middling industrial city on the Atlantic coast, a mailbox stuffed with papers is powerful reassurance that one is not alone. The reprint privilege permits new papers to feed off their more secure and journalistically established brethren, and editors everywhere to draw on the richness of other scenes. UPS provides a weekly newsletter too— the *Free Ranger Intertribal News Service*—that reprints largely cultural materials from other papers. Thomas Forcade, for several years a leading UPS figure, also has propagandized for the underground press in his rococo psychedelic prose. ("The underground press is crouched like a Panther, dollars and days away from daily publication and thus total domination in the print media. In the past 20 years over 400 establishment dailies have died. After the underground press goes daily, they'll die like flies.")

Happily, all this takes place without a party line or rigid mandates from on high. UPS coordinates national advertising, publishes a periodic list of UPS members, and an annual UPS directory. As for other functions, UPS remains full of just-over-the-horizon promise that has yet never been quite realized.

One of the reasons UPS has not developed more is that late in 1967 another service organization, Liberation News Service (LNS), was founded by Marshall Bloom (Amherst, '66) and Ray Mungo (Boston U., '67), who had met when they were radical editors of their respective college papers. Bloom had been scheduled to be director of the United States Student Press Association during the 1967–68 year, but at a summer editor's meeting he was purged. He was considered too freaky, too irresponsible. He just did not fit into those carefully contrived categories of "leadership" and "maturity," the stuff out of which most of these promising young editors were made. Bloom had neither time nor temperament for remorse, and he and Mungo set out to form a competing news service free of cloying liberal taint and the patterned techniques of journalism schools. They were a curious duo—dope-smoking, hip, full of far-out incredulousness, yet terribly concerned about Vietnam, the urban crisis and politics. To begin their news service, they simply sent out letters to underground and college papers and Movement groups announcing what they were up to.

The initial organizational meeting initiated Bloom and Mungo into the circus of circa-1967 Movement politics. It was held in Washington on an October afternoon, the day before the March on the Pentagon. Mungo recalls that Bloom began in solid academic fashion by outlining how LNS hoped to unite underground papers and provide solid coverage of Movement affairs, when up jumped Walter Bowart in Indian headdress, cheered on by the rest of the *EVO* tribe, to read a poem about the underground and to propagandize unashamedly for the Underground Press Sydicate, which at that time was run by *EVO*. Up jumped other editors to charge *EVO* with the embezzlement of UPS funds. Eventually, Allen Cohen of the *San Francisco Oracle* managed to get the floor to read *his* poetry.

"And so it went," wrote Mungo much later. "The college editors were interested mostly in campus revolution, the pacifists in the war, the freaks in cultural revolution and cultural purity. . . . A few fist fights broke out between warring factions of the antiwar forces. . . . Our glorious scheme of joining together the campus editors, the Communists, the Trots, the hippies, the astrology freaks, the pacifists, the S.D.S. kids, the black militants, the Mexican-American liberation fighters, and all their respective journals, was reduced to ashes. Our conception of LNS as a 'democratic organization' owned by those it served, was clearly ridiculous; among those it served were, in fact, many whose very lives were devoted to the principle that no organization was desirable." [3]

"Do your thing, do your thing," someone shouted at the meeting. "If we like it we'll send you money when we can." After licking their wounds, this is exactly what Bloom and Mungo did and how the underground press reacted. By early 1968 LNS reported that its thrice-weekly news packets were going out to over 360 newspapers, magazines and radio stations, most of them only sporadically paying the monthly fee, which then was fifteen dollars. The LNS list included a far broader range of publications than just the membership of the UPS. A little over half were college papers (183) and among the others were such non-youth-culture publications as *Viet Report, Jewish Currents* and the *Militant.*

Liberation News Service, then, had closer relations with the political movement than the Underground Press Syndicate. During the underground press's first years, the political movement had not taken the papers seriously. This had not bothered those early editors in the least, since for the most part they gave their allegiance to a highly cultural radicalism.

Bloom and Mungo tried to straddle these two worlds, balancing their cultural and political radicalism like carnival jugglers. However, the Pentagon march, escalation in Vietnam, draft resistance, and militant student protests forced a new seriousness on much of the underground press. The political radicals at LNS just had no use for packets that gave articles on LSD, missives from Allen Ginsberg, nature poetry, and groovy recipes equal billing with political and Movement news. And they were not about to compromise. "Many [underground-press people] had been flower children," wrote Vicki Smith and Thorne Dreyer in a heavily political analysis of the underground press. "Their prophetic insights had been clubbed to the ground by the cops and had been marketed to the populace by the masters of cooptation. But though the trappings proved cooptable, the vision was not. It was how you achieve that vision that demanded reevaluation. It could not come [the lesson was being pounded home] in isolation from society. You could not escape external reality—it would bust you sure. And even if you could create a heaven-on-earth, a pocket of utopia, what about the rest of the world? What about those who did not start from a position of material privilege, for whom doing-your-own-thing was unthinkable?" [4]

In June 1968 an LNS badly splintered between the cultural and political radicals moved to New York City to try to start anew. Here the political radicals could muster overwhelming strength. In secret midnight meetings, hushed debates and ugly denunciations, the conflict between what Mungo dubbed the "Virtuous Caucus" and the "Vulgar Marxists" crescendoed. Instead of convincing Bloom and Mungo, the constant pressure only pushed the Virtuous Caucus more into a hardline hippie position. The Vulgar Marxists weren't about to budge either. They had historical necessity on their side. Finally, one morning in August the "Virtuous" staff backed a large rented truck up to the office, filled it with the press, collator, files, typewriters, mailing list, addressograph, and everything else that wasn't indisputably personal or worthless, and in a little caravan of cars left for a farm in Vermont bought with a five-thousand-dollar down payment from an LNS benefit.

Late that night a Movement posse of Vulgar Marxists and their allies arrived in Vermont. After roughing up Bloom and several others, the New York LNS faction got a six-thousand-dollar check signed over to them. (Ironically, the money ended up in the hands of the state of Vermont for legal disposition.)

For a while the underground press had two LNS's—one in Vermont and the other in New York City. At first, Vermont LNS put out their packets twice a week, then once a week, then sporadically, until by February 1969, without benefit of clergy or mourners, the "Virtuous" LNS died, a victim of the times as much as of the exigencies of life on a farm.

Eight months later Mungo came out of his Vermont haven, where he lived what he called a "postrevolutionary life," to visit LNS in New York City. He was sickened by the workaday hustle-bustle. "I wanted to scream, 'There are no answers! There are no systems! This is not my salvation! Leave me alone!'" The LNS staff looked pale and flabby, dressed in rugged work boots, fatigue jackets,

FREE BOBBY NEW HAVEN MAY 1

LIBERATION NEWS SERVICE

old denims and chinos, their urban pallor increased by the yellow fluorescent lighting and the grim, humorless nature of their writing.

That visit seems to have been enough to have severed Mungo from the Movement—any movement. "I no longer have *any* kind of program to save the world, let alone nineteenth-century Marxism, except perhaps to pay attention to trees."

Mungo's recent book, *Famous Long Ago: My Life and Hard Times with Liberation News Service,* is dedicated to Marshall Bloom, who late in 1969 killed himself, leaving Mungo, as he writes in his dedication, "confused and angry, lonely and possessed, inspired and moved but generally broken." The pages of Mungo's book are washed with lyricism and melancholy, and the book stands as a testimony both to the beauty and spirit of this anarchy-laced radicalism and to its self-indulgent frailties.

Mungo admits to no ideology and says that he and Bloom decided to start LNS not because of any deep conviction but "because we had nothing else to do." "Most of us in Washington didn't really believe in 'The Revolution' to come," he confesses, "or else we acted like the revolution was then and there; we tried to enjoy life as much as possible, took acid trips, went to the movies, and supported people because they were fun or well-intentioned or in need." To a certain extent this is one of those rare tidbits of candor that refuse to fit into those categories labeled "commitment" and "purpose" so laboriously constructed by sympathetic scholars and reporters and Movement activists themselves. Of course, Mungo is alienated, and it is out of this alienation that he builds his life. But he certainly had

more commitment and concern than in retrospect he cares to give himself.

Mungo and his friends simply believed that the Movement should be groovy. When the LNS people could no longer grow high on each other, and comradery dissipated into bitchy political discussions or undisguised hostility, Mungo tried to exorcise his ill feelings. "We were possessed of dark spirits in those days," he writes of the LNS schism. "Some of us, alas, remain so, but many others have freed themselves." The great beauty of this earthly paradise of cultural radicalism is that evil and violence are always out *there,* far from the groovy reality of us. In this there is a kind of folk Manichaeanism. The duality between good and evil is the distance between "Woodstock Nation" and straight society. What happens, though, when evil and violence intrude in a world where their very existence is denied. What happens, say, at Altamont raceway in California during the Rolling Stones' free concert when Hell's Angels start clubbing people, allegedly killing one black youth. A picture in *Rolling Stone,* a rock newspaper-magazine, shows two husky Hell's Angels brutally attacking an obese naked man with pool cues. In a semicircle around the Angels stand the children of the New Culture. Their faces are filled not with anger or horror or mere indifference but with mild curiosity —*this* is not *their* world; this cannot affect them; this must be the exotic rite of some other tribe. "I was standing two feet away," says Greil Marcus, formerly associate editor of *Rolling Stone.* "People reacted by saying 'wow, violence, far-out.' Nobody did anything. Hundreds of kids raised their hands in the peace sign, and I felt like throwing up."

Sometimes the reaction to violence takes other turns. After a protest at the University of Wisconsin, Dr. Seymour L. Halleck, a psychologist, examined three students. They had all witnessed police violence. Two had been victims of that violence. And they had all suffered psychotic reactions. Writes Dr. Halleck: "Faced with a situation in which anger was entirely appropriate and in which feelings of rage could no longer be suppressed, they were both confused and horrified by their own aggressiveness. They had not learned to accept anger as a part of their personality and when they could no longer deny its existence they were overwhelmed by anxiety." [5]

The political radicals, on the other hand, did not try to suppress their anger or to deny the reality of evil. Often it infused their lives with a fierce and constant energy. At LNS the Vulgar Marxists were *serious*. They set up an office manager, regular hours, et cetera. "Their method of running the news service was the Meeting and the Vote, ours was Magic," writes Mungo. "We lived on magic and still do, and I have to say it beats anything *systematic*."

This debate between the Virtuous Caucus and the Vulgar Marxists may have been couched in hip jargon, but it is as old as the nineteenth-century debate between Marxists and anarchists. The lesson of modern radical history is that the Vulgar Marxists are correct *in terms of strategy*. You don't successfully overthrow a government by dropping out and denying the existence of the authoritarian state. You don't bring change by seeding tiny utopias on ground controlled by the government. According to the Marxists the anarchists and antiauthoritarian Leftists simply deny social reality. "Have these gentlemen ever seen a revolution," asks Friedrich Engels. "A revolution is the most authoritarian thing there is; it is the act whereby one part of the population imposes its will on the other part by means of rifles, bayonets and cannon—authoritarian means if such there be at all; and if the victorious party does not wish to have fought in vain, it must maintain this rule by means of the terror which its arms inspire in the reactionaries." [6]

The American Left went through those same arguments itself after the free-form, highly cultural radicalism of the *Masses* and the pre-World War I period had failed to bring a revolution. Many radicals simply could not stomach the narrowly political, ideological radicalism that was the result. John Dos Passos, for instance, wrote into the *New Masses* to ask why the magazine didn't continue the *Masses* tradition of exploring regions without ideological baggage or rigid editorial stance. "Friend John," replied Mike Gold in an early issue, wasn't Dos Passos merely counseling a bland and impressionistic revolt that would end, once again, in "pessimism, defeatism, and despair"? Wasn't it better to slip "Moscow and revolution into the pilot's compass box" instead of navigating by "doubt and introspection." [7] (The tragedy is that such a Marxist revolution takes a terrible toll of the very ideals and energies and structures that would be required to create a utopian society. It is not a question of whether the end justifies the means; it is that sometimes the means employed changed the ends. Of course, this historic irony is often used in support of the most repressive of governments, and this is the crudest intellectual dishonesty.)

On an unconscious level, the early hip cultural radicals seemed aware that the moral complexities of the contemporary world are such that only the young can die good. They reveled in their youth and avoided the staggering, stultifying contradictions of modern society. Their great achievement was to create the consciousness of a new kind of world—in Haight-Ashbury's short summer, in New York's East Village hippies, in Be-ins, smoke-ins, free stores and pocket communities across the country—but they believed that consciousness and reality were the same, not realizing that consciousness is conjured out of the spirit, while reality is forged out of sterner stuff, out of social forces.

What was needed, then, were underground papers that would help forge that hip consciousness into reality or at least help understand why it was impossible to create a counter culture within the bowels of contemporary America. But the early cultural radicals were constitutionally unable to fill that role. "We're no community paper," Allen Katzman, by then managing editor of the *East Village Other*, told a reporter in 1967. "We're a worldwide movement for art, peace, civil rights, morality in politics." [8] And, so, *EVO* kept right on creating images, reinforcing the hip consciousness long after the urban utopias of the hip world had dissipated, strung out on too much reality. Eventually *EVO* became highly political, but by then the East Village community had grown far away from the paper. Now half of *EVO*'s circulation reportedly is out-side New York City. Even the East Side Bookstore, right off St. Mark's Place, the hub of the East Village, sells over three times as many *Village Voice*'s as *EVO*'s.

In San Francisco, too, in the fall of 1967, when the tourists left Haight-Ashbury, the national journalists went off in search of still brighter stories, and the harsh life of the ghetto reasserted itself, the *San Francisco Oracle* fell into rapid decline. The *Oracle* would not peddle tarnished visions, and it could not deal with the ambivalent and difficult realities of Haight-Ashbury. The *Oracle* had been almost too beautiful. The paper was a vision, selling as much to tourists as to hippies, and the staff could not easily hack away at that vision to leave room for the ambivalent and difficult realities of Haight-Ashbury. Next to a magnificently intricate drawing and scroll alluding to the wonder of drugs, they could not really place a grim story about a murdered drug dealer. Beside a wandering allegory on love, how could they write about new arrivals who were having their money and belongings ripped off. From a high of 100,000 in August, the circulation fell to 50,000, and the *Oracle* folded. The *Oracle*'s creative genius was debased and diluted, turned into gaudy psychedelic posters, the weak commercial art of Peter Max and others, flashy advertising campaigns, and all the endless paraphernalia of the hippie business. Now San Francisco even has a *Haight-Ashbury Tribune,* a paper ostensibly in the tradition of the *Oracle*. It is a 25-cents-a-copy sex sheet full of nude young long-hairs, peddled to tourists longing for a souvenir of the Love Generation.

5
Post-Mortem on the First Generation

Underground papers are not neatly rationalized instruments of information and politics able to don the latest fashion in belief or life style. To one degree or another, papers remain wedded to the vision of youth culture and Movement politics that brought *them* into the world and onto the streets. One of the distinctive features of the first-generation papers was that for the most part they operated with that libertarian truism: "Everything is all right as long as it doesn't hurt other people." The papers had no restraints on language or content, and when many Americans first picked up an underground paper it was to chuckle over an occasional four-letter word or gasp at the picture of a naked girl. In truth, *EVO*'s slum goddesses, the *Oracle*'s romantic pictures of intertwined bodies, and the *Barb*'s accounts of Sexual Freedom League activities weren't terribly titillating. The early underground didn't intend that they should be, for the sexual aspects of the papers were simply natural counterparts of their other broad radical interests.

This radical libertarianism carried over to advertising policy. In *EVO*'s "Wheel and Deal" classified section, for instance, the hip community could advertise just about anything it chose to. In the January 1966 *EVO*, these were the first four items under the "Personal" heading:

Man, 25, on his way to the top in the newspaper trade, is interested in meeting young woman, tolerant, square, and not necessarily beautiful. Object matrimony. EVO Box AA1

Lessicks Kid, go home and blow stories from "In the Bronx" by Jack Micheline.

Available at Phoenix, 8th Street and Tompkins Square Bookstores.

LITERARY CURIOSITIES. Peace Eye Bookstore, 383 E. 10th St. Open odd hours.

RICHARD REYNOLDS BEARD. Handsome blond with a tint of red, curly beard worn by champion Go player. Will sacrifice for $100. EVO Box 1RR

It would have been unthinkable for writers and artists championing freedom of expression to tailor advertisements to fit even hip niceties and as the weeks passed "Wheel and Deal" grew weirder and weirder and less and less related to the East Village community. By late 1967 "Wheel and Deal" had become a sexual supermarket patronized by a nonhip audience turned on to a multitude of activities and dropped out of anybody's attempt to form a counter culture. Here are the first four items under the "Personal" heading in the December 13, 1968, *EVO*.

DELICIOUS Kosher salami attached to 32-year-old handsome married me. If you're female, young, lovely and "hungry," let's meet for "something to eat." 685-1541 weekdays.

CALIFORNIA couple visiting New York mid-December. Desire meeting others interested in leather, rubber, bondage and discipline. Photo exchanged. Box 5247, Sherman Oaks, Calif. 91413

MAN, white, suave, Continental style, would like to meet girls 18–27 who are interested in the French, Greek, and Italian culture. Must be clean, shapely and sophisticated type. Everything kept confidential. Call BE 3-1111, ask for Gerald.

BEAUTIFUL MEXICAN GIRLS needing American boy-friends, "free details," Mexico, Box 3973 MEVO, San Diego, Calif. 92103.

All through 1968 and early 1969, page after page of "body ads" and sex-oriented advertising remained tucked in the back of *EVO* making the paper an enviable 50 percent advertising and helping to bring circulation up to a high of 65,000 in early 1969. Justified by the editorial staff in the name of freedom, and purportedly ignored by the hip community, the ads became absolutely necessary to the economic well-being of the paper.

The financial success of many other undergrounds, including the *Berkeley Barb* and the *Los Angeles Free Press* also depended on such sex ads. Jack Harris, the *Freep*'s classified-ad manager, estimates that a third of the readers buy the paper primarily for the sex ads. In the *Free Press* the commercial purveyors of erotic promise moved in en masse announcing their heterosexual and homosexual films, topless and bottomless nightclubs and sex-book stores in display ads featuring graphic pictures of their wares. This was yet another rich lode of advertising revenue for the *Free Press* and something of a crowd pleaser as well. Coupled with the more prosaic hip advertising similar to that found in the *Village Voice,* the sex ads made the paper 50 to 60 percent advertising, and helped the *Freep* to gross an estimated one million dollars in 1969.

The *Free Press* remained very much Kunkin's paper. This was not that unusual, for most of those first-generation editors—men like Walter Bowart of the *East Village Other* and Max Scherr of the *Berkeley Barb*—had nurtured and shaped their papers with the almost proprietary zeal and self-confidence that later would be deemed "capitalism" and still later "male chauvinism," and created the not improbable impression that they and the paper were one and the same. They and their coteries dominated the creative aspects of their papers and left the "shit work"—the typing, advertising, bookwork, et cetera—largely to the women. Eventually the *Free Press* staff, men and women who at first had worked as unpaid volunteers, became bloated with success and grew away from the paper. "We're a bunch of middle-class hippies," says one *Los Angeles Free Press* staffer who earns over $200 a week. "Nobody identifies with the paper any more," says another employee. "It's a job, a well paying job at a minimum of three dollars an hour where you can wear long hair, come in and out as you like, and have temper tantrums." Kunkin, himself, lives in a large house overlooking the city and for business purposes has found it necessary to install a telephone in his convertible.

In the past two years, the *Free Press* has related less and less to the world it seeks to serve and write about. "It used to be that the *Freep* was a bridge between the hip and the straight worlds," says Alex Apostolides, the former *Free Press* art-scene editor. "It served a real function. I can remember two years ago when three Panthers were killed. The wife and mother showed up at the office because they were sure they'd get a fair hearing. That wouldn't happen anymore. The advertising has helped kill the paper. How can you editorialize about not exploiting people when you have eight pages of exploitative sex ads?"

The *Free Press* has not retreated back into left-liberalism. The paper has published material that many undergrounds would not have dared touch. Three times the offices have been the target of fire bombs, and the newly fortified building remains a prime potential target for right-wing terrorists. The paper has not been rationalized into a smooth, self-sustaining business enterprise like the *Village Voice*. Nor has the *Freep* in any sense become an accepted part of the Los Angeles liberal establishment. The problem largely is that the *Free Press* represents the fullest flowering of the contradictions implicit in the early counter culture or radical-youth culture. As Art Kunkin points out, drawing on his excellent command of radical history, the *Freep* has the faults of such early-1900's Socialist papers as *Appeal to Reason*. It is privately owned and doesn't relate to a unified national movement. Kunkin's explanation did not for a moment mean that he was about to divest himself willingly of his paper, his three bookstores, and his mortgaged $250,000 4-color Mergenthaler press. The counter culture has yet to devise working counter institutions of a truly modern institutional size, and Kunkin believes that a "utopian" structure for the *Freep* might mean the end of the paper.

As it is, the *Free Press* has grown into the most incongruous and unwieldy of giants. That gigantic offset press, bought with a down payment in case repression shuts off outside printers and secreted in a spacious building in a Los Angeles suburb, had to be fed daily if Kunkin was not to go bankrupt. And so this socialist intellectual was forced to print "shoppers" and other papers he really had no business dealing with. The *Freep's* internal structure is another central problem. The main offices sit on Beverly Boulevard directly across from CBS Television City. CBS's squat series of windowless rectangles have all the grace of a modernesque bomb shelter; the *Free Press's* squat windowless building—with a "Smothers Brothers Censored" sign over the door—is little better. The large building is divided into a labyrinth of corridors, cubbyholes, and tightly spaced rooms, all painted as brightly as a nursery. The effect is to cut off any sense of communication or common concern among the more than thirty staff members.

There is a cavernous gap between the workaday life of the paper and the idealistic, movement-building job the *Freep* is presumably doing. The office bristles with all the backroom skullduggery, cliques and maneuvering common to any bureaucracy. Intrigue has a special impetus here, for the paper's hierarchical structure is as flexible as soft plastic, a perfect setup for a hip Julien Sorel. There is just no sense of togetherness and common purpose among those well-paid scions of the middle class with their Mercedes-Benzes, good dope, calfskin vests, Volkswagens, mountain-climbing equipment, and even a swimming pool. (During a financial bind in early 1970, the *Free Press* temporarily stopped paying free-lance contributors their customary $20. The staff took no cut in pay.) There is a vague sense of unease in the office. "Some days I'll get up feeling fine," says one staff member, "but by the time I get to the office, I'm physically sick." Usually the tensions are restrained, but this writer happened to be at the *Freep* one evening when a staff member broke a wooden plank over the back of a former staffer.

The *Freep* has a whole history of staff squabbles and attempts to unionize, a history that is as complex as it is obscure. During one such conflict in the fall of 1969, the bulk of the paper's more creative staff members left. Many of them went on to form *Tuesday's Child*, a short-lived underground. For a while the *Free Press* faltered editorially. It seemed to have reached a plateau in circulation, and during the first months of 1970 the Los Angeles readership actually declined, although circulation increases outside the valley took up the slack.

Kunkin was not discouraged; the picture frame would fill up again, and it was true, too, that in the last months of 1970 and early 1971, the paper was displaying renewed editorial vigor and the circulation picked up. Nevertheless, during those very months when all the external signs of newspaper health were improving, the *Freep*'s financial position was steadily deteriorating. Kunkin did not, indeed could not and would not, *rationalize* his paper into a smooth-running enterprise similar to the *Village Voice*. Despite the bitter gossip of former staff members, Kunkin was no businessman. He had thought the printing press a good and necessary innovation. It had been his proud toy at first, but the press was proving a deadly drain on the paper's resources.

The printing press was being managed in a manner that might charitably be called casual. For the *Free Press* to continue to publish, it became imperative that the printing plant at least break even, and by the end of 1970 Kunkin was spending all his time out at the plant. It was no use. Kunkin was disliked by much of both the business and Movement worlds. To many Movement journalists he was Kunkin, the pig publisher, and they were happy enough to rip him off for printing bills. On the other hand, those business people with impeccable credit ratings were not about to give radicals any printing jobs; of course, those sleezy, marginal operators who always subsist on the edges of publishing had business to give, but as the recession deepened they had no cash to pay their bills.

The book stores were faltering also, and Kunkin decided he would have to sell out. Among rumors of how, all along, he had been earning an income substantial even by establishment standards, Kunkin sold the *Free Press* to Barry Bernstein, a local attorney who had been writing a legal column in the *Freep*. When this fell through, ownership of the paper passed to Therapy Productions, a rather shadowy outfit indeed.

Kunkin retained editorial control, but what could be made of these readers, these disaffected bourgeois, tourists, homosexuals, radicals, hip youths, swingers, closet Leftists, and curious? Even Mao or Che or Lenin would have had trouble molding anything out of such motley stuff spread out there in the sprawling urban village that is Los Angeles. And, it still seemed possible that the *Freep* might yet deteriorate into an updated example of yellow journalism, pandering not to the jingoism of the working class but to the indulgences of the "liberated" middle class.

That is the fate that was in store for the *Berkeley Barb* as well, a paper that has had some formidable labor problems of its own. In June 1969, the *Berkeley Fascist*, a satirical sheet, did some simple arithmetic and figured out that with 90,000 circulation and fifteen pages of ads, Scherr was netting $5000 a week. Even Scherr will admit that he was making "a hell of a lot of money"—very little of which was going to a staff still subsisting on tiny Movement wages. The *Berkeley Fascist* article led to six weeks of negotiations between Scherr and his staff—first for wage and other benefits, and then, finally, for Scherr to sell the *Barb* to his staff. It was to no avail, and on July 11, 1969, the 12-page *Barb on Strike* appeared. It featured as its logo not Don Quixote but Scherr spurring his mount onward with a spear to the buttock, dollar bills trailing off behind the galloping editor.

"Capitalist pig Max Scherr has locked us, some 40 members of the *Berkeley Barb* staff, out of our office and fired us for trying to turn the *Barb* into a model of the people's revolution," wrote Steve Haines in the *Barb on Strike*. "We felt that it is sheer hypocrisy for the *Barb* to mouth the words of revolution while lining Max's pockets with the people's cash. We felt that *Barb* profits should go for bail funds, legal-defense funds, medical clinics. . . . For us, the staff, we wanted enough bread to pay our rent and groceries. . . . Max refused to give us anything substantial. Max refused to commit anything at all to the community."

A Movement scenario for the bitter melodrama would have had Scherr realize that the *Barb* belonged to the community and step down, letting his staff turn the paper into a cooperative. Scherr, however, was the product of a previous Bohemian era. The *Barb* was very much *his* dream. Even Scherr's former staff gives him credit for having seen "the importance of developing our media . . . and almost alone having had the willingness to make the effort." Scherr was a member of the first generation of editors. Perhaps some of the others could change and accept the cooperative and communal forms. Scherr knew that he could not. And, too, basically the *Barb* was not socialist, anarchist, utopian, Movement, or radical; basically, the *Barb* was capitalist and Scherr was the owner.

Scherr did make some concessions, even offering to sell the paper to his staff—now reconstituted as the Red Mountain Tribe—at a remaindered price ($140,000), payable over a lengthy period. At first the Red

Mountain Tribe accepted, only at the last possible moment to back down. These euphoric sons and daughters of the *Barb* were not about to let a piece of paper entrap them, their free spirits, and in some cases their private incomes, especially when they realized that all those entangling legal responsibilities would not disappear even if the *Barb* were suppressed or lost its circulation.

Almost immediately, Scherr found another buyer, thirty-eight-year-old Allen Coult. For his $200,000 Coult became the owner of the "scab *Barb*." Anyone who owned it, worked for it, wrote for it, sold it, or even read it, risked social ostracism. Unable even to get handouts from Movement groups, and himself something of a hippie-come-lately, Coult dedicated his paper to the "New Revolution." "This revolution asks nothing from the Establishment," wrote Coult in his initial editorial statement. "It will allow the Establishment to perish in its own greed and corruption. The New Revolution will build a new world out of the love, work and knowledge of those who participate in it."

As it turned out the "New Revolution" was fueled on sex. When *Rolling Stone* cast its eye on the Berkeley/San Francisco underground scene in October 1969, it noted wryly: "Very roughly, the *Berkeley Tribe* wins on the bulk of news, the (San Francisco) *Good Times* wins on depth and variety of its content . . . and the *Barb* wins on tits (a total of 22, as compared with four, plus one cock, in the *Good Times:* no titties but one artful copulation photo in the *Tribe* . . .)" [1]

After several months Scherr managed to buy the *Barb* back. When he finally returned to his scarred-up desk in the summer of 1970, after recovering from a heart attack, the *Barb* was still a listless, sexed-up version of its old self with a third the circulation. It was put out now by people who all earned more money than the best-paid old staffer ever had, whom Scherr didn't even know, and who treated "Max." the granddaddy of the underground, with the respect and deference he neither wanted nor could tolerate.

Scherr tried to rejuvenate the *Barb* with his flamboyant mishmash of radical news, opinions, ideas and rumors. It was difficult, though, since Scherr had lost most of his radical or left-leaning audience; moreover, it was apparent that Scherr and his people could scarcely tolerate the new direction of the Berkeley Movement. Max, who had done as much as anyone to popularize the word "pig," did not care to see policemen shot down in the street. In August, when Ronald Tsukamoto, Berkeley's one Japanese-American policeman, was shot to death the *Berkeley Tribe* ran a two-page spread entitled "Why NOT Tsukamoto" listing the names of "brothers killed by the Berkeley police." The *Barb*'s article was entitled "Don't Chortle over Dead Cops." "Don't keep urging the blacks, the browns, the poor, the women, to go get guns then sit back and state: 'The movement has reached a new level of struggle.'" Instead, "the full force of the community—especially the youth and street people—must be brought to bear on the Berkeley Establishment and its Chief of Police, Bruce Baker."

To many this might seem like wisdom, but published in the *Barb,* the article could have little impact.

The RAG is
enjoined from
selling on
campus.

THE RAG

Vol. 4, No. 33
July 20, 1970
20¢ in Austin
25¢ out of Austin

2330 Guadalupe, Austin, Texas 78705   Phone—478—0452

"I envy you. You
North Americans
are very lucky. You are fighting
the most important fight of all -
you live in the heart of the beast."

6
The Arming of the Cultural Vision

The second generation of underground papers has not stagnated among fading psychedelia and hippie hyperbole or become the casual plaything of the alienated middle class. Now almost all papers have politically radical concerns, and it is only the crudest shorthand that allows one even to talk about *the* politically radical and *the* culturally radical papers. This cross pollenization has studded the landscape with hybrids that defy categorization. This is as true of people as of papers. After all, where can one place Abbie Hoffman, who grew up out of the civil-rights movement and now leads the Yippies as a self-styled "cultural revolutionary." Or Jerry Rubin, another political activist, who has let his hair down and become a Yippie. Then there is the *National Guardian,* now reupholstered as the *Guardian,* a journal of the New Left, and yet still highly Marxist, bragging that it "will not blow your mind." And the Weathermen, mixing acid, anarchy, Marx, rock and terrorism, and issuing proclamations ringing with all the moral certitude of a Cotton Mather. Just where do we place them and the papers that are their supporters. The best we can do, then, is to say that while this spectrum is hopelessly blurred, some papers are more Marxist and political in nature while others identify heavily with a youth-based radical culture and politics.

The culturally radical papers, direct descendants of the *Oracle* and early *EVO* began to cast off their kaleidoscopic politics of joy and good vibes well before the political radicals started marching with the banners of Marxist revolution. The earliest second-generation paper was

Austin's *Rag*, put out by members of "the left-wing love, flower and freedom sect anarchistic division of S.D.S." Austin was as logical a birthplace as any, since—be it 1965 Berkeley, 1966 Austin, 1968 Atlanta, or 1970 Gulfport, Mississippi—whenever the conscious nucleus of a radical-youth culture exists, an underground paper is born. Not a party, an organization, a cause, but a paper. The mere act of putting out that paper is the most valuable kind of radical organizing possible, and for a few months the paper *is* the Movement.

In the fall of 1966, while the *Berkeley Barb* was still proselytizing in its extravagant way and the *East Village Other* neared the peak of its creative powers, Austin, Texas, had its introduction to youth culture. It went under the name "Sweet Thursday"—a day when all the scattered freaks, hippies, and other radical flora and fauna were supposed to come out of hiding and just *be* on the West Mall of the University of Texas campus. The day seemed doomed to failure. At the beginning of the 1966–67 school year, Texas was still undisputed crew-cut country, hip culture just a minor sect. Sweet Thursday wasn't even sponsored by the university. It was an S.D.S. event publicized in a tiny new underground, *The Rag*.

On the appointed day they began to show up—hippies, folk singers, profs, dogs, frat rats, politicos, high-schoolers, Beats—until there were hundreds and hundreds spread out across the lawn, the most mind-boggling spectacle of hip culture's potential that Austin or the South had yet seen. Someone painted an old World War II plane in front of the R.O.T.C. building with the slogans "Make Love Not War" and "Fly Gently Sweet Plane." Others wrote graffiti on campus buildings, distributed helium-filled balloons and lollipops, and ran a balloon up the flagpole to fly triumphantly above the American flag.

It was a sweet Thursday, indeed, for S.D.S. and *Rag*. In those days they were very much the same people. Taking their highly cultural politics and a special set of enthusiasms, they turned *Rag* into what would become one of a few legendary undergrounds. *Rag* owes its reputation to having been probably the first totally Movement paper and having been singularly successful in creating a politically and culturally radical community in Austin. (*Rag* served its own community very well, and partly because of this it was rather boring to the outsider.) Many of its editors have gone on to play prominent roles on other undergrounds. Jeff Shero, a former vice-president of S.D.S., founded *Rat* in New York City. Dennis and Judy Fitzgerald and Thorne Dreyer moved to Houston and began *Space City!*

Rag's early days are looked back upon with justifiable pride and undisguised melancholy. "When I came to Austin in September 1966, the Movement was small," says Dave Mahler. "The number of radicals was so small that everyone knew everyone else. There were only fifty people or so. The people who were doing S.D.S. were doing the paper, and were doing Sweet Thursday. The people would go out and have a demonstration and then come back again and write about it. It was sort of easy. You were the Movement. There was a lot of creativity, because there was such instability. It was exciting also because things were so new. We could write about the Vietnam war without worrying about boring people. There wasn't much factionalism either."

The Movement is not a creature of any paper. It grows uncontrollably in directions underground editors can neither divine nor channel. In the mid-sixties Austin radicals were lucky to get two hundred people out for their antiwar demonstrations. Several years later, on May 8, 1970, what was perhaps the largest parade in Texas history marched through the city. There were an estimated 10,000 to 25,000 persons walking two-by-two along downtown streets to protest the Vietnam war and the deaths of four students at Kent State. "One campus politician guessed that half of the persons who marched in the parade had never participated in a protest march before," wrote the *Texas Observer,* and certainly most were not radicals or readers of the 3,500-circulation *Rag.*

That May peace march was dominated by liberals, but Austin has a large radical community. Texas Right-wingers can quote chapter and verse on the "radicalization" of U. of T.; they offer as prime evidence Jeff Jones, the 1970 student president, a radical, a *Rag* staff member, and thanks to the media something of a household word in Texas. The streets offer their own evidence filled with hundreds of long-haired dropouts, teeny boppers, high-school freaks, hips passing through on the great American road.

The *Rag* has not evolved to take in this enlarged, amorphous radical community. The circulation is 3,500 but that is a paltry total compared to the 1,500 figure in 1966–67, when there were so few radicals. Part of that potential readership has gone to the *Daily Texan,* the student paper, that now covers the news with a decidedly left-liberal slant. And part is not interested in the uneven mishmash of articles and information the weekly *Rag* provides.

At the beginning the *Rag* had an editor—or "funnel," as he was called to differentiate him from the preeminent editor of traditional publications—and assorted staff positions. After the first year Thorne Dreyer, the first funnel and an instrumental force in shaping the paper, left to go to New York.

The *Rag* set out to develop a paper that would truly be a radical institution itself, and this is one of the fundamental distinctions between the first- and second-generation papers. On all the earliest papers there had been a clear distinction between "shit workers" and the creative staff, and an equally clear distinction between the idealism of the articles and the offensive tenor of much of the advertising. The *Rag* takes no advertising that might be considered sexist or dishonest. Moreover, the paper has broken down its hierarchical structure to such an extent that by 1970 the *Rag* had by far the most anarchistic structure of any underground.

The *Rag* developed the egalitarian structure not to assuage bruised egos or pay out a few tokens of prestige to all members of the volunteer staff, but to develop a community. These Texas radicals were trying to create an organism healthy and developed in all its parts, with a commitment and discipline growing organically out of the community, not out of any formal structure. They had gone beyond the spiritual utopias of *EVO* and the *Oracle* and were seeding a kernel of utopia in the Texas heartland.

The *Rag's* administrative work is done primarily by the "bureaucrat," the one paid staff member ($35 a week). The paper itself is put out literally by whoever shows up for the weekly editorial meeting and layout night. The "staff" ranges from six or seven people to about forty, with an average of fifteen or twenty. There are grad students, freshmen and upper-classmen, a couple of high-school students, even an assistant professor. Few of these people look on the *Rag* as their primary outside interest—or, to use the circa-1960 term, "extracurricular activity."

Layout night is—well—weird. It is functional anarchy. People keep wandering in and out of the bare little office in the "Y" above Somner's Drug Store across from campus; occasionally looking in on the Y.M.C.A.'s "bad-trip" center next door, where counselors talk people down from their paranoia; laying out a page; rapping; drinking soda; showing a story to that week's "copy coordinator," the one rotating position and the person responsible for seeing that somehow or other everything gets together and is sent to the printer. "When I first came to the *Rag* in the summer of 1969," says Gabbin Duffy, "it took a couple of weeks before anyone would even talk to me." This can go the other way. One first-time visitor found himself typing stories; after a couple of hours people started asking his advice on this and that story or how to manage one function or another.

The staff box in the June 29, 1970, *Rag* suggests the inexplicable,

helter-skelter manner in which the paper is put together:

Staff

. . . And it came to pass that many were called but few were chosen . . .

. . . but fewer showed up . . .

Dave wrote about Traffic and Music and the RAG/YD suit plus did the Rag Rag, Phil wrote about the Food Coop and laid out page 4, Mike was around all week and forgot to buy layout sheets but laid out page 12 on the back of a Traffic poster and Jon laid out pages 14 and 15, Bill did News Briefs, Jude and Joanie did the Center Spread. I laid out page 2 and Michele.

A lot of people dropped by during layout and Dave attacked Phil with an aggressive glass of Chember's Ice Tea. Jim gave his legal opinion on the Cartoon and I laid out that page too.

Joyce typed the whole thing and Nick did some ads and Alan did the photos and Amber laid out page 5 and just because I walked into the meeting late Monday I was the coordinator.

And Gavin is back already and Amber, Mike, Dave, Phil, Berry, Michele and a lot of other people typed and made this RAG possible for you to enjoy and hold dear to your heart until this very next time next week.

JOHN

It is no mean achievement to put out a weekly newspaper without any hierarchy of tasks and obligations. For many new *Rag* staffers that is the most vitalizing and original aspect of working for an underground paper. At first, it is somewhat unnerving. Trained to work under the omnipresent eye of authority, many people simply don't know what to do. Eventually, though, most learn to maneuver in their freedom and make a contribution to the *Rag*.

The paper is able to roll along—

never more than $100 ahead, scraping together the $60 rent each month, arguing to be allowed to sell on campus, parceling out *Rag*'s to anywhere from half a dozen to over thirty street sellers, hassling with printers—because it is not raked with sectarian political squabbles. Of course, there is that inevitable split between political and cultural radicals, but it has not turned into a knock-down-drag-out contest between Champions of Absolute Truth as it has in New York and Berkeley. Like the anarchist workers of nineteenth-century Spain and Italy, so far removed from the schisms and divisions of London and Geneva that they remained united, these Austin radicals do not pay much attention to distant disputes. "We're the freaks section of the Movement," says Duffy. "By freaks I mean we're people not hung-up on petty ideological things." They are not hung up primarily because, even now, they profess a highly cultural radicalism.

When Jeff Shero left the *Rag* to found New York's *Rat* in the spring of 1968, it was inevitable that the new paper also would become part of "the left-wing love, flower and freedom sect anarchistic division of S.D.S." But this was no longer 1967, and many of the flower children had grown thorns. *Rat* consciously set itself up as a political alternative to the *East Village Other*. Gone was *EVO*'s and the hippies' heady optimism; *Rat* was as interested in survival as in apocalypse. Shero called the paper "subterranean" rather than underground and imbued the sloppily laid-out pages with a sense of a grubby, yet irrepressible youth community—a community of the Lower East Side and of New York in gen-

eral, rather than simply of the psychedelic world of the East Village.

The paper melded personal accounts of demonstrations and protests including a special Chicago Convention issue with a long article by Tom Hayden ("We are coming to Chicago to vomit on the 'politics of joy,' to expose the secret decisions, upset the nightclub orgies, and face the Democratic Party with its illegitimacy and criminality"); articles on rock that helped popularize such stars as Jeff Beck, Frank Zappa and Phil Ochs; perceptive reviews of movies and plays; political articles; intriguing graphics and collages; and featured as its symbol a rakishly posed rat armed with a machine gun, saying in the first issue, "Watch out, Punch Sulzberger!" It was not only rock musicians that *Rat* brought to consciousness of its audience but ideas about ecology, women's liberation, imperialism and other concepts that would soon grow up out of the underground.

Rat set out to speak for New York's radicalized hippies who made fists not peace signs. Several months later they would pop into the nightmares of Middle America as the Yippies—the dirty, vulgar, profane, unpredictable, unreasonable Yippies, who ran wild through the streets of Daley's Chicago and tried to nominate a pig for President. From the first issues *Rat* actively politicized the hippie community.

"Society moves as the 'movement' moves," wrote *Rat* in April 1968. "The kids on the Lower East Side who had survived the winter didn't need the organizing experience to know the same things the organizers had learned. They knew it in their guts. They knew where the hippie entrepreneurs were at. They knew all about the media-inspired 'Flower Child' phenomenon and its equally mythological 'East Village.' " *Rat* had already realized that turning on, tuning in and dropping out were no longer so terribly radical. Soon everyone from account executives to teeny boppers would be turning on to marijuana. Soon the aboveground media would be so fully tuned into the counter culture's ideas, music, and styles that little of that mind-blowing quality would be left in the underground press.

Whatever faith these politicized hippies may still have had in youth culture pure and simple was soon dissipated. *Rat* had been enthusiastic when Bill Graham, the rock impresario, opened the Fillmore East. Graham seemed honest, ready to give full value to the rock audience. He even passed out hot chocolate on the cold opening night. When Shero interviewed Graham he gave him every opportunity to talk about the revolutionary aspects of rock. Graham, however, was not about to have radical motives imputed to what was essentially a business enterprise. He spoke with the mature wisdom some might consider tainted with cynicism:

RAT: People say that rock music is maybe a revolutionary expression of a new generation. And that it's kind of the cultural manifestation of a whole new set of ideas; a new art form for the young people. Do you think that that is a correct description?
GRAHAM: No.
RAT: You think it's just music?
GRAHAM: No, it's good music; it's following along progressively. Why wasn't it said when be-bop came in or modern jazz or the Modern Jazz Quartet began,

or when Szabo plays or Coltrane? Why weren't all these people a new art form, a revolutionary movement? [1]

Graham was just a businessman, but Janis Joplin, the late blues singer, was something else. *Rat* had praised her extravagantly as a part of their culture, as one of them. So during the summer of 1968 Shero and Thorne Dreyer went to the Chelsea Hotel to interview their fellow Texan. She told them that in the past two days she had talked with *Life, Look, Time,* and *Holiday.* "What do I want an interview in a little old hippie publication?" she said. "Look, if you can convince my publicity manager it's important, I'll do it." The two underground journalists never bothered to try.[2]

It seemed, sometimes, as if every aspect of their culture—from clothes to music to language—was being dismantled, crated up, and shipped into the outer room of the Establishment. To remain radical these Yippies would have to invoke the territorial imperative, to protect the hip culture that they thought was theirs. They invigorated their anarchistic, highly cultural radicalism in another and, for them, a highly logical way—by almost methodically beginning to rip off the system. At first this was a different concept to get across to young Americans whose day-to-day morality consisted of familiar homilies learned in home and school, plus the fear and expediency learned in the streets. In March 1968, when *Rat* published an article on how to sneak into the subway ("The first rule is never to stop if anybody says something to you, or calls out 'Hey!' "), the reaction was immediate and overwhelmingly negative. Two weeks later in the next issue, *Rat* felt compelled to offer a small lecture: "Once you break through the news-speak rhetoric of the Great Society, it becomes not only moral but liberating to throw a monkey wrench into the machine. Not to pay for the subway; not to buy from the A&P; not to think in their terms, and therefore, not to speak their language. Then we do everything we can to destroy their system, and in the process attempt to build something new based on humanity." In future issues *Rat* detailed how to cheat corporations, how to get free medical help, and how to get on welfare ("You just have to show up at your local welfare center, broke, and with some touching explanation, and the city will give you enough money to stay alive").

By 1970 the new ethic was taken for granted. This was especially evident at gatherings of youth culture. Rock entrepreneurs from Atlanta to San Francisco approached their concerts with trepidation. As likely as not, young long-hairs would stand massed at the entrances shoving and screaming to be let in free, effectively gumming up the mechanisms of once lucrative businesses. Thousands arrived at rock festivals without tickets or any intention of buying them, and the brief epoch of the gigantic rock melas seemed likely to end not because of the mean and often vicious opposition of the middle-aged Establishment but because young radicals had turned these dues-paying meetings of Woodstock Nation into invitations to bankruptcy.* Shoplifting, already *le vice Américain,* has become a way of living. Welfare is popular, and in Berkeley food stamps are even an occasional means of exchange.

Rat's journalists not only passively attacked the system, but actively participated in the most militant demonstrations, courting arrest and bodily injury. At the Columbia University revolt in the spring of 1968, *Rat* staffers were inside the buildings taken over by students, and the paper's "Heil Columbia" issue gave an accurate account of what it felt like to be taking part. Here, spread across the pages, were incriminating documents that had been taken from President Grayson Kirk's office. Here were richly evocative accounts and pictures showing the police coming in through the windows.

The Columbia revolt profoundly changed the lives of hundreds of students and the course of the entire student movement. To understand that, one must go to the underground press rather than to the cartoon realities of *Strawberry Statement* or the tepid objectivity of the Establishment press. Here, for instance, are

---

* *Never underestimate the ingenuity of the American entrepreneur. In August 1970 at the Goose Lake Rock Festival, in Michigan, 200,000 youths parked their cars in lots officially named "Layolot," "Astralot," "Tripalot" and "Takealot," and walked down "Kilo Road," "Freak Street," "Zonked Avenue" and "Do It Street" to the entrance, where after paying fifteen dollars they continued past uniformed guards with guns or clubs, mounted guards, a "mobile unit" of bikers, an electrified fence, barbed wire, and a ten-foot brick wall into the 390-acre private part for three days of sun, dope and rock. "Like you feel like you're in a concentration camp back in Germany," one participant told Changes, a rock magazine. "Like it isn't really America."*

LIBERATED
DOCUMENTS
PAGE 8

may 3-16, 1968

n.y.c. 15¢ outside 25¢

RAT

SUBTERRANEAN NEWS

HEIL COLUMBIA

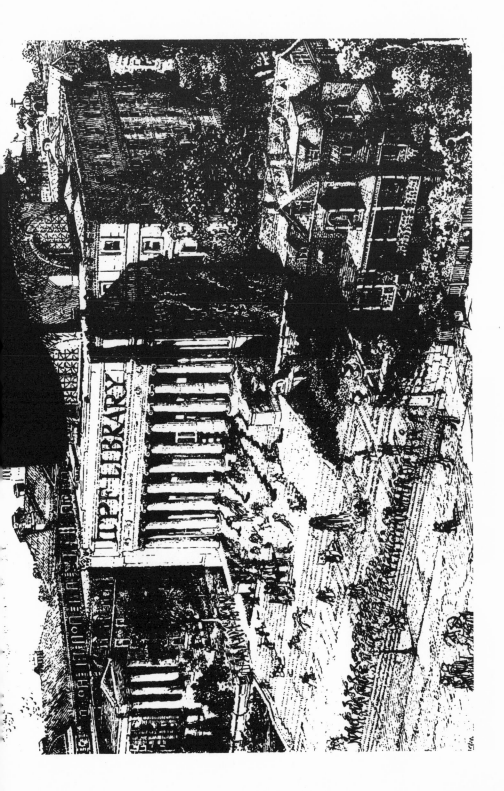

excerpts from Jeff Shero's story dealing with experiences inside Low Library:

. . . Segmented time lost its normal meaning, sleepless hours blurred into sleepless days. While events crashed, racing through the minds of the participants changing them more swiftly than months of arguments ever would, certain movements, sometimes inconsequential, stand out like rays of clarity in the jumbled joy and strain of the time. . . . A Negro sargeant [sic], supposedly guarding the ledge outside the Presidential suite, made friends with the window watchers and when he got too cold gladly took a glass of the President's imported sherry. . . . Sir Stephen Spender, the elderly British poet, climbed through the second-story window to greet the students. Some, unaware of their guest's fame, demanded forcefully to know if he was a reporter. Reporters weren't allowed. . . .

The Vignettes are pleasing, they give a certain reassurance that everything is the same, that the status quo oscillates and then returns to normalcy. But during the first few days new political precedents slowly formed and solidified. Participants by the hundreds realized new concrete possibilities in their lives and were forever changed. Alliances between black and white, between the campus and the community, the exaltation of people over property and the unchallenged participation of outsiders in the struggle—ideas found only in radicals' fondest pot dreams slowly emerged into realities.

During the siege, whites and blacks held separate halls, with little communication, yet the blacks refused deals for amnesty just for themselves, instead they told the mediators and the public—amnesty for all and not only an end to gym construction, but get rid of IDA as well. The distrust woven into the minds of whites and blacks for hundreds of years, unraveled just a little.

The press screamed about the disrespect for property and the destruction brought about by the demonstrators. Then the Administration called in the Police, which spread more destruction in hours than the demonstrators did for days. The demonstrators began to work on a new principle. If the cause is just, if we are right that Columbia's role in the counter-insurgency of the IDA means more efficient death for Vietnamese, and its seizure of property in East Harlem perpetuates crippling racism, then we should hold our position as effectively as possible. Tear off a door of Grayson Kirk's cabinet to build a stronger barricade or smash a window to get desks to block up a basement; it's judged much better than smashing another person's skull.

A third precedent was set, a problem which is still a matter of great debate at Berkeley. During the blockade nonstudents from both the black community and the white radical community joined in, and no students bothered to raise the issue of outsiders. It became as legitimate for a radical to go to Columbia as to the Pentagon. The University was no longer seen as a protected island, freed from outside involvement and participation. Just as the administration works with the corporate leaders and fronts projects for the CIA and the military, so the students work with forces outside their narrow community.

The development which held the most pathos was the tortured, self-searching role of the faculty. Except for the handful of radical professors who backed the political demands, most of the faculty attempted to save their position by being mediators; protectors of order. But the conflict was polarized. Those who wanted to maintain harmony in a discordant atmosphere had no real power or position. The faculty became more faint-hearted after the initial leftward surge, as employees of the University they identified with the institution they had learned to live with. Maintenance of the institution was repeatedly stated as more important than the issues at stake. Most blockaders felt the University was an integral part of an oppressive system, an idea which the professors who built their lives on academia could not accept,

The conflict still unfolds. It seems the Administration made the fatal mistake of overplaying its hand, and has done great damage to itself. But then another possibility exists. Steve Weissman during the Berkeley Free Speech Movement observed that the Administration saved the Movement time and again from extinction through its blunders. Good luck? No, he would respond, the bureaucracy is so rigid, unresponsive to the needs of the community, and subject to a system of outside control that it couldn't help but blunder into mistakes which outraged an academic community. He argued it was the nature of the system.

And so may it be now. Leaders like Mark Rudd are singled out as instigators, but the crises are much more thoroughgoing. The struggle at Columbia has sparked new dreams in students throughout the country. It's now only time before "Columbia" is imitated with new intensity throughout the country.[3]

One did not have to be a radical or a liberal sympathizer to appreciate the Shero article and *Rat*'s Columbia coverage in general. A reader might disagree violently, but at least he would learn what the students felt and how the protest had affected them and their lives. No aboveground medium even came close to conveying that reality.

There was another special kind of protest that grew out of this resurgent cultural radicalism, a protest that had nothing to do with either conning the system out of goods or actively demonstrating. This was media manipulation. Since cultural radicalism is based on the concept of a spiritual-youth nation ("Woodstock Nation"), media manipulation was a

logical weapon. Thomas King Forcade, who radiates a fierce Yippie joy and anger and who is by far the most outspoken spokesman for the Underground Press Syndicate, is one of this new hybrid of hippie and radical. A minister in the Church of Life, a small hippie sect, in March 1970 the Reverend Forcade interviewed Abbie Hoffman, a master at the art of media manipulation, for the UPS news service. It was a rare exchange since Hoffman—a Movement superstar, a Yippie, and one of the Chicago 8—usually plays the media game with such as CBS and *The New York Times*. As often as not he ignores the underground press:

FORCADE: Tell me how you've been so successful in using media.

HOFFMAN: Get them to promote an event before it happens. Like the thing about Washington, Chicago, the Pentagon demonstration, uh, to get them to write about an event. In other words, to do an ad, you know, to make an advertisement for the event. . . . You gotta study the techniques that they use in advertising, and the one thing they don't do is have very straight press conferences. Chicago in a way was a hype. It was a lot of bullshit about what was going on. But, out of that, because of what happened there, not in the sense of the way we predicted it, but still it was a very offensive and important event in American political history, especially as far as we relate to it. The people that got involved had a certain strange kind of power. We didn't have it then. . . . Now I think in terms of television. All we can do is create certain kinds of images, and get people to react to those images. Make yourself visible. That's the way I relate to television. I'm more interested in what goes on in prime time than what goes on Meet the Press and those things on Sunday. That's totally irrelevant. All those fuckin' pigs they parade there. That's irrelevant.

FORCADE: What do they watch?

HOFFMAN: Well, I'll tell you what they do watch. Every fifteen minutes there comes an ad for Brillo. And they say, you want Brillo? Brillo will get you laid. Brillo will. You can brush your teeth with Brillo. It's the greatest thing in the twentieth century. . . . At the end of the fucking show, nobody's bought any of the ideas the people are putting forth on Meet the Press, or any of their education. They're buying fucking Brillo. Because that's what TV's for. It's all shit. That's why they spend $150,000, $200,000 on a three-minute commercial. That's why they do it. They spend more on the commercial than on the show. And the best talent goes into that. Sometimes I feel much more rapport with people on Madison Avenue in terms of them understanding that whole rap. You know, that whole difference between education or rhetoric and information. People don't understand it.[4]

In May of 1970 Forcade and several friends, themselves practitioners of media manipulation, drove down to Washington to use Yippie principles to ridicule the President's Commission on Obscenity and Pornography. Forcade, who was scheduled to testify, had costumed himself with theatrical good taste in a black suit and clerical collar and a broad-brimmed black hat. His companions were dressed in kind; the two twin schoolgirl daughters of a lady in the UPS office in black leather jackets, jeans and berets; another young girl in a granny dress; and several others wearing their everyday hip best.

Inside the hushed hearing room, the group spread out among the spectators and reporters and passed out underground papers, mimeographed handouts, mirrors inscribed "this is pornography," and "joints" rolled out of oregano instead of marijuana. No sign of irritation crossed the resolutely impassive faces of the commission, and they remained full of their unrestrained dignity and seriousness of purpose, even when Forcade launched into his testimony:

The Constitution of the United States of America says "Congress shall make *no* law . . . abridging freedom of speech or of the press." This unconstitutional, illegitimate, unlawful, prehistoric, obscene, absurd, Keystone Kommittee has been set up to recommend advisable, appropriate, effective, and constitutional means to deal effectively with such traffic in obscenity and pornography. To this we say, fuck off, and fuck censorship . . . Either we have freedom of the press, or we don't have freedom of the press.

The Underground Press Syndicate has repeatedly encountered your brand of political repression in the thin but transparent guise of obscenity, despite the obvious fact that the primary content of Underground Press Syndicate papers is political and social writing. This becomes even more obvious when underground papers are compared to the millions of tons of specifically salacious and prurient four-color crotch-shot magazines which are readily available in the same cities where underground papers are repeatedly busted for "pornography." We know where you're coming from. Besides, arousing prurient interest in America IS a socially redeeming value. So fuck off, and fuck censorship . . . The Underground Press Syndicate has been harassed unrelentingly since it was founded in 1966. . . . The following papers have been victims of censorship in the last three years. Beware of them, for they are the free high-energy source that will drive us wild into the streets of America, yelling and screaming and tearing down everything that would keep people slaves.

Now Forcade turned on his cassette tape recorder to Bob Dylan's "Ballad of a Thin Man" with its taunting refrain: "You know something's happening, but you don't know what it is, do you, Mr. Jones?" And he read the names of forty-five underground papers in a voice full of tense, tightly controlled anger:

". . . *Fifth Estate, Distant Drummer, Dallas Notes, San Diego Street Journal, San Diego Door, Rag, Space City News* . . ."

Even after the last name was read, Dylan continued singing. "I'm sorry, Mr. Forcade but I don't understand what's happening," said the commission chairman, Dean William B. Lockhart of the University of Minnesota Law School. Forcade smiled.

When the music stopped, Lockhart asked for questions.

"Would you mind explaining to me how we have engaged in 'McCarthyesque witch hunts and inquisitional hearings'?" asked Otto N. Larsen, a commission member, and professor of sociology at the University of Washington.

"I think I have the material in my box to explain that," Forcade said and walked over to Larsen at the semicircular rostrum. Reaching into the box Forcade pulled out a cream pie and—SPLOSH—threw the pie in Larsen's face. The pie slithered down the professor's face and came to rest in his lap.

Larsen maintained his composure. No outrage. No cry of disbelief. "Don't bug me, I'm asking you a question," Larsen said.

Forcade's face paled. Where were the inevitable police? Nobody moved. He had totally freaked out the commission. "You're violating the Constitution," he said.

"Mr. Forcade, I guess we've had enough from you," said Dean Lockhart. The UPS representative and his friends packed up and hurried out.

"I just wish they'd reacted more," Forcade admitted as he walked out. The commission had been totally incredulous. They had hardly reacted at all. It had been almost embarrassing. But it wouldn't matter if the pie throwing got good coverage in the media.

Several hours later tooling up the New Jersey Turnpike, the front-seat passengers took turns fishing across the radio dial to catch news of the hearing. Nothing. Nothing. Nothing. ". . . Forcade, a youthful Yippie leader, threw a . . ." It was magical. Coming out of that loudspeaker was an event created and packaged by the media guerrillas. Just as Abbie had said, Forcade had power. ". . . and in Washington, Thomas Forcade . . ." It was working.

In New York the *Daily News* had a dramatic front-page photo of Forcade flinging the pie. The headline over the story itself was pure Yippie stuff: "A PIE SMEARS SMUT PROBE Underground Press Arises." Wow! *The New York Times* and the *New York Post* were good too, and all over the country the story got a big play, almost always with pictures.

No one can maintain his dignity in the face of a cream pie, and no matter how objectively journalists may have tried to write their stories, only one message got through the chuckles and guffaws—that this swashbuckling Yippie hero had completely bamboozled the President's commission. Never mind that the largely Johnson-appointed commission was

A LIBERATED NATIONAL PUBLICATION/NEW YORK/MAY 23, 1970/25¢

LIBERATED *Guardian*

against obscenity laws. Never mind that the commission was attempting the first significant research into the nature of pornography and obscenity in this country. Never mind that the American public is hopelessly misinformed about obscenity. That story was not told in the American media on May 14, 1970. It was lost somewhere, victim not only to a cream pie but to the formulas of daily journalism.

The cultural guerrillas had succeeded, but their very success pointed out the limitations of media manipulation. Their dramas can fill the television screen, magazines and newspapers with evocative and symbolic vignettes that erode the myths, rituals and truths on which the American society is based. The cultural radicals, however, cannot put forth their counter myths, rituals and truths with such impunity. Rational discussion is not among their weapons; neither can it be given the flashy, transient nature of what we have learned to call "news." Thus, never will the media guerrillas be able to say, "If only they had listened!" Their message is seen and felt rather than heard.

The cultural radicals are able to put forth their ideals and myths in their papers and in their lives. The *Chicago Seed,* for instance, has done away with its editorial structure and replaced it with an admittedly imperfect collective of nine people plus a score of others who come in and out of the office. "It's an editorial amoeba that oozes toward putting the paper out," says Abe Peck, the former editor. Most of the core collective live together in two houses and they are all paid fifty dollars a week.

There is such human richness in these communes—even if they fail. Now that even resolutely conservative couples live together and chastity has become a kind of fool's gold, communes are perhaps the one radical life style left. Each one has an organic life of its own. Each one is the tender bud of community in a society of almost intolerable loneliness. Fully realizing this, most underground papers have tried to evolve in an egalitarian and communal way. Sometimes this had involved the creation of a new paper, as with the *Berkeley Tribe* or the *Guardian,* the old-left weekly that is not even a part of the underground. In the spring of 1970, many young workers struck the *Guardian* charging that the twenty-two-year-old newspaper had a traditional hierarchy and had grown isolated from the Movement. They went on to form the *Liberated Guardian,* a highly political paper that does have close ties with LNS and the underground press.

Working on the *Seed* or any underground paper can be the most magnificently vitalizing experience. "You see, man, on the *Seed* people enjoy their work," says Abe Peck. "No matter how great a fuck-up it is. Like Linda, she's a shy kind of person who went through America being told she couldn't do a fucking thing, that she had to be a secretary. But her life became insufferable at that fucking *Playboy* building on Michigan Avenue. She just couldn't do it anymore. So she came to the fucking *Seed,* man, like she came in a very draggy way as a typist. Even that was better for her. Like it was her paper too. And now she's taken over as advertising manager. She takes such pride in it. I mean like before, just

SEED

CHICAGO   VOL. 5, NO. 4   35 CENTS

SPECIAL THANX ON THIS COVER TO THE
DISNEY ESTATE & THE SAN JOSE RED EYE

for her to make a phone call was colossal. And like now she's just written an article for the paper.

"She's changed because we've all changed. We learned that dominance wasn't the only way you could be a man. We learned that there ain't that much time to go running around doing bullshit things that subjugate people, and women in particular."

On the *Seed,* women are very definitely rising up, not only demanding equality, but stimulating the paper in new and important ways. This was only natural, since the underground press began talking about the women's liberation movement long before the mass media took it up, and underground journalists have begun to incorporate the ideas into their lives well before they will profoundly affect society as a whole. One paper, *Rat,* was even taken over by women in early 1970. And when two male editors of San Francisco's now defunct *Dock of the Bay* decided to put out a sex magazine "to make money for the Movement," the infuriated women staffers ripped up the proofs.

Nothing like this has happened on the *Seed,* and the *Seed* is much more than print content, be it women's lib. or anything else. More than any underground since the *Oracle,* the *Seed* transcends those arbitrary boundaries between print and graphics. Each page is printed in a different color, almost every issue has an extraordinarily beautiful centerfold, and there is an incredible attention paid to finding original or unusual drawings, pictures, cartoons, wood-

cuts and designs for every page; graphics that enhance the print content of the paper just as the print content enhances the graphics. The *Seed*, quite simply, is the most stunning-looking paper in America.

The *Seed*, with a circulation of over 40,000, is probably the most heavily cultural major underground in America. Almost no one of the staff has actively worked in the political Movement. "We're dropouts," says Peck. "Like I come from dropping LSD and dropping out from graduate school. Linda dropped out of working at *Playboy* as a secretary. Someone dropped out of high school. A couple dropped out of speed. Another dropped out of junk."

For all its bright colors and hippie veneer, the *Seed* is surprisingly political and highly radical in its analyses. An October 1970 issue (Vol. 5, No. 11) contained articles on high-school revolts; a piece on ecology; an analysis of Third World developments; articles on the Black Panthers; a long story on women in advertising and another on lesbianism; a nuts-and-bolts article on the radical use of communes, liberally quoting John Sinclair, the White Panther leader; plus a number of cultural articles. The *Seed* has grown increasingly radical over its three years of publication. "We used to think that rock and dope was the fucking revolution," says Peck. "That's the hippie thing. Now we're still hippies, a new kind of hippie. We've come to realize, man, that culture and politics are inseparable. It's all one ball, a ball of fused elements. That's the jump. And like people have followed us. Our circulation has gone up. Our feedback has grown up. Hip culture has grown up. It grew up like peni-

cillin grew up. It grew up in the corner, nobody saw it, and suddenly it was a miracle drug. And people said, "Penicillin, far out, far out.' But then something showed up in the disease that was resistant to penicillin. Everyone went into a funk and they went back to the laboratory. Eventually they got other drugs too. So penicillin's like dope, music, fucking in the streets. We need that, but we need something else too. Now when we have the big cure it's going to be culture and politics all fused together."

Another paper to have fused these elements with particular success was the *Berkeley Tribe*. The paper began in August 1969 during the strike against Max Scherr's *Berkeley Barb*. Scherr's former employees, reconstituted as the "Red Mountain Tribe," took Scherr's training in the who-what-and-whys of the journalistic craft, and adding a communal life style, and a ground swell of euphoria and energy, they created a paper that fairly pulsated with vitality and soon reached a circulation of 53,000. It was clean-looking and graphically exciting. It was a Movement paper, most of the staff considering themselves nonsectarian radical-revolutionaries, and yet the *Tribe* sustained that feisty Berkeley spirit, merging the life style of cultural radicalism with New Left political radicalism.

On the cover of the first *Tribe* stood nearly the entire Red Mountain clan—naked, fists clenched to the sky, faces radiating unabashed, unashamed communal joy. Inside Stew Albert wrote: "I think it was necessary for us to first love and then to hate Max, and now we must learn to understand him. Max had a dream of something beautiful, but his soul had a broken slave at its center telling him the dream was a lie and he and his brothers were certain to fail. The dream was true but the slave chained us all. The *Barb* never really existed except in the printed word. Max's slave was the master of us all. Now we are free and the dream will be honored in the flesh. Max Scherr was a corrupt prophet, but the Tribe has at last come out of the wilderness."

The Red Mountain Tribe carried out of the wilderness many habits learned at the *Barb*—including much of the paper's structure. The *Tribe* listed some forty names on the masthead in helter-skelter, egalitarian fashion; nevertheless, there was an editor, assistant editor and business manager, all of whom had held similar positions on the *Barb*. The joy was something else. It was very much *their,* the Red Mountain Tribe's paper. It was *their,* the Red Mountain Tribe's, Movement as well. And although the early *Tribe* never covered Berkeley with the *Barb's* comprehensiveness, its articles had an intimacy of concern that feared neither humor nor self-criticism, and a style, a series of styles, unhampered by journalistic conventions.

The special meld of print and graphics that is an underground paper beggars description. This is especially true of the *Tribe,* which managed to balance articles on the Weathermen against analytical pieces on the Rolling Stones; somber pictures of David Hilliard, the Black Panther Minister of Information, against brilliant caricature by Ron Cobb, the Movement's Daumier. It is impossible to describe; but several excerpts from articles, chosen because they typify that blend of culture and

politics, can perhaps suggest what the Red Mountain Tribe was getting at. There was, for instance, a piece by "Marty" in the October 10–16, 1969, *Tribe* telling "The Truth about Telegraph Avenue":

Telegraph Ave. is constantly besieged by professional media people with their cameras, tape recorders and notebooks in a futile attempt to satisfy this country's hunger for insight into the "hippie phenomenon."

Although they are able to photograph, tape and write about all the varied street scenes, they are plagued by an inability to understand the condition, the situation and the future of the people and the street as viewed by those who live and work there. These newsmen don't see kids barfing in the street at 3 in the morning from smack, or two friends walking someone who took too many reds.

They don't see people sitting in front of Cody's late at night listening to a guitarist singing folk songs. There is a lot they don't see, but most of all don't feel, because they are not part of the street they are trying to capture on film, tape and in notes. . . .

The term "street people" includes a lot of different kinds of people. I will not attempt a definition, for I believe we defy the basis for definition. Each person is an individual, and as a group we cannot be joined together as a class.

Dislike and hate for the street people is not confined to the straight world. Many "successful" hip people come down hard on us too. We are called anti- or counter-revolutionary, yet we are played with like pawns in the revolutionary chess game by both sides, and the hip capitalists want us to get paying jobs. We are claimed to be hateful and self-centered, yet I have seen more love and sharing and less egoism, between street people than in other areas of the hip community. . . .

Every species has its predators, and

BERKELEY TRIBE

PUBLISHED BY THE STAFF OF THE FORMER BARB

PUBLISHED WEEKLY BY RED MOUNTAIN TRIBE — P.O. BOX 9043 BERKELEY, CA. 94709 — 122 WALLER PRESS — VOL. 1, NO. 13, ISSUE 13 October 3-9, 1969 — **15¢ BAY AREA** 25¢ ELSEWHERE

the people of the street have more than their share. The police are the most vicious of our enemies. . . . Another predator stands safely on the street beside the cops, with his long hair blowing in the breeze—the pusher. Steppenwolf said in a song, "God damn. I said God damn the pusher man," and a lot of people on the Ave. are starting to agree. . . .

There is a beauty to the street, and this is where the failure of words, or the ability to relate experiences, comes into the picture. How can I communicate the feeling of a clear warm night at two in the morning on the street rapping as if we were old friends with someone I have never seen and will never see again. Or the freedom of living on the street, or the people who are close to me. This friendship can't be put down on paper, for everyone to feel as I feel it. . . .

We don't have leaders because we are all leaders. We are from a thousand different places and on a thousand different trips and we're getting closer together because we are tired of being prostituted by those seeking gain at our expense.

Then there was Stew Albert's piece on the Chicago conspiracy trial entitled "At the Flick" in the December 5–11, 1969, issue:

The Conspiracy trial is two movies being shown at the same time to a jury that must select its favorite. Both films cover the same historical event—the Democratic Convention, but the style and plot are so different that each film's aficionados are willing to go into the streets over a matter of taste.

"Establishment Unlimited" has made a Grade-3 black-and-white pro-police flick of the early 1950's. Its stars are selfless pigs who seek to head off the destruction of a great, patriotic and prosperous city. Through dint of tireless and very dangerous undercover work, the police are able to locate the perpetrators of criminal anarchy, discover their plans and, after a spectacular and violent chase scene

covering all of Convention Week, foil the plans.

Finally, a court of very Christian law throws the culprits into the dungeons they deserve for ten years. . . .

Things are harder for Establishment Unlimited because of the groovy underground flick being shown at the defense table. And what's being shown has only been the trailer for the spectacular to come.

The underground flick has no script. It is heavily spontaneous and tries to convey to the jury a sense of what things are really like. It tries to show that the Establishment production is bullshit despite its brand name. It tries to convince the jury that guys into this kind of underground-movie trip could never conspire to do anything except smoke dope and fuck—or in a quick pinch—defend themselves. . . .

The festival award will be presented by people who were raised on Establishment Productions products and tend to see everything through its myths. But lately they have been getting bored with the same old thing and are looking around for something new. . . .

Maybe their repressed desires for adventure will lead them to vote for us and tell the pigs to go fuck themselves.

Nobody really knows what is going to happen, but Foran is getting shaky. He knows that in a theater of freedom we have all the style.

For a few short months the *Tribe* was one of the most exciting underground papers in America, the most vivid evidence imaginable that radical politics and radical culture could be merged—even if only in the youth ghetto that is Berkeley. In 1969, however, the *Tribe*s and the *Seed*s were in a decided minority. The self-conscious political vanguard of the underground press considered hip culture something of an indulgence if not an outright fraud.

Volume Three, Issue Seven   Copyright/Atlanta Cooperative News Project/1970   February 16, 1970

great speckled The·BIRd

15¢!

25¢ outside Atlanta

"THE WALLS, THE BARS, THE GUNS AND THE GUARDS CAN NEVER ENCIRCLE OR HOLD DOWN THE IDEA OF THE PEOPLE. AND THE PEOPLE MUST ALWAYS CARRY FORWARD THE IDEA WHICH IS THEIR DIGNITY AND THEIR BEAUTY."

Huey P. Newton

7
The Arming of the Political Vision

Mass struggle plays hell with your poetry.

— JOHN REED

ip culture seemed self-indulgent and inbred, particularly to those who had organized in the heartlands of the South, sat-in at draft boards and taken an active part in the civil-rights or antiwar movements. These radicals, too, were discouraged by the failures of their basically reformist efforts. But when they looked for new tools to end racism in America and bring the GI's home from Vietnam, they were drawn inexorably not toward a revitalized cultural radicalism but to Marxism and political revolution. These ideas could not help but affect the underground press, and by 1971 there were many papers that thought of themselves as propaganda weapons in the struggle for worldwide Marxist revolution.

To liberal intellectuals, who have lived through the Cold War, this transformation is the epitome of stupidity and sheer intellectual dishonesty. There is no need here to tell once again the grim litany of Stalinist abuses that so thoroughly disenchanted that generation of intellectuals and writers from Marxist theory and leftist ideology generally. The legacy of that disenchantment was such that in the early 1960's, Movement intellectuals and journalists would brag about the New Left's lack of ideology, and its direct existential quality. This was more than adolescent prattle to get on with the job without thought or scheme, for these young Leftists had inherited an intellectual tradition that had soured into near scholasticism. Neither was it simple anti-intellectualism. It was, as Carl Oglesby, a former S.D.S. president writes, "a necessary defense against the power of an exhausted but nonetheless practiced ideology, the net effect of whose truths might easily have been to send the activists packing to the socialist clubs, where they would have been made either skillful at writing themselves off as change agents or bored. They wanted neither. They wanted instead to go south and get their hands and their heads—their lives—into the dangerous, the moral and, therefore, the authentic. The instinct from the beginning was to discover the streets, and there was nothing at all antiintellectual about this. It embodied rather a refusal to tolerate the further separation of thought from its consequences: books argued with each other and lied and in any case did not make much of a difference; only direct experience was incontrovertible." [1]

Unfortunately, improvisation is as limited a form of politics as it is of theater, and by the late 1960's, as the Movement burgeoned into this country's first mass radical movement since the decade from 1910, it was obvious that the politics would have to take a more substantial form than that unfettered, free-flowing one of the early days.

The Movement's basic critiques had become widely accepted in many communities—thanks in good part to the underground press. The *Barb,* for instance, had weaned thousands of young people away from traditional American patriotism. Yet once that jump in faith was made, where was one? The *Barb* represented no party, ideology, religion or cause. It was a scribe for the Movement's many manifestations, neither inventive nor profound. In Berkeley, now largely a community of the "saved," the *Barb* had no one left to proselytize. "They're banging on the heads of those who already are convinced," says Terry Hill, who edited the *California Daily* during the summer of 1969. "All the exposés in the world don't have to do with a thirty-two-year-old cripple being beaten by four T.A.C. patrolmen."

The underground press and the New Left generally have had to develop other forms to remain highly relevant to such highly politicized centers as Berkeley. But why Marxism, a belief that in this past half century has been abused and warped almost beyond recognition? Don't these radicals realize, as George Lichtheim writes, that "few things are more pathetic than the 'practical philistinism' which fails to see the connection between thinking that animates a movement and the practice allied to, and largely dependent upon, the thinking"? How can anyone not see that Marxism is morally and intellectually bankrupt?

In the first place these New Leftists did not come upon Marxism as a historical tradition or as an active part of their intellectual heritage Indeed, in the mid-sixties, when the New Left and Movement papers occasionally presented an article that unblushingly applied Marxist analysis, an article as often as not written by European radicals, it seemed as incongruous as a piece by a dietitian in a gourmet magazine. Not only did these young Americans reject Marxism on their own, but Marxism had been so thoroughly and self-righteously expunged from the intellectual life of our universities, that these young radicals knew almost nothing of it; moreover, the very fact that the New Left had had no ideological underpinnings had often been considered by academic and journalistic supporters as a sign of undisputable virtue and—need one add—proven Americanism. Thus, when young radicals, in their search for tools to create a truly radical New Left, came upon Marxism they came upon it not as one of those essential but limited tools for understanding contemporary society, but as the ultimate font of wisdom.

Some members of this new generation grasped at Marxism with the same religious fervor that earlier cultural radicals had shown to such concepts as "rock and revolution" and "the hippie revolution of the spirit." For them, the result may well be the same—that Marxism will recede back among the potpourri of ideas and sentiments that is radical-youth culture, as an added and necessary element but not as the sole bearer of the truth. For the Movement as a whole, Marxism will probably provide the essential metaphor, the basic structure and class analysis on which the Left will build. Marxism's contribution, then, will be to have given the Movement a tradition, a revolutionary tradition, for the self-conscious vanguard of the Movement and the underground press are now avowedly revolutionary.

One result of all this is that the distinction between the more political underground papers and traditionally radical papers such as the *Guardian,* the independent Marxist weekly, or the Trotskyist *Militant* is no longer enormous. Both the New Left movement and the underground press are less and less "movement"—ideologically unhampered politics, flowing and ebbing with events. There are fixed points, a catechism of belief. "People at the (S.D.S.) convention understood that the political

stakes have been raised," wrote *Movement,* a national S.D.S.-oriented newspaper, in the summer of 1969. "Either you're for the N.L.F. or you're for imperialism, you're for black liberation or you're for racism." Once unfurled, these banners of belief have led New Leftists to struggles among themselves over strategy, theory and ideas. By January 1970, *Movement* was printing fewer and fewer personal accounts of political struggles. That had always been the guts of the paper, and an editorial analyzed what seemed to be wrong: "This, we think, is mostly due to the political problems that the movement in general faces: fragmentation, the inner directness and changing priorities of collectives, and correct-line-ism (people become afraid to make even tentative evaluations of their struggle, for fear of being labeled 'racist,' 'Economist,' etc., etc.). . . ."

Liberation News Service's allegiances have long been with the most Marxist side of S.D.S. "S.D.S. led the way during the important struggles in the student movemvent," LNS's Allen Young told John Burks of *Rolling Stone.* "It has been really important in helping the Movement develop its ideas and its growth. On the whole the growth of the Movement is largely attributed to S.D.S. LNS also believes that organization and collective action are necessary, and that the best organized force—the best white organized force—has been S.D.S. S.D.S. has always rejected escapism, as have we—going off to live in the hills or on the farms, or excessive use of drugs, like speed in particular."

LNS generally accepts the S.D.S. analysis that the primary conflict in the world today is between United States imperialism and the oppressed peoples of the world. This transfers the Marxist class struggle into an international conflict between the capitalist, exploitative United States and the revolutionary forces of the Third World, including the oppressed minorities of America. This thesis is all the more compelling since during most or all of their adult lives, the LNS collective and other radical editors have daily seen, heard and read of the Vietnam war, where, against all odds, logic, predictions and precedents, the Viet Cong and the North Vietnamese have fought the world's greatest power to an apparent standstill. They have read revisionist history and social science to buttress their view of America as an imperialist power in a foundation of fact. Some LNS people and many underground editors across the country have even seen at first hand a Third World revolutionary society—in Cuba as members of the Venceremos brigades. As often as not, such a visit infused the word "revolution" with credibility it cannot have living in the United States, where revolutions run the gamut from cars to cassettes.

In their revolutionary struggle the LNS collective displays a kind of dedication that is rare among underground papers. Twice a week they write, print, and mail out 20- to 40-page packets of articles, Movement information and graphics. For this service, the five hundred or so subscribers are supposed to pay $20 a month. However, most can manage to send in their money only sporadically, and the LNS collectives are lucky to get their full $35 subsistence pay each week.

LNS is not a terribly groovy environment. The office is not located in the East Village but on the crumbling rim of Harlem adjacent to the northernmost extension of the Columbia University campus. There, in the basement of a soot-stained apartment house, behind barred doors, shaded windows and a double-locked door, the LNS collective put in their five-day, mid-morning-to-late-evening weeks.

The main room, the print shop, and the cluster of tiny offices are dank and austere. The office is lighted by the steely-cool glow of fluorescent tubing. The walls are bedecked with pictures of Che, Fidel, and Song My; the tables and chairs are covered with papers, pamphlets, and all the various clutter one might expect in a busy, unpretentious newspaper office.

The LNS collective is promiscuous neither in sex, nor in emotion, nor in ideology. Their lives are so involved with one another's and with LNS that it is difficult for anyone without a partner in the collective to become a real part of it. Most of them live together in several apartments in the Columbia area. They do not live with the spontaneity and unpredictability of the old LNS. They attend demonstrations and actions together. They eat together every weekday evening. They are by no means purely political. They try to root out elements of male chauvinism. They condemn anyone who is "ego tripping." They watch carefully to see that no one becomes "the leader." They struggle to create a truly egalitarian collective.

As often as not, the LNS packets are bare of cultural materials, and they seem light-years away from youth culture. The content is generally a meld of international stories dealing with radical advances anywhere from Uruguay to Guinea; news about demonstrations and actions throughout the United States; and internal news about Movement affairs in the United States. There may be articles by LNS correspondents in Beirut, Berkeley, New Haven or Vientiane; during the summer of 1970 there were special reports from LNS writer-photographer teams in Africa and Latin America. The packets are charged with Movement-building uplift. On a regular basis they provide a sort of tally board of latest actions, past and future demonstrations, trials, riots, repression, uprisings, bombings and achievements. This is a compilation that no traditional paper or news service would ever provide and that creates the inevitable impression that day by day the United States is moving closer to revolution. "Our journalism is designed to propagandize," says Allen Young, once a leading LNS spokesman. "We're trying to demystify the word *propaganda*. We think that our political movement is based upon truth. We try not to be shrill and full of jargon just as we try to eliminate bad spelling."

When LNS articles are based on solid reportage and intimate knowledge, they can be as startling politically as the early underground papers were mind-blowing culturally. LNS presents a vision of a world so different from the one set forth in most American papers that the reader is practically forced to accept the account either whole cloth or not at all. Here, for instance, are excerpts from a story that Sheila Ryan and George Cavalleto, LNS correspondents in the Middle East, mailed out

of Amman during the hijacking crisis in September 1970:

AMMAN, Jordan (LNS)—TWA, BOAC and Swissair jets lay glittering whitely under the desert sun like three huge, delicate sea gulls that had lost their way. A long line of gracefully undulating camels threaded their way between the planes and the squat, mottled bugs that were the camouflaged Jordanian Army tanks encircling the area.

This was Revolution Airport on Thursday, Sept. 10. The airport, a long strip of hardpacked desert, was guarded by a large force of commandos from the Popular Front for the Liberation of Palestine; they had dug slit trenches for defense. "PFLP" was emblazoned in red paint, in English and Arabic, on the bodies of the planes, and Palestinian flags hung over their open cabin doors. Delighted Palestinian children in small khaki uniforms were brought out to see the airport.

On Sunday, Sept. 6, the PFLP had hijacked three planes. (A fourth attempt, on an El Al flight, failed when a security guard shot one commando to death and captured the other, a young Palestinian woman named Leila Khaled.) One of the hijacked jets, a $24-million Pan American jumbo jet, had been flown to Cairo; minutes after the passengers and crew had safely scrambled from the plane, it was blown to bits.

The other two aircraft were flown to Revolution Airport in the desert northeast of Amman; the PFLP had occupied the barren area and improvised landing lights. On Wednesday the Swissair and TWA jets were joined by a BOAC plane hijacked by the PFLP during a flight from Bahrein, a British colony on the Arab Gulf.

The Pan American jumbo jet was captured and demolished, the PFLP declared, because "The USA is responsible for the poverty and inhuman conditions of the Palestinian people, because it gives Israel all the support it needs to expel the Palestinians from their home-land. . . ."

In hijacking the planes, the PFLP reached up into the sky—where the stewardesses were serving martinis to passengers on their way back to the U.S. after a summer in Europe or Israel—and pulled 409 people and the attention of the world down to the Jordanian desert, on whose perimeters Palestinian refugees have been living for 22 years.

There was great concern about the passengers being held in the desert heat —though they were supplied with port-able air-conditioning units. Not too far away from Revolution Airport, at Schneller refugee camp, Palestinian fami-lies are packed sometimes ten to a room in tin houses that are ovens in the summer sun.

At Revolution Airport during press conferences reporters inquired anxiously of passengers held in the planes about the stench of the toilets; open sewers flow through the refugee camps, and every summer hundreds of children die of diarrhea, as flies spread disease from the sewage.

As the hijacked passengers ate cheese, bread, jam, butter, meat and sometimes chicken dinners, the press worried lest the food supply run short. In the refugee camps, people are subsisting on UN ra-tions of less than 1500 calories a day.

When the water supply at Revolution Airport was rationed, the media pitied the passengers; in many refugee camps in Jordan, the central water taps are turned on for a few hours daily, and they stop flowing before all the families have filled their jars. Some days there is no water at all. . . .[2]

The LNS graphics are a perfect counterpoint to the articles. No cute cartoons. No psychedelic drawings. No bright caricatures. But pictures, posters and drawings charged with militancy and political statement. The photographs are probably the most successful creative aspect of LNS's journalism. For over a year, they were the primary responsibility of David Fenton, an eighteen-year-old high-school dropout. A brilliant craftsman, he is the most widely reprinted photographer in the Movement. "I have a special thing I want to do photographically," Fenton told

one reporter. "I go into normal everyday oppressive situations and photograph the alienation and despair—in high schools, like, and clerks in stores—the corruption of American society." He photographs a high-school student slouched beside a row of urinals taking a private drag on a cigarette. He pictures a lithe slim youth running from a mammoth horse and mounted patrolman. In New Haven, at the May 1970 pro-Panther demonstration, Fenton—dressed in a fatigue jacket and crash helmet with film containers taped to his camera strap—wended his way through tear-gas-laced streets, often within reach of bayonet-carrying soldiers, crouching, ducking, running, retreating, snapping scores of pictures, getting a few extraordinarily poignant and evocative photographs.

In the fall of 1970, Fenton and Allen Young, the two best-known and most professionally competent collective members, left LNS after being accused of "ego tripping" and "male chauvinism." LNS announced it would be printing only one packet a week for a while to allow time for the collective to evolve a new structure and underground editors who wanted to visit were asked please, please, to call a day in advance and set up an evening appointment.

Most papers, be they primarily politically or culturally radical, have something of an internal split or tension between the cultural and political forces. *The Great Speckled Bird* in Atlanta presents a particularly clear example of this. *The Bird* is something special, as befits a paper that takes its name from a Southern spiritual that in turn comes from the Old Testament ("Mine heritage is unto me as a Speckled Bird the birds round about are against her: come yet, assemble all the beasts of the field, come to devour"). Despite its namesake, *The Bird* has no use for that heavy, well-wrought, Biblically inspired Southern prose. There is a casual sophistication to much of the writing and a cool graphic brilliance that gives each issue unity and clarity. Doubtless that has helped the paper in its rise to become the largest paid weekly in Georgia (circulation 18,000).

Success or not, *The Bird* has remained completely and uncompromisingly devoted to the Movement. The paper was born in March 1968 and was an antiwar, antiracist newspaper. There were twenty or twenty-five people involved. These included Tom Coffin, a graduate fellow in English at Emory University and a Reed graduate; Gene Guerrero, Jr., and Howard Romaine, both working with the National Student Association (N.S.A.) to start a free university in Atlanta; Jim Gwin, a Harvard grad and former Vista volunteer; other grad students, young professors, a lawyer, and several other Vista volunteers.

Just as in Austin two years before, the 1968 Atlanta Movement was small. No more than ten or fifteen people considered themselves organizers and the primary antiwar organization was the Atlanta Workshop on Non-Violence. *The Bird* could define,

almost become, the Movement; and those first "Birdmen" saw no reason to dilute their message with liberal *ifs, buts* and *howevers.* In that very first issue *The Bird* took on the one sustaining symbol of Atlanta's white moderates, an ikon liberals carried forth to combat like Italian peasants with their plaster saints, the legend of Ralph McGill, the editor and publisher of the Atlanta *Constitution.*

What's It All About, Ralphie?

—DON SPEICHER

Died. Ralph McGill, editor, publisher, early civil rights advocate, pragmatic realist, manipulator and leading exponent of U.S. Imperialism and deception; of pronounced self-righteousness and senility, compounded by both the Red and Yellow perils; in Atlanta, Washington, Saigon, Newark, Hanoi, Detroit.

Born in Tennessee around the turn of the century, McGill soon learned the ways of gun totin' (he called it his spare pencil) and corrupt political machines. Although a onetime supporter of progressive civil rights causes, albeit not unfalteringly, McGill later denounced these ties and began to re-bait the progressive camp himself.

More recently when his sense of southern guilt, sentimentality and maudlin self-preoccupation along with his credo of "objectivity" proved unable to cope with contemporary political realities, McGill withdrew to the nuclear-powered, riot-controlled tower of liberal reason and rationality, from whence he never returned.

He is survived by his daily column, nationally, but most certainly, syndicated.

Thus the Great Liberal passes from

us. Who will forget his courage, his leadership and his clear wisdom?

"We are in Hanoi for many reasons—including a treaty. But we are also there because the security of the future demands we be there. We are there, too, because we are the only world power able to do what must be done."

And: "We are very close to the necessity to use the small strategic nuclear weapons. We cannot put massive armies to the task if the task comes.". . . Here lies the crux of the Liberal method of argument, McGill's method, that of the Pragmatic Realist, the "Objectivist." The invocation calls for reason, reality and rationality, and presumes those qualities to be possessed by only one side, his side. With this method such blatant evils as the Ku Klux Klan may be condemned. But so also may the insane use of nuclear weapons against a peasant people be suggested—with, of course, reason and rationality. . . .

Less than a month later, Martin Luther King, Jr., the one sustaining symbol of black liberalism was assassinated at a motel in Memphis, Tennessee. *The Bird*'s cover for the third issue pictured Joe Hill, the I.W.W. leader, with the words "Don't Mourn Organize IWW Joe Hill Murdered Nov. 19, 1915" a wreath around the portrait. At the bottom of the page were the words, Martin Luther King, Jr., April 4, 1968. On inside pages were excerpted portions of Dr. King's recent essays calling for a unilateral cease-fire in Vietnam and a deadline for United States withdrawal; and his remarks that "A nation that continues year after year to spend more money on military defense than on programs of social uplift is approaching spiritual death." Gene Guerrero, Jr., the first chairman of the Southern Student Organizing Committee (the Southern radical organization), a draft resister and a former textile-union organizer, wrote the lead article, "I Have a Dream . . .":

Martin Luther King's dream of creative nonviolence which would be able to move America has been slowly dying for several years. With his death the dream has probably died as well—killed not by some poor white Southerner, but by American liberals.

Watching the television coverage on the night King was shot it seemed that white America might be shaken into some positive action. One of the most striking images was that of Chet Huntley on NBC, genuinely shaken by the shooting, speaking again and again of how the rest of the world must think that the United States is a nation of killers.

Next day, however, Huntley was back to his old self, as white America. The front-page editorial by Eugene Patterson in the ATLANTA CONSTITUTION stated, "It is now that he must depend on the people he loved and died for to honor his life by living its lesson and not forsaking him for the violent men he fought. This is the great memorial Dr. Martin Luther King, Jr., most wanted his people to raise. Let him not have lived in vain."

At the same time Ralph McGill attacked poor white racists burdening them with the responsibility for racial violence.

These men and their brothers have buried King's dream. Martin Luther King was not the simple, gentle, riot-preventing moderate these men would have us believe. Nor is the racial crisis in the U.S. a conflict between poor white racists and Black Power advocates.

King was a gentle man who spoke of love and of nonviolence, but he spoke even more often of the deep sickness gripping this country. Throughout his struggle King tried with success to maintain a militancy which spoke to the heart of the problem while allowing whites

GREAT SPECKLED BIRD

Volume One, Number One   A Publication of the Atlanta Cooperative News Project © 1968   March 15 - 28

What's It All About, Ralphie?

-- don speicher

Died. Ralph McGill, editor, publisher, early civil rights advocate, pragmatic realist, manipulator and leading exponent of U.S. Imperialism and deception; of pronounced self-righteousness and senility, compounded by both the Red and Yellow perils; in Atlanta, Washington, Saigon, Newark, Hanoi, Detroit.

Born in Tennessee around the turn of the century, McGill soon learned the ways of gun totin' (he called it his spare pencil) and corrupt political machines. Although a onetime supporter of progressive civil rights causes, albeit not unfalteringly, McGill later denounced these ties and began to red-bait the progressive camp himself.

More recently when his sense of southern guilt, sentimentality and maudlin self-preoccupation along with his credo of "objectivity" proved unable to cope with contemporary political realities, McGill withdrew to the nuclear powered, riot controlled tower of liberal reason and rationality, from whence he never returned.

He is survived by his daily column, nationally, but most certainly, syndicated.

Thus the Great Liberal passes from us. Who will forget his courage, his leadership and his clear wisdom?

"We are in Hanoi for many reasons--including a treaty. But we are also there because the security of the future demands we be there. We are there, too, because we are the only world power able to do what must be done."

And: "We are very close to the necessity to use the small strategic nuclear weapons. We cannot put massive armies to the task if the task comes."

And: "Unless reason and realism come to North Korea and Hanoi, those who advance the squalid theory that only their country is to blame will be able to choose the moral war of their choice--a grisly choice, to be sure, but a possibility, unless reason and reality can be invoked."

Here lies the crux of the Liberal method of argument, McGill's method, that of the Pragmatic Realist, the "Objectivist." The invocation calls for reason, reality and rationality, and presumes those qualities to be possessed by only one side, his side. With this method such blatant evils as the Ku Klux Klan may be condemned. But so also may the insane use of nuclear weapons against a peasant people be suggested--with, of course, reason and rationality.

The liberal's insistence on Reason is the source of his power and the center of his deception. He says, "Let us put aside moral stands and emotional outcries and consider the situation objectively by carefully examining all the facts. Let us reason together." This guise is used to make his conclusions appear to be the only rational ones, thereby making all objections and disagreement irrational. This is the big lie.

As practiced by McGill and other liberals born of the Cold War, the approach assumes that they alone have a monopoly on reason. cont p. 7

 CHIRP

Greetings. We're here. Part and parcel of the Great American Scene. The Great Speckled Bird. Hear, hear.

"So how come?" you ask (or maybe you don't, and maybe you don't care. In which case we may well ask the same of you.) But we're here, as they say, to do our thing. Which being: to bitch and badger, carp and cry, and perhaps give Atlanta (and environs, 'cause we're growing, baby) a bit of honest and interesting and, we trust, even readable journalism. A rare thing, you must admit, in America today.

But above and beyond, we are also trying to offer some alternatives to what some call "The American Way of Life." Enervating plasticity. A depressing lack of meaning. And the fear is frightening. Ah, we say, systems are not sacred. People are sacred. And if a system is dehumanizing, destroy the system, not the people. For somehow we must learn to live with one another, or die. We

must discover new ways to solve our problems, or die. We must acknowledge that change is inevitable, or die.

But: To criticize in America today is "unobjective." To protest is "irresponsible." To dare suggest the need for basic change, radical reform, is blasphemous. And the labels are ready: Nigger, Hippie, Commie, Peacenik. The whole bit. On one day peace demonstrators may be attacked by such men as Ralph McGill, publisher of the Atlanta Constitution, who next day very rationally determines that the use of nuclear weapons in Vietnam may well become the only "reasonable" and "responsible" course for us to pursue! Insane? Obscene? And American.

So we live in this nation of steel and concrete, plastic and glass, bombs and bullshit. We are led by men who wish to control but who are themselves controlled, for they live in an age long past. We are talked at by media which explains everything, understands no-

thing. We eat our tranquilizers, drink our alchohol, and curse those dirty Commies (or niggers or hippies) who so threaten "Our Way of Life." We are a nation not of sheep but of puppets, repeating the old slogans, using the old formulas, knee-jerking through life, afraid of tomorrow, afraid of today.

But men are intelligent when they try to think and understand, honest when they can be, courageous on principle. And people, especially the young, are now tired of the pap-feeding, the absurd sloganeering, the lies, the bullshit. With the discovery that our plastic civilization is hollow and void, these the "turned on" seek meaning. Through involvement. Political activism. Art. Drugs. Involvement.

So that's how come. That's where we are. Learning to live despite America. And to the gentlemen of HUAC, we are indeed subversive.

Tom Coffin

opportunity to respond creatively. He tried to serve as a bridge between the younger militants and the "concerned" white community. His success may be measured by the statement made by Stokely Carmichael following his death that King was the only man in the older generation of Negroes that his generation would listen to.

But King's greatest problem was the attempt by America's liberal leadership to make him one of their own—a "responsible" leader. They tried to do this by emphasizing King's nonviolent approach to rather than his critique of the problems in America and his programs to change the country. While King was alive he was able to elude their grasp by speaking forthrightly about racism and other problems. To the distress of the Patterson-McGill liberals he opposed the Vietnam War, which he viewed as the basic stumbling block to peaceful and nonviolent change.

But now that Dr. King is dead, his dream is smothered by those who have been making pious sermons on nonviolence, gentleness and heart-searching, but who offer no meaningful programs to end the burning and the killing both in America and in Vietnam. Their assumption of nonviolent posture without King's critical understanding of the American sickness is a blasphemy on his name.

The Bird had broad intellectual concerns as well—long reviews of books that wandered in and out of ideas in a manner familiar to readers of *The New York Review of Books;* first-rate film criticism; interviews with musicians and artists; coverage of art shows and local theater. In its politics the paper sought to create a uniquely Southern radicalism based as much as anything else on dormant populist tradition and directed primarily at a student audience. These were largely the views of S.S.O.C.,

taken up by *The Bird* because S.S.O.C.'s first three chairmen—Guerrero, Gwin and Howard Romaine—all were *Bird* staff members. "What alternative to electoral politics is posed to white middle-class students (and professors) who every year flock to the Stevensons, Kennedys and McCarthys," Guerrero asked in the May 24–June 6, 1968, issue. "The alternative is becoming ever more clear; build a movement based on the personal exploitation of middle-class students (and professors) and from that base attempt to relate to the needs of the black movement, the Chicano movement and the labor movement." It was a middle-class politics, but after all that was *The Bird's* natural turf; the paper probably had the highest proportion of master's-degree holders, grad-school dropouts, and Ph.D. candidates of any underground in the country.

That original vision, nurtured and neatly trimmed in the groves of academe, did not last. In the first place the *Bird* house, a rambling old building about to be torn down, chanced to be on 14th Street near Peachtree. Soon "14th and Peachtree" came to have much the same meaning as "Haight and Ashbury" or "Saint Mark's Place." It became Atlanta's and the South's prime center of hip culture. Of course, in 1968 there were only fifty-or-so hippies, freaks, Beats and Bohemians; nevertheless, a symbiotic relationship developed between the paper and the community, *The Bird* needing the hips as street sellers, and the hips needing to sell *The Bird* as their surest source of income.

The local media, seeing long-hairs peddling the strange tabloid on the street and sidewalks of the city, dubbed *The Bird* "the hippie paper" and after a few months summarily pronounced the hippies dead. "The last really visible sign of the community," wrote Reg Murphy in the Atlanta *Constitution* in December 1968, "is a troubled tabloid newspaper, *The Great Speckled Bird.*" This was long before the paper considered cultural radicalism as one of its prime concerns. By 1970 the main white "mass struggle" in the South was between the hips and the straights. It fit no textbook pattern, yet no radical media could possibly ignore it, and *The Bird*'s cultural and political coverage evolved to serve the new audience.

The original politics did not last either. There was much that was callow and self-serving in those early views. Still, such a politics contained an openness and humanity that might serve well even today. Immediately after the 1968 Presidential elections, Tom Coffin, then the editor, wrote an essay that suggests that humanity.

Election eve, 1968, on the Georgia Capitol Lawn: 50 young people, arms outstretched, fingers in the V-sign; separated (and protected) from 6000 Confederate and United States flag-waving Wallace supporters by a double blue line of Georgia State Patrolmen. A meaningful tableau.

On the outside of the police frame, surrounding the Speaker's platform are the "rednecks," Wallace supporters . . . and also, of course, the Working Class: hardhat construction workers, department store clerks, secretaries, grade and high school teachers—taking their lunch hour to cheer the man who speaks for them. Hard-working people, 8 to 5, five days a week, to whom overtime is an economic blessing. Racist probably, and anti-communist certainly, for that is what

they have been taught. Racism is ingrained in the white American psyche, it is an integral part of the white American system, taught in the schools and in the streets. . . .

Facing them, inside the police frame, are militant blacks, white students, bearded peaceniks: they are educated and hip. They recognize the intellectual vacuity of the threats either of Communism or Black Power, fearing rather the aggressive militarism and the destructive racism increasingly out of control in this nation. They see, that is, the other side of the coin.

But theirs is now the Politics of Alienation, of Isolation. They stand incommunicado in this group, scorned and scorning, surrounded by a police force they neither respect nor trust—but on whom has fallen the duty to preserve peace in a potentially explosive situation, which duty they performed, for the most part, with efficiency, restraint, honor. And they were called pigs indiscriminately. . . .

Can we convince them that the war system is ultimately not in their favor by mocking chants of Fascist, Fascist, Fascist? or the 8-to-5 working people, from whose families most of us came: does our long hair and liberal profanity convince them of our Freedom, does it make our Alternative attractive, does it question their beliefs or merely mock them? If we are serious about revolution, these questions we must ask ourselves. For we need allies in revolution, active and supportive, and we need neutrals, especially the police and the army. Now we must find these allies, create these neutrals. We have taken the first step in a 40-year war; that first step must not be the last. . . .

Funeral services for *The Bird*'s loose, folksy radicalism were held at Mount Beulah, Mississippi, in June 1969. There at a weekend conference, under intense S.D.S. pressure, S.S.O.C. was dissolved and the mantle of white Southern Movement leadership passed to S.D.S. and its Marxist internationalism. *The Bird's* Bob Goodman attended the meeting and wrote about such national S.D.S. figures as Mark Rudd and Mike Klonsky with respect, even awe. They were

more rigorous in their analysis, more serious, more willing to accept both personal and organizational discipline, more conscious of the necessity to take security measures, more inclined toward theoretical thinking but also acutely aware of the danger of divorcing theory from practice. Their outlook is national and international rather than regional. In their willingness to postpone the benefits of the revolution until after the revolution, and in a tendency toward single-minded rationalization of one's whole life toward making the revolution, they are already second cousins to Godard's Chinoise. Their immersion in Marxism has permeated their outlook and might transform their practice. They would rather be correct than numerous, and they do not hold to the view that any kind of movement is better than none.

There was a purism, even a preciousness to this sort of analysis. It foresaw a day when those bearing the True Dialectic could retire to mountain or garret to await for the revolution to spring full-blown from their foreheads. It was not the tonic *The Bird* needed, though the staff followed doggedly alone. The kind of Marxist analysis S.D.S. stood for had no more interest in the idiosyncrasies of an individual or region than a biographer has in the history of his subject's arm and legs; and so, *The Bird* could no longer flaunt its regionalism with such impunity.

The Bird has found itself in a political and psychological limbo, unable to relate to any of the competing radical organizations of 1970 Atlanta and spread-eagled between the pulls of the cultural and the political radicals. *"The Bird* is not relevant to any one group," says Ted Brodek, an instructor of Central European History at Emory and an original staff member. "This may be pleasing to intellectuals, since it's such a potpourri. Intellectuals can read *The Bird* and learn just when various ideas came into currency. It's like a catalog. When did the Panthers become prominent? When did Women's Lib become important? The paper is terribly neutral and diffuse, even in its coverage of the Movement itself."

Many staff members are profoundly threatened and insecure as *The Bird* struggles to break out of its aloofness, to take that second step. No one offers his allegiance to other institutions, other dreams. No one leaves the paper. There simply are no alternative institutions. Success has brought its own kind of failure. Fourteen full-time staff members earn $40 a week, a pittance but enough to provide individual apartments, cars, movie tickets, records, and all the other artifacts of the *haute* hippie life style. "There's just no struggle like in the old Movement S.S.O.C. days, when everybody lives together," says Charlie Cushing, a long-time staffer. "Now it's a pretty good job. The whole system works with the idea of working hard to earn money. And that's just the way *The Bird* works."

Even the new *Bird* house conspires against change. It is a spacious warehouse in a diffuse business-residential area miles from the hips or any other community. Here, among partitioned offices that reach only part way to the curved roof and hangarlike steel struts, is a fit setting for the intense psychological and political conflict that was the primary preoccupation of the 1971 *Bird*. No hierarchical superstructure exists to channel and refine personal and editorial conflicts, since the paper long ago moved into the more egalitarian, collective or communal work structures. In fact, as far back as March 1969, Tom Coffin, who had edited *The Bird* with literary distinction and executive airs, stepped down to be replaced by an editorial committee with a rotating managing-editorship.

Since then, Bob Goodman, universally acknowledged as something of a "structure freak," has developed a finely tuned system of rotations that include not only the top editorship, but all "shit work" positions. The system gives each staff member a specific area of editorial responsibility and control—ecology, racism, military, Women's Lib, hip community, culture, imperialism, Movement, militarism, political economy, sexism, reactionary right, housing, communications media. This leaves each managing editor *pro tem* with the thankless task of coordinating copy, acting as a time clock and occasionally a pest.

Such egalitarian and frankly utopian structures demand individuals filled with a sense of common struggle and common goals. This simply is not the case at *The Bird*. Gone is the invigorating, unifying danger of publishing in the radical hinterlands that so enlivens, say, the *Kudzu* people in Jackson, Mississippi. Gone, too, is the challenge of standing in the self-declared forefront of the struggle, a challenge that infuses Berkeley's *Red Mountain Tribe* with

a tolerable measure of self-importance. What is left is that familiar cultural-political split, but here tenfold more prominent and fought over with the weaponry, energy and deviousness of a group-therapy marathon.

Staff meetings often are monstrous, headless, amorphous blocks of time. They are subtle, highly stylized plays for power, male-dominated for the most part. The women, however, are heard with increasing regularity since they formed their own weekly caucus in the latter part of 1969. "Women traditionally acted against one another backing *their* man," says Stephanie Coffin. "We decided that we would stop all the endless gossiping and backbiting. Of course, the same divisions are found in the women's caucus that are found in the paper as a whole. But we have developed a rare solidarity. We've been able to stop many of the power plays by standing up and saying what's going on. It has brought our discussions up from the level of personality to one of real issues and politics." By the summer of 1970 the men had their weekly caucus as well, but the debilitating tensions and the basic cultural-political split remained.

The political radicals want the paper to see beyond hip culture. They hope to look out at Atlanta's white working class, whose most repressed elements are sullen and inbred, measuring out their lives in beer and babies. They think of muckraking articles, flashy exposés to erode the uncertain liberalism of many college-educated Atlantans. They imagine alliances of common interest and purpose with black groups. And they envision cultural coverage that once again might in-

Volume Three, Issue Sixteen

April 20, 1970

The
great speckled
BIRD

now 20¢!

25¢ outside Atlanta

Free vietnam Apr.18

Free the Earth
Apr. 17-24

clude art galleries and plays and jazz and country music. In all this the idea would be for *The Bird* to serve as an organizing tool. Ideally, these journalist-activists would write their weekly articles out of deep-felt knowledge, achieving a telling intimacy, concern and radical-logic. For a political radical this is a compelling vision. Yet somehow this faction of *The Bird* has not been able to move out on any of this, to dare to try.

To cultural radicals, *The Bird* itself *is* the primary organizer. Their argument is that already and almost despite itself *The Bird* has become a symbol to youth across Georgia of "our" media, the one sustained product of noncommercial youth culture. The paper has provided income for hundreds and hundreds of hippie youths, and it has been the one natural advertising media for such hip enterprises as boutiques and rock concerts. Wouldn't it be the greatest folly, the cultural radicals ask, to seek out some other constituency and to jettison the most radical and dynamic element in Atlanta? What must be done, is for *The Bird*, first of all, to develop communal-living structures. Only then can the paper be the thing of harmony in content and personnel that it must be to serve as a hip organizing force. (Unfortunately, the few small *Bird* communes that have been tried have not worked well or long.)

"Living in a commune develops a strong sense that underneath the difference lies a very strong common sense," says one *Bird* staff member, who goes by the name of Harry. "It's less contradictory. It's like sharing a collective consciousness."

"What the Left has never done in this country is organize itself," says Steve Wise. "We're trying to do that here. We're trying to get people more communal."

It is difficult to arrive at some halfway house between the cultural and political forces. Miller Francis, Jr., the most articulate of the cultural radicals, believes that the ideal solution would be for *The Bird* to split into two papers; but Atlanta just isn't big enough. Francis maneuvers the symbols of cultural radicalism with the subtlety and sureness of Marx working with the tools of economic determinism. "I don't say that rock *is* the revolution," Francis says. "I say that rock is the manifestation of the revolution. It's a metaphor for energy and change. It's also a thing you can focus on and learn how this generation differs. This is the first generation in the West to have a real potential for genuine change. We get letters from fourteen-year-old hippie kids in nowhere Alabama who get hassled and read *The Bird*. In Atlanta, these are working-class kids from the rural South. I've just never understood why Marxist-Leninists never picked up on all this."

Francis writes about rock and youth culture with a kind of magical insight that looks suspiciously like wisdom:

As far as media are concerned, so many young people, especially student radicals, still have one foot planted in the world of their parents and of their parents' parents. They feel that to trust any medium besides print—film and music, most importantly—is to lack force; they have no understanding of and no faith in media, which, ironically, have in our world an impact and influence of staggering proportions compared with that of the printed word. Worth pondering is the fact that underground newspapers are often supported primarily by record advertising, and that young Atlanta dropouts sell *Birds* they don't read to buy records they can't live without. To literates it isn't a comforting thought that a Top-40 record album—produced with the help of businessmen with roots in the corporate system of exploitation and manipulation—may be much more effective as radicalizer of the 'young people in a community than their local underground press.

The current split between radical theorists and activists and non-political dropouts is in many ways a division into different awareness of political forces ("politics:" the total complex of relations between men in society—Webster.) It is true that "hippies," especially in the South, are generally demoralized, and suffer a great deal because they have a very naïve grasp of the institutional forces that control and affect their lives (the Movement naïvely classes them as "problems" not solutions); it is just as true that the effectiveness of activist organizers suffers because they too fail to understand other equally (or more) powerful forces that determine the quality of our lives. The success of the Movement depends on both groups sharing their awareness. It is infinitely more *political* significance that Johnny Cash and Bob Dylan can form a musical alliance, or that *Sweetheart of the Rodeo* was recorded at some conference for radicals. . . .

The Great Speckled Bird
March 19, 1969

As convincing as all this sounded, it was no simple matter for *The Great Speckled Bird* to gear over to serve the hip community. Most street sellers don't even bother reading *The Bird,* and it is rare to find hippies with a good word about the paper or political activism. When the April 1970 peace march passed through Peachtree Street, the protesters called out, "Come and join us."

"Come and join *us,*" the stoop sitters and strollers answered. "Come and get high and join us."

Haight-Ashbury, the East Village, and the hippie sections of most Northern cities have all passed through such apolitical phases. To reach the hippies *The Bird* has emphasized the political aspects of cultural matters —pointing out, say, that capitalists are the motive force behind rock festivals. It has not been an unqualified success. In the summer of 1969 an article appeared stating that the free Sunday events in Piedmont Park were more than music, love, peace and dope. They were the beginnings of a revolutionary movement. Almost as soon as the issue hit the streets, a group of thoroughly incensed hippies arrived at the *Bird* house. They simply had no use for such militancy, for ruining *their* good vibes, *their* good times. "It erased any illusions in my head about writing for them," says Francis.

In recent months many members of Atlanta's hippie community have moved out of their antipolitics of peace toward a Yippie-like hard line. Police are finding it difficult to arrest people on Peachtree Street unless they are in full force, and the air is charged with a new militancy. This is not due to those subtle thrusts of politicized culture that have appeared in *The Great Speckled Bird.* The paper just cannot relate to young hips ."We're a different generation," says Francis. "In many ways the same things hang us up that hang up those older than us. We all have intellectual backgrounds. In fact, my interest is an intellectual one even in intuitive things."

Even those few *Bird* staffers of an age that would allow them to relate to the hip community are shunted aside. "People here don't take me too seriously," says Tom Dodamead, fifteen, the youngest staff member. "I haven't even been able to talk to most of the people. I don't even know what's going into the paper until I see it in the layout room."

The irony in all this is that the one person who does go into the hip community is twenty-six-year-old Gene Guerrero. He is a hulky, good-natured, old-fashioned sort of a person, one of those humane socialists whose musical tastes run from blue-grass to blues, and who had not the least pretensions to being terribly hip or groovy. There is a second level of irony here, since it is Guerrero who most fiercely believes that *The Great Speckled Bird* must get out of its "class bag" and increase its working-class concerns, and yet he spends most of his time among the hippie youths of Peachtree Street.

In recent months *The Bird* has become increasingly Marxist in its analysis. More attention is paid to international radical news. The paper is also featuring tough investigative reporting of the local Atlanta scene. These latter articles are by no means sharply rhetorical, charged with fiery homilies, and *The Bird,* really despite itself, retains that sense of elegant cool. Miller Francis, for one, has left the paper and *The Bird* no longer even atempts to speak authoritatively about the "hip revolution."

To find papers that manage to satisfy both political and cultural radicals, one must travel to the backwaters of American radical life—to nowhere Alabama, Mississippi, or even Houston, America's sixth-largest and possibly fastest-growing city. In less than a decade, Houston has shot up out of its Texas provincialism to become a sophisticated center of industry, space and medicine. Houston's middle class has gone through this change with little of that psychic disintegration familiar in other cities, and these good citizens fairly bubble with a Junior Chamber of Commerce pride. There is another Houston though—a world of black, Chicano and poor-white ghettos; of business and political leaders manipulating Houston's future like a Monopoly game; of drugs and ennui in the suburbs; of hippies and assorted long-hairs building lives within the confines of the city limits. This is the Houston that *Space City!* has covered since June 1969.

Space City! began just two months before Houston's first real antiwar march, a gathering of no more than three hundred people, and an indication of the city's ranking on any continuum of Movement activity. Here again, then, is the typical pattern of an underground paper forming at the start of Movement activity. *Space City!* is unabashedly radical. Among its founders are Dennis and Judy Fitzgerald and Thorne Dreyer, native Houstonians who cut their teeth beginning Austin's *Rag.* The *Space City!* layout pays obligatory obeisance to McLuhanism, but the paper remains highly print-oriented. There is a solid intelligence to the reviews and cultural articles, an intelligence that doesn't pose as brilliance, draping itself with literary flourishes or obtuseness. It is a radical journalism grounded in fact. There have been major muckraking and numerous articles challenging the conventional wisdom, either above or underground —"The findings presented on the dangerous effects of these hormonal drugs (birth-control pills) are highly inclusive; a cause for concern, to be sure, but certainly not for panic. The underground press has been guilty as the commercial media in blowing up these findings as absolute proof that oral contraceptives are lethal."

Space City! is structured in an egalitarian fashion that leaves little room for unfettered flights of ego. There is a copy editor and a layout editor, positions rotating with each issue, plus one person who does the bookkeeping over a sustained period. On the surface, then, *Space City!* appears as anarchistic as Austin's *Rag*, yet the Houston paper is a hundredfold more resolved and balanced in content and full of common purpose as well.

This togetherness is due primarily to a core collective of four couples who live together in a splendid house in slow decline from its days as a residence for a wealthy doctor, and who make ends meet by selling the 10,000-circulation *Space City!* on city streets. Nothing is particularly awesome or revolutionary about the commune. These are simply people, radicals at that, whose workaday worlds and free time mesh perfectly, eight Americans living in what can only be called a hostile community. At first, Dennis Fitzgerald had doubts about the commune—"I was skeptical. I figured that when you live 15 hours a day together that's enough. But when we work there's only a certain level of communications. So what you need is not to get away from each other but to fall apart together, to get into each other's heads. At 11 or 12 we go home, make a pot of coffee and talk for a couple of hours. All the hassles we may have

had during the day get talked out. We have a fairly structured situation at the house. We try to break down role relationships—things like cleaning up, cooking, we take turns, men and women, and you know in advance. The main problem is that it's very difficult for other people. We're too tight. It screens out weak personalities. Two kinds of people get through and continue working on the paper—those who are very insensitive to what's going on and those who are very strong."

Space City! has had a special importance in Houston since the city is a sprawled-out, Texas version of Los Angeles. The paper holds the radical community together. To do this it avoids the hairsplitting ideological politics of other prominent radical forces such as the Trotskyist Young Socialist Alliance (Y.S.A.) and the R.Y.M. II, S.D.S. faction. "They're deadly," says Judy Fitzgerald. "They call us revisionists, because we're for rock concerts and speeches."

Space City! is cocksure of itself, confident it is building a strong radical community out of Houston's disparate youth and radical cultures. "We're the only radical group in the city working to relate to the people in a broad way," says Dreyer. "At this point what we're doing is one of the most needful and essential things."

An amorphous radical community is developing in Houston. Militant black and Chicano organizations are arising, and their activites are covered religiously by *Space City!* Large numbers of hippies and other long-hairs come together at the several commercial hip areas and in the park on Sunday. Despite *Space City's*

space city!

·formerly space city news·

20¢

25¢ out of town

vol 1 no 21 May 23–June 5, 1970 houston, texas

Jane Fonda Interview ... P. 10

Jackson and Augusta ... P. 2

heavily political orientation, many hippies think of the Houston paper as theirs. "It has the balls to say things nobody else will say," says David Joshua, who calls himself a hippie. "*Space City!* is written for the heads."

The paper has helped lead the hip community out of its beliefs in peace symbols and good vibes into a militant stance that directly threatens entrepreneurs and business people dealing with youth. In July 1970, for instance, Dennis Fitzgerald wrote an article entitled "Up Against the Wall Culture Vultures" about the appearance of Traffic, the rock group, at the local auditorium:

Traffic tickets were selling for $6.50 a head at Hayes (nee Hofheintz) Pavillion last Thursday night. And a lot of people were translating their indignation into action: a message for local promoters. . . .

When I arrived 30 minutes early, a bundle of *Space City*'s under my arm, a crowd of several thousand was milling around in front, waiting for the doors to open. The scene was low key, stoned, meeting friends unmet since the last concert.

Shortly after 8 P.M. they began letting in ticket holders. Almost immediately you could see this wasn't going to be a concert like other concerts. There are always a few penniless malcontents hassling to get in free. But this night there were more than a few, and they were being uncommonly aggressive. One source of anger was that there were no low-priced tickets being sold, $6.50 only.

Within a half hour the lines had formed. The doors were shut and locked. Outside a thousand people (of whom maybe a tenth had tickets) were pushing and chanting, demanding to be let in.

It was often like the spirit generated by a hard-fought football game. The people were digging on each other and

on this sudden solidarity. It was fun. The cause was clearly just: all the money that was to be made had already been made; inside there were still many empty seats; and outside there were people who wanted in. But such logic runs counter to a promoter's ethic, so the doors had to be defended. . . .

Just when it seemed that the cops couldn't hold back the crowd any longer, a dozen reinforcements arrived and regained control of the doors. . . . At least twice . . . the cops used mace on the crowd. That cooled it quick. Everyone fell back, eyes and noses burning. . . . . As the hours passed, the battle surged and waned. It was always a game, but it grew increasingly more serious. Towards the end, lots of people were smoking dope openly, even tauntingly, in front of the cops. There was that much togetherness; people knew the cops couldn't bust anyone. By 10 P.M. about the only people flashing peace symbols were the promoters. The people responded with the finger, the fist, and an occasional dixie cup packed with ice. . . .

As Traffic began their second number, the promoters relented, and the crowd surged in, cheering, fists high. . . . Concerts in Houston have become increasingly a time for energy outpouring, for kicking out the jam. But promoters and people who own things want concerts to be shows where other people pay for their tickets, stay in their seats, and applaud and go home quietly at the end. That just ain't gonna work. . . .

We need to regain control of our culture. Liberate the Pavillion (or get our own place). Support our local bands. . . . . Don't watch the world, build it. Create what needs to be created; destroy the old forms which restrict us. Now, because tomorrow they may have *you* under contract. *Do it!* [3]

Space City's radical journalism has taken on a new seriousness since late July 1970, when Carl Hampton, the twenty-one-year-old chairman of

Houston's People's Party, a revolutionary black organization, was shot down by police. The police said that a black militant had opened fire on them, but the circumstances were certainly suspect. What is indisputable, though, is that Hampton and his fellow party members were armed revolutionaries living in a proud, prosperous city that finds even the patriotism of mild liberals suspect, and that has absolutely no use for radicals. In that sense at least, the bloody confrontation was inevitable as are others in the future. Immediately after the murder, Victoria Smith wrote in *Space City!*

You know, we really have a movement in this city and it's happened in little more than a year. Before that there was nothing, virtually nothing. It should be clear by now that the power structure in Houston doesn't want us around—any of us, black, brown or white. And don't doubt for a minute that the Houston pigs are ready and willing to kill any or all of us.

Right now the police are continuing to harass our people. Whirlypigs fly over our houses and our offices daily. A number of movement organizations, including *Space City!* have been under police surveillance.

If there was ever a time to get serious, it's now. If there was ever a time to get together, to suspend our ideological differences for a while, it's now. That does not mean that individuals or organizations need or should compromise their organizing style, or suddenly desert their constituencies. But we need to re-recognize our common struggle, if any of us are to long continue in that struggle at all. . . .

One thing that really hit me, something I have known for years but hadn't thought much about lately, is that if I, if we, don't live our lives fighting this American monster that killed Carl, that

is killing people all over the world, that is destroying the planet, that is twisting people's minds—well, then our lives aren't worth shit.[4]

In little more than a year, then, *Space City!* arrived at that most critical of junctures. The paper had helped to create a radical-youth movement and now it had somehow to move out of its isolation. "We've decided that we'll have to get out and get involved or just become journalists," Dreyer told one visitor during June 1970. That summer the paper did go out and start "Of Our Own," a place where on weekends, for a couple of dollars, young Houstonians could go and dance and groove to rock music. The staff tried in other ways to involve itself more with the community. But it did not seem to be enough, and in their February 14, 1971, issue, *Space City!* announced:

This is the last issue of *Space City!* until

This is serious.

In the past, we've made occasional appeals for money, equipment, energy. Sometimes you've responded, and sometimes you haven't. Either way we've managed to keep on happening, doing some good things and some things not so good, but surviving. (And that's no small feat in Astroland as you're probably aware.)

Now, however, we've come to the end of something. This issue of *Space City!* will be the last issue for . . . well, we're really not sure. Whether this ending will be a death, or whether it will only be the quiet before a new, better rebirth depends mainly on you.

We don't want to stop. But we can't go on in the same way either. In the last year and nine months Houston has changed. What used to be good enough (and incidentally all we could manage) is no longer sufficient.

If it were just a matter of raising a little more money, adding a few more pages to every issue, and getting the whole thing a little more together, we could probably do that, just like we've done it before. But it's not that easy.

If you want it we're stuck in a rut and freakin' out. Also we're broke like we've never been before.

So we stop, take it apart, and try to put it back together again. Hopefully better, maybe bigger, maybe weekly, maybe . . . We can't do it without you. We need more of you making *Space City!* happen. We need advice, criticism, love letters, writers, do-gooders.

And we need money. We need at least $3,000. We could make that if every one of you gave a quarter. If everyone of you gave a dollar, we could have a newspaper that'd knock you on your head.

Hey, one last thing. While we're gone there's something people got to remember: that there's high times and low times, but the way to make it every time is to keep on trucking all the time.

That's how you'll know us next time you see us.

—The Collective

Except for the Pollyannas of the right, no one thought for a moment that *Space City!* had printed its last issue. However, it did take three months before the paper published again. In their first new issue (April 6, 1971) a "Letter from the Collective" described how *Space City!* would be trying to deal with the sort of problems that have affected all of the second-generation papers:

. . . for those two reasons—financial and existential—we quit printing for a while. And once we didn't have all the frantic busy work to occupy our every waking moment, we had a little time to take a good look at ourselves. And we figured

out some things. A master plan. A way to get out of our rut. That plan involved a lot of things, many of which we can better communicate by *showing* you in these and future pages than through trying to rap it all out in words.

But we can give you some hints. One: NEWS. Lots more news. Local news. Raking the hometown muck. Filling the cavernous void left by Houston's dailies. That's what we really wanted to do. Less bullshit. Less rhetoric. Less long rambling analytic this and that. More hard information.

To do this we needed, Two: RE-ORGANIZATION. In the past everybody on the full-time staff equally shared responsibility for everything. That meant: everybody equally shared in *freaking out collectively* about everything. This meant that nobody could get deeply enough into anything. You couldn't really dig in, follow through.

The answer we found was specialization. Novel idea? People on the staff picked areas in which we wanted to function and swore on a stack of Roget's Thesauruses that we would stick to those areas and stop spreading ourselves so thin. Areas like local news reporting, distribution, production, advertising, photography. . . . So we worked that all out.

And then came, Three: WEEKLY PUBLICATION. We decided to double our burden, double our fun. . . . For several reasons. First, we could be more of a *newspaper,* more immediate. Get the word out twice as fast. And we also figured it would help us financially in the long run, as well as giving vendors a better deal.

There was nothing apocalyptic about the changes but they were enough to revitalize the paper and the staff collective and to make *Space City!* unquestionably one of the strongest underground papers in America.

Volume 2   Number 21   [Issue 47]   May 29 – June 5, 1970   15 CENTS BAY AREA 25 CENTS ELSEWHERE

BERKELEY TRIBE

"WITHIN THE NEXT 14 DAYS WE WILL ATTACK A SYMBOL OR INSTITUTION OF AMERIKAN INJUSTICE"
—WEATHERMAN, MAY 21, 1970

8
Post-Mortem II

The second generation of underground papers can see their success in the streets and in the mass media. They have helped forge and publicize a truly revolutionary youth movement that can bust Timothy Leary out of jail, blow up buildings, bring thousands of pro-Panther demonstrators to New Haven, meet with the Viet Cong as a serious political group, and hold revolutionary conventions. They have brought such ideas as women's liberation and ecology up into the consciousness of Americans, and they have helped turn the hip subculture into a mass youth culture. On the papers themselves they have largely done away with private ownership and editorial hierarchies, and they refuse to take ads that would demean women or in any way cast doubt on their ideals. Despite their many successes, many underground journalists have grown more and more outraged, even despondent, for the Movement itself still stands on the far fringes of American political life (despite a President who in his 1971 State of the Union address called for "power to the people" and described the general malaise in terms reminiscent of the 1962 S.D.S. Port Huron Statement).

Many of the papers have turned harshly militant, identifying with a worldwide revolutionary struggle. They print pictures and diagrams of rifles, pistols and other weapons. In this there is a conscious attempt to break out of bourgeois youth culture and forge ties with the lower classes, but ironically, the pictures and diagrams are telling evidence that such underground papers are as middle-class as ever. Guns are very much a part of lower-middle-class and work-

111

ing-class American culture. A boy grows up with them. He respects them. He knows how to use them. And if he reads a radical paper, he certainly finds pictures or diagrams of guns superfluous or downright foolish. It is only these scions of the middle class, schooled in a tradition that considers guns illicit and somehow almost sensual, who need such elementary instruction.

In early 1970, some "heavy" Berkeley politicos assumed the leadership of the *Tribe*. They thought of themselves as Marxist ideologues, but it was all mere dressing for their revolutionary exhortations, and the *Tribe* settled in for a highly stylized revolutionary struggle, a struggle fought out more on the pages of the paper than anywhere else. Of course, upon reading the 1970 *Tribe,* the uninitiated might imagine that the storming of the White House was only hours away. Here were enthusiastic accounts of trashing ("The Safeway store buckled under our attentions. Their garden-supply store got it first. Soon the windows were busted and we were standing there with shovels from the store, bricks from the wall . . ."); occasional pieces on guns and dynamite ("If you're gonna mess with explosives, keep the primer and the main charge separate up until the last possible minute"); a "Statement of Lao Patriotic Front on the Great Victory of the Plain of Jars"; a centerfold picture of Bobby Seale, the imprisoned Panther leader; a series on the Urban Guerrilla ("familiar with the avenues, streets, alleys, ins and outs, and corners of the urban centers, its paths and shortcuts . . . the urban guerrilla safely crosses through the irregular and difficult terrain unfamiliar to

the police, where they can be surprised in a fatal ambush or trapped at any moment"); and a picture of Kim Il Sung of North Korea, with the caption "Whatever the adversity we should protect our mimeographs and other printing equipment and materials even at the risk of our lives." Although each issue of the *Tribe* became more militant, more strident, more laced with revolutionary expletives, the Red Mountain Tribe were largely "paper" tigers—paper-medium radicals who created gigantic images of themselves that overshadowed them and their accomplishments and in which they could only half believe.

Marxists, the *Tribe* politicos may have called themselves, but they were really anarchists of the word, having conveniently forgotten the connection between word and deed. Albert Parsons had been one too, when in 1884–86 he edited the Chicago *Alarm* and advised: "Workingmen of America, learn the manufacture and use of dynamite—a weapon of the weak against the strong, the poor against the rich. Then use it unstintedly, unsparingly." Chicago authorities convinced a jury that Parsons must have had a part in the 1886 Haymarket bombing and sent him to the gallows—almost certainly innocent of all but his literary anarchism. Laurent Taihade, the French poet, provides us with our primary moral parable on such anarchism of the word. In December 1893, after a bomb exploded in the Chamber of Deputies, wounding several members, a journalist asked Taihade his impressions. *"Qu'importent les victimes si le geste est beau?* (What do the victims matter if it's a fine gesture?)," he answered. Four months later

Taihade happened to be sitting in the elegant Restaurant Foyot when another bomb exploded the *"beau geste"* putting out the poet's eye.

There is no need to go picking through the bone pile of nineteenth-century history to point up the weaknesses of the *Tribe*'s radical-revolutionary journalism. Even in comparison to the *Masses,* the 1930's Communist-line magazine that in many respects was narrowly political, the *Tribe*'s journalism seems decidedly weak. Its critics called the *Masses* naïve and self-serving, yet there was an energy and vividness to the reporting and writing that far transcended any secular political lines. The best of the *New Masses* reportage was, as Tom Wolfe has suggested, perhaps the earliest example of the New Journalism. It managed to combine the old-fashioned gritty journalism that builds details into facts, and facts into stories; the literary techniques of the novel; and the insights of the essay form. When Richard Wright wrote about Negro reaction to Joe Louis' victory over Max Baer—*"Something* had happened, all right. And it had happened so confoundingly sudden that the whites in the neighborhood were dumb with fear"—he created a world. When Albert Maltz tells of a sit-down strike in a Fisher Body factory, the reader is transported there:

. . . The police kept shooting. There were twenty to thirty reports, only some of which were followed by bursts of flame. The others were riot guns at close quarters. But the gas had less effect than hoped for. Three things were against its success: the water from the fire hoses, which cleaned the air; a cold night with a slight wind so that the gas did not rest heavy on the ground; and, most of all, the flaming courage of two hundred men who didn't care a damn about gas or police.

And through the twenty minutes or so that the attack lasted, there was one steady, unswerving note: the strikers' loudspeaker. It dominated everything! The voice of Victor Reuther, organizer of the union, rose to a tremendous pitch. It was like an inexhaustible, furious flood pouring courage into the men. That voice never stopped for breath, for thought, to escape gas or bullets. And it won. The police ran back. . . .[1]

In their passion, the *Tribe*'s revolutionary journalists had forgotten that fundamental distinction between rhetoric and reportage. The *Tribe* had little room for articles based on substantial reporting and no room at all for novelesque techniques. The paper was full of the casual invective that calls a cop a "pig" and thinks that it has said something, but few on the *Tribe* would bother writing articles to show specifically why Berkeley police are so notorious. The *Tribe* spelled America with a *k* or a *kk* or a *kkk,* but it did not bother to spell out some of what the Red Mountain Tribe considered the horrors of this society. The paper had become, as one Berkeley revolutionary admitted sadly, "impressionistic jargon."

The *Tribe* applauded guerrilla warfare and terrorism, not only because of their backgrounds, but because they were ideas that had grown up out of the New Left not as vicious mutants but as legitimate offspring. From the beginning the New Left had depended on a kind of moral witnessing. The sit-ins were "a kind of mass vomit against the hypocrisy of segregation," Jack Newfield wrote in *A Prophetic Minority.* "Today, most of the movement's demonstrations retain this quality of retching upon a system that literally makes many young people sick to their stomachs. . . . The sit-ins, too, were a spontaneous, unplanned activist contagion. They gave people something to do immediately to show their feelings about segregation. They required no ideology, no politics, and no scholarship—just one's body and a certain set of ethical values." [2]

Such moral witnessing translated brilliantly into media terms. Two minutes of national television time—say, Bull Conner's dogs attacking demonstrators—appeared to accomplish more than two years of political organizing. The logical outcome of this was the mass moral witnessings of the Washington demonstration from the then astounding 20,000 who showed up at the S.D.S.-sponsored antiwar rally in April 1965 to the hundreds of thousands who made the journey in the late 1960's. In the October–November 1969 Moratorium, liberal politicians usurped the peace movement transforming it into their symbolic, emotive and inconsequential ritual. To millions of Americans wearing of a black armband could

PEOPLE GE

HELMETS

A helmet is a must for street actions, especially if you are short. I am 5'2" and not a fast runner, but twice the pigs have passed me by while swinging their clubs. Remember, the pigs are out for blood and gore; they want to go down on unprotected heads. Don't give them the chance!

The cheapest helmet around is a steel tank helmet with ear protection, important if you are taller and more likely to be side-swiped. Advantages: Price ($1.50), has built-in suspension (needs no liner), is bullet and shrapnel proof. Disadvantages: It is very heavy and although adjustable, may still be too large for some women's heads.

The next up in price is the white O.C.D. (Officer Civil Defense) steel helmet. Advantages: Price ($7.95), lighter weight, shrapnel proof. Disadvantages: No ear protection, white color too visible for night actions, Paint it.

Next are the U.S. Army issue "pot" helmets, the best of which are the M-1 steel helmets as used by "our boys." Advantages: Bullet and shrapnel proof, dark color (Army drab), some ear protection. Disadvantages: Price ($9.95 "like new," $6.95 "excellent, used," $4.95 "good, used.") All require plastic helmet liners ($4.95 new, $3.50 "excellent," $2.00 "good.") LINERS MUST BE WORN UNDER POT HELMETS, as these contain the suspension webbing that keeps the pot from making contact with your skull. Some used helmets lack chin straps. Don't attempt to run in a helmet without this 75 cent accessory.

"Hard hats" (construction helmets) are made of aluminum or fiberglass and are extremely lightweight. Hard hats are one-piece helmets with built-in suspension (no liner needed). Advantages: Price ($5.00-8.00), extremely light weight, and is adjustable because of built-in webbing. Disadvantages: No ear protection, it is not bullet or shrapnel proof, it may crack under repeated blows (it will protect your head even if it does crack) and you will have to improvise a way to attach a strap which must be bought separately ($.75).

Crash helmets are the most commonly seen head protection at demonstrations. They are made of plastic or fiberglass and are fairly light weight. Crash helmets have a foam rubber padded interior and a removable visor or bubble shield made of clear plastic. Advantages: Fairly light weight, built in strap or chin guard, and they fit snugly. Disadvantages: Price ($11.95 upwards through $34.95!) None of the crash helmets have built in suspension webbing which insulates your

STREET WAR

If you are into street fighting, the most important thing is to keep your head together. The best way of doing that is by wearing a helmet. This should be common sense, understood by everyone, but the Left likes to ignore such practical trivialities. While you are searching for a new soft spot on your head of rhetoric, the man is searching for a new piece of your head.

I have been stopped at street actions by many people who have been freaked by my "preparedness." Two highschool boys informed me that I was inciting the pigs to riot by wearing a helmet. Bullshit! The main rule which should motivate your choice of defenses is to be adequately protected without being so encumbered that you cannot see, hear, or move easily.

When we go out into the streets unprepared, our asses exposed to the wind, we are inviting trouble. Self defense means making ourselves as invulnerable as possible without cutting down on agility or effectiveness. Following are some recommendations for dealing with the man's technology piece by piece so that we can stay alive while tearing down the Amerikan empire piece by piece. Consider it street insurance.

GAS MASKS

If you can't afford a gas mask, don't want to be weighted down, or don't want to sacrifice your peripheral vision, a fairly effective gas mask can be made out of several 4x4 gauze pads soaked in water or vinegar placed inside a paper hospital surgical mask (both easily obtained from surgical supply houses). These masks are light, easily carried, easily hidden or disposed of, and cheap. With these, you can wear goggles, obtainable in ski shops or the navy surplus store.

The cheapest of the really effective gas masks is the O.C.D. gas mask which was made for civilians in case of gas attack. They are virtually the same as those used by the National Guard and local pigs; Advantages: Price ($8.00) brand new, one-piece and lightweight with the cannister built on. These are guaranteed brand new (the only way they're sold) and take it from me, they work! The mask is adjustable and easy to run with. It comes in its own carrying bag. Disadvantages: There are no replacement cannisters. These are attached only at the factory, and contain enough chemicals to protect you for four hours of heavy gas. This is really a blessing in disguise, because people throw them away when they are exhausted, there is no way for a store to sell you a used mask. If you have a very narrow jaw it may not make an airtight fit, but even then it will filter out 99% of the tear gas.

U.S. Army gas masks also offer full face protection and are adjustable. Advantages: Comes with bag and fresh cannister. Disadvantages: Price ($14.00),

cannister is connected to mask by long rubber hose, making it difficult to run. There don't seem to be any replacement cannisters available.

Navy masks are similar to Army masks. Advantages: Adjustable, snug fitting, fresh cannister and bag. Replacement cannisters are available for $1.50 each. Disadvantages: Price ($15.00 new). These have TWO hoses connected to the cannister. If a pig slashed either one you would be breathing pure gas. Worse, he could spray a chemical weapon up the tube. Don't get too close!

U.S.A. Protective Field Mask M9A1. Advantages: Full face protection, easy to wear, cannister screws directly onto face of mask. Comes with its own bag and anti-slim cloth. Disadvantages: Price ($16.00 new), no replacement cannisters available that I know of.

All gas masks have plastic goggles which fog up as you breathe. This can be remedied by getting an anti-fog cloth for 25 cents.

WALKIE-TALKIES

The walkie talkie, or "transceiver," is your telephone when you are in the street. The pigs have their own Motorola walkie talkies with a special pig channel. Any pig on the street can contact another to find out where the action is. When we get dispersed and separated by pigs at an action it is very hard to regroup. This is partly because we have no way of finding our where our people are. With a few people carrying walkie talkies tuned to the same channel that problem would be eliminated.

To get a good pair of walkie talkies that will carry a fair distance within a city you have to shop around. Don't be freaked by the variety of designs and makes on the market. Keep these few basic facts in mind while searching. Any pair of walkie talkies under $25.00 is probably a toy. You won't need a pair unless you want a friend to definitely have one. Hopefully, a lot of people will soon have walkie talkies equipped for Channel 9 and you'll be able to talk with or listen to any of them with your single unit. It should have at least nine transistors and 100 milliwatts. Five watts is the most powerful walkie talkie made. Over one watt requires an FCC license. There is no test involved, you just buy the license for $8. The FCC license application form comes with the transceiver, you don't need a license first to buy the walkie talkie. And nobody's going to beat down your door if you don't file the application. Whether or not to get the license is strictly up to you.

Don't be taken in by gadgets or fancy streamlined designing. A beeper for alerting your partner is useful although she will not hear it unless her unit is on anyway, but if it already comes with the unit and the price is reasonable, take it. Buy in a reputable shop where you can ask questions and know that you are getting honest answers. In the electronics field there are no real "bargains." You might hit a sale, but you get what you pay for.

The Civilian Band (C.B.) on which all walkie talkies operate has 23 channels. Less expensive units have one set of crystals which are tuned to only one channel, usually Channel 9, or sometimes Channel 11. If you wish to use a different channel you have to take those crystals (1 for transmit, the other for receive) out and plug in the proper crystals for the channel you want. Some units have

CHOPPERS

The executive's toy, a build-it-yourself one woman helicopter, is now within the financial and practical reach of anyone with a little "chutspah." The copter will carry a 200lb weight, which means one 110lb woman and 80 or 90 pounds of food, messages or what have you. Its uses are as infinite as your imagination, especially during an imposed curfew like the one in Santa Barbara. The copter itself weighs approximately 250 lbs and is small enough to land on almost any flat roof in the city where it can be stored with just a tarpulin thrown over it. There are probably all sorts of city, state, federal and aviational ordinances against using a one-woman copter in the city but what do you care? If you want to try it legally the plans come with all the right forms. For three dollars you can get photographs, fully illustrated plans with lists of components, and flight instructions from the following companies: Bensen Aircraft Corp. Dept. PS-20, Raleigh-Durham Airport, Raleigh, N.C. 27602; Rotor Way Inc., P.O. Box 1096, Mesa, Arizona 85201; and for two dollars from Helicopter Development, Box PS-147 Washington, New Jersey 07882 and for one dollar from Compcop, Box 1267, Redwood City, California 94064.

O.C.D. MASKS

PROTECTION AGAINST MANY NASAL AND EYE IRRITANTS

NEW!

The eyepieces are made of clear, transparent plastic.

These are the head straps. Each is adjustable. They make the mask fit tightly when adjusted.

IN CANVAS

This is the faceplace

signify full commitment, the carrying of a candle in an evening march full penance, and attendance at a demonstration an act of great moment. The radical outrage, condemnation and critique was nowhere to be seen—least among the momentary flurry of doves, peace signs and feelings of good brotherhood. In such a situation, given the New Left as it had developed and the continuing direction of American policies both here and abroad, sabotage proved attractive—and not only to the *Tribe.* After all, what were bombings but "retching upon a system that literally makes many young people sick to their stomachs. . . . They required no ideology, no politics and no scholarship—just one's body and a certain set of ethical values."

The bombings would serve a purpose as an organizing tool only if, as Andrew Kopkind wrote in *Hard Times,* they forced the middle class to make an existential choice—either for or against the revolution. At very least one would imagine Berkeley radicals committed to the revolution would support the *Tribe.* However, many of them have grown disenchanted. "It's ironic," says one revolutionary feminist. "Some of us were discussing how we'd like to have a paper that at least sometimes covered stories with the 'objectivity' of CBS. The *Tribe* just doesn't give us the news we need to know." Even street sellers have few good words to say about either the *Tribe* or the *Barb.* "They sure aren't books of eternal truth," says Chuck Berdhiaume, who makes his living on Telegraph Avenue selling up to three hundred papers a day. "After you've been in it for six years or so, there's nothing in the papers. It's all sensationalism." All during the summer of 1970 the *Tribe* continued to exhort the youth masses to immediate revolution, but as the paper's circulation fell to below 30,000, its exhortations risked becoming acts of self-flagellation.

A belief in bombings and guerrilla violence is the exclusive prerogative of neither the cultural nor the political radicals. It is certainly easier, though, for nonideological cultural radicals to accept terrorism than for political radicals, who bring to their beliefs an ideology and a historical perspective. Terrorism is a happen-

READY ...

...HING

...othing you wear to a ...ould also be plain ...the equipment in the ...the rest of your body ...otected. For instance, ...d by the pigs today is ...tear gas which only ...ory system. Pepper gas ...t which burns any ...n. Therefore, standard ...e tightfitting cuffs and ...gh sneakers and gloves. ...other uses besides gas ...are excellent for ...ood for running, and ...r picking up hot tear ...throwing them back. ...always reflect the ...onditions. Plan to be ...r extended periods of ...warm in the winter, ...r in summer. August ...l, and you'll probably ...eat. Pants, of course, ...should be of tough ...enim are best. ...should also be as ...ible, so that you're ...and not easily ...your outfit from day ...ana around your neck ...our face or hair, plus ...other methods of ...cannot be recognized ...r films. Another ...r an empty shopping ...mewhere on your way ...to get away, place ...gear (gas mask, ...ag and blend in with ...owd.

...vier a bullet proof ...vestment. You can ...uminum vest that ...for $14.95. If an ...to far out for you ...ster in Puerto Rico ...ction from a bullet

SOURCES

Walkie Talkies are available from Lafayette Radio (Berkeley, S.F.), Radio Shack (Albany, Oakland, SF, San Leandro and more) and Olson (SF). Radio Shack has a $30.00 plain-and-simple one watt unit which is probably the best buy. Crystals for channels other than 11 cost about $5 per set. Make sure you get the "T" and "R" crystals straight. Never rely on the batteries packed with the set—they are Yokahama specials. Get Duracells for the real thing.

Helmets are available at Henderson's Surplus, 1941 San Pablo, Oakland, and Globe Sales Co., 1156 E. 12th St., Oakland.

Gas masks can be had from Acme Surplus, 8th St, between Washington and Clay, Oakland, and Henderson's. Acme's are cheaper.

High band police receivers (pigs here operate at around 155 Mhc) are available from Lafayette Radio, Radio Shack, and Olson for $17-$35. They will drift and aren't too strong (using their own antennas) but are good for operations within one mile of the cars.

Bullet proof vests are available by mail from Surplus Distributors, 6279 Van Nuys Blvd., Van Nuys, Cal. 91401. They'll send you their very hip catalog (which gives almost no information) for free.

FIRST AID

Medics have found from hard experience that anything which may identify you as a medic (white coat, red cross, medical bag, etc.) only increases your chances of being singled out for a beating. Ideally, EVERYONE in the streets should be carrying enough supplies and have enough knowledge to give at least rudimentary first aid.

Anytime you are going to a potentially dangerous situation, you should be carrying (preferably distributed throughout your pockets, rather than in a bag) the following:

One or two sterile gauze pads
Several (10 or 20) 4x4 clean gauze pads
one or two kling or kerlix rolls (2 ply gauze rolls for securing gauze to wounds)
a bottle of eyewash (such as Murine, or any commercial eyedrops), boric acid solution, or water.
a roll of adhesive tape
bandaids
a small plastic bottle with some cleansing disinfectant agent (hydrogen peroxide)
a small plastic container full of mineral oil to dissolve gas clinging to your skin
cotton balls
DO NOT carry glass bottles or anything sharp (even scissors) as the glass can break and hurt you and anything sharp or pointed can be construed as a deadly weapon. The gauze and kling should be carried in baggies, as these can also serve to seal off a chest wound if necessary. You can also carry, in baggies, cotton balls soaked in water, boric acid solution, etc. instead of a bottle of eyewash.

ing. It even appeals to Timothy Leary, who before anyone else, more than anyone else, and after practically everyone else had given up, propagandized for a nonviolent psychedelic revolution. "Turn on, tune in, drop out," he told young Americans in lectures on college campuses and in his column in the *East Village Other*. Police arrested Leary at least fourteen times in the past five years on drug charges, and in March 1970 he began serving a six-month-to-ten-year sentence for drug possession. Despite all this, he maintained his belief in nonviolence.

In September he escaped, with help from Weathermen, and soon afterward a letter from Leary appeared in *EVO* and other undergrounds. "Listen. There is no choice left but to defend life by all and every means possible against the genocidal machine." Many radicals simply refused to believe the letter, for if the "high priest of drug culture" had become a militant revolutionary then there could scarcely be a single nonviolent radical left in America. It was true, though. As Leary wrote *EVO* from his temporary haven in Algeria, "We were profoundly moved by the Weathermen. They represent an old dream of ours —acid revolutionaries, holy liberation saints. To begin with—they are physically beautiful. They radiate pure God energy that the hippies possessed in 1967—young men and women certainly in touch with their internal Godhood. . . . The Weathermen are the soul of white young America. We urge all young Americans who are still alive to life—to emulate and support." [3] Leary had not changed that much. "Tune in, turn on, drop out," was the perfect

slogan for the psychedelic radicals of 1967 and it is the perfect slogan for the Weathermen of the 1970's as well.

The Weathermen have even issued many of their proclamations through Yippie auspices in New York rather than give them to politically radical groups. However, there is always a veneer of Marxism. Bernardine Dohrn's "Declaration of a State of War" said in part: "We are adopting the classic guerrilla strategy of the Vietcong and the urban guerrilla strategy of the Tupamaros to our own situation here in the most technically advanced country in the world."

The Weathermen, then, accept the Third World analysis of S.D.S. There may be brilliantly compelling arguments in its favor, but the theory provides the most insidious justification for a politics and an underground journalism that relate neither to the lives of those involved nor to the lives of their friends, nor to the lives of anyone they can talk with or understand. At least partly because of this analysis, the LNS collective is imprisoned in that Claremont Avenue office behind walls papered over with ideological justification. During the summer of 1970 LNS sent writer-photographer teams to Latin America and Africa but none to travel around the United States to talk to underground editors and to learn about this country. LNS reports regularly about oppressed black people, but they don't even try to get into the hearts and minds of the white working class, the middle class, hip youths or young radicals.

The LNS collective consider themselves Marxist revolutionary journalists, but they are a different breed from their counterparts during the 1930's. Then André Malraux commanded an aviation corps in Spain. Waldo Frank accompanied Earl Browder to a Terre Haute prison cell. Rockwell Kent assisted marble strikers. Others aided miners in Kentucky, worked with strikers in Detroit, and fought in the trenches of Spain. LNS, however, generally gets out into the community only during demonstrations. They do very little active reporting and only rarely do LNS articles achieve the intimacy of concern and sureness of detail that rivals the best of past radical journalism.

Part of the problem is the very enviable tightness of the LNS collective. In trying to organize itself in a utopian manner, LNS has not developed an organization well suited to relate to the outside world. On the contrary, working communes are the most subtle of organisms. They do not function well far from the hothouse centers of their existence; neither do they ingest outsiders well. Ironically, then, in struggling to create a pocket utopia in a cellar on Claremont Avenue and to avoid elitism within their ranks, the LNS collective as a whole has become a self-centered elite that related only to itself.

LNS is by no means alone in having such problems. The paradox, in terms of that traditional conflict between cultural and political radicalism, is that the underground press strives to have it both ways. These are cultural radicals demanding, in Engels' words "that the first act of the social revolution shall be the abolition of authority." Thus, *The Great Speckled Bird,* the *Tribe,* and practically all second-generation papers are trying to develop the most egalitarian and utopian working situations. At the same time these underground journalists seek to create papers and ways of life that will bring radical change.

The *Rag* in Austin probably has the most "postrevolutionary" structure of any paper. The paper has no week-by-week feel or quality. No one takes particular care with the layout, and sometimes the paper is difficult to read. A blotched layout ruins the effect of a good poem. A fine piece of political analysis stands next to a shoddy mishmash of reporting and opinion. "It's all sort of sporadic," says the *Rag*'s David Waddington. "With this structure people get half-assed and sloppy, and then the next issue everyone does well." What's left unsaid is that in the amorphous, ill-defined radical community in Austin, the *Rag* is no longer very important.

Another part of this structural problem is that despite the sacred revolutionary trilogy of *liberté, égalité, fraternité,* liberty and equality are often at odds. Whenever the meaning of equality is pushed so hard that it must mean absolutely equal participation, absolutely equal work, and absolutely equal say, the meaning of liberty is soon debased. At LNS two of the staffers, Allen Young and David Fenton, were considered ego trippers and left. Young, particularly, had taken it on himself to see that things got done, and he had become, in the eyes of the outsiders, LNS's leading figure. He was what another generation would have called a "natural-born leader" and many of the other LNS people considered this not only unhealthy but unworthy.

This sort of political radicalism

often calcifies into a moral absolutism that can be shattering—both to the Movement and to individuals. In late 1970, *Old Mole,* Boston's highly political underground, published an article about the paper's experience in the Movement, and it summed up parenthetically why *Old Mole* would be going out of business:

Life in the Movement

AN ARTICLE ABOUT OURSELVES

The Old Mole
Liberation News Service

WHO ARE WE?

This article is mainly about ourselves. To criticize the movement is for us self-criticism, since we have been part of it for a long time. We have learned from the women's-liberation movement that the surest antidote to rhetoric is speaking out of one's own experience. Secondly, this article is about our friends and people we know, and thirdly about people we don't know who share the main points of our social background and experience.

We are people who have been in the Movement some years, and taken an active role in it. We are mostly middle-class and college educated. We are all white. We have changed our style of living a lot from our parents' styles, but we still have some profoundly middle-class attributes. We could talk you to death. Sometimes it seems as if we could never get up off our asses and stop talking long enough to do anything. At other times we struggle against these bad tendencies by flying into frenzies of unanalyzed activity.

We are typically the children of indulgent parents and we think a lot about expressing ourselves. We are uneasy about subsuming our personalities in a mass movement where their originality might not be noticed. We find it difficult to be followers, and we are expert at finding fault with whatever concrete proposals for action might be made. On the other hand, many of us love being leaders, without having any disciplined conception of what good leadership means. We can be awfully elitist and competitive.

All this is very middle-class. We don't mean this as self-flagellation, we think that middle-class people can become good revolutionaries. But in order to do this we have to think seriously about our faults and try to change. That means that we have to give up the delicious egotism of seeing our faults as charming eccentricities of our individual personalities, and see them instead as social attributes, products of our class, race, and sex position in late capitalist society—faults which can be overcome as many other revolutionaries have done.

Who are we? If the shoe fits, wear it. There is a growing part of the movement that is not so much like us—that is younger, less intellectual, more working class. There is the most militant and (we think) advanced part of the movement that is black and brown. Undoubtedly these comrades have problems too, but they are somewhat different and we can't talk about them from experience.

HOW DO WE FEEL ABOUT OURSELVES?

Many of us came into the movement because we were what they used to call "maladjusted." Since there are so many of us they can't call it that any more. We were lonely, unhappy, and torn by attacks of self-hatred. We still are.

It's not surprising. Look who we are, look where we come from. Our past embodies everything we hate about America —isn't that how we became radicals, by realizing what we'd been through?—but our past is still part of us. We are its product. When we look inside ourselves, we can find everything we hate about

OLD MOLE

25¢ NUMBER 38   A RADICAL BI-WEEKLY   BOSTON, MASSACHUSETTS   MAY 1–MAY 14

NOAM CHOMSKY ON LAOS
NEW HAVEN PANTHER TRIAL
THE LIVES OF CHILDREN

Capitalism—competitiveness, criticism, alienation, fear of other people, individualism, loneliness, and despair of making it different. Because of these things, and where we come from, we feel illegitimate as revolutionaries. And so we feel guilty—the old liberal trap.

The most minute differences make us unable to work together, because we are so insecure that any difference is threatening to our whole political identity. We often spend as much time attacking each other as the system, but it is the frustrations imposed on us by the system that make us so insecure.

We also are stuck up. We can even convince ourselves that our clarity with words provides us with a clear view of reality, and that we know more about how to make a revolution than other people. Many of us secretly look down on the people we profess to save—they don't read the papers, they are so inarticulate, they shoot up. Our secret snottiness is perceived by those who profess to organize. We are so well-educated and so clever with words that they often don't see why they resent us and feel put down by us, but they do, and they are right.

It is no excuse, but is important towards changing ourselves to realize our intellectual arrogance is primarily a defense. We spend most of our time clinging together, afraid of the world we must convert. It is hardly an irrational response. We do live in the belly of the monster and its power over us all can be quite terrifying.

Linda: I began to learn some of this from the Cubans. On the one hand they would say to me: "The trouble with you Americans is that you don't really have faith in the people." And on the other hand they would say, pausing from their 12-hour-a-day backbreaking labor, their 24-hour-a-day readiness for U. S. invasion, with genuine sympathy and even awe, "You are so brave; it must be hard to live under capitalism." Both are true. Our comradeship and our vision of the future are hardly enough to sustain us, and on bad days we are kept going mainly by our hate. Hate is dangerous. It is a very cold kind of fuel; it turns too quickly to cynicism and despair, and it is always too close to our own self-hate.

Meredith: I know where that hate comes from. I went to the same school as one of the heaviest Weathermen, and believe me, that high school was as close to hell, to a meaningless bourgeois hell that destroyed the humanity of everyone in it, as I want to get.

We cannot and should not stop hating. The world is hateful, on the whole, and our anger makes us keep fighting. But there are also germs of the new world around, in ourselves and others; and we can't let our anger block our awareness of that. We have to keep open.

HOW DO WE BEHAVE?

What is your picture of a full-time political activist? The traditional Movement stereotype is a kind of human machine—white and male, of course—going about from group to group; dispensing advice, propaganda, and organizing plans; never sleeping and hardly eating; ceaselessly talking; never relaxing or letting up; and regarding even his recreation talking to friends or making love or listening to music—as work, as something competitive, as something by which he has to prove himself. He has no friends—that is, there is no one to whom he truly opens his heart, although he may complain to his wife or girl friend. Perhaps he never looks into his heart at all. Perhaps he never looks back.

It's no kind of life for a human being.

Sometimes it seems like we all gave up what made us most human when we went into the Movement. One of us feels she mustn't paint, it's bourgeois and not contributing directly to the process of making a revolution. Another would always go to a boring, pointless meeting rather than do something she really loves doing. Others, who got into the movement younger, have never even found out what they would really love to do, what they would be doing in a post-revolutionary society.

Surely these excesses of personal deprivation aren't really necessary! Are they even helpful? How can we make a human revolution by torturing ourselves, by giving up all we care for in our past?

We are always going to extremes. I don't mean extremes in the bourgeois sense of actions that are violent or shocking. I mean we figure out some principle, carry it to its farthest-out logical extension, and then act on it. We think this is revolutionary purity. Only the most extreme statement of any idea sounds revolutionary to us, though in fact it may be a distortion.

The idea that exclusive personal relationships like bourgeois marriages are bad politics has been sometimes transformed into the idea that nobody should live in couples; or that people should smash monogamy by sleeping around regardless of the emotional damage this may cause them or their friends; or that people in a political collective should all sleep together in rotation. When you think of the human consequences of such ideas, which have all been put forward on some occasion or other as the only really revolutionary cause of action, it's appalling. But most of us don't stop to think of that. The purity of an idea is more appealing than our own self-preservation and we confuse ways of changing ourselves with ways of destroying ourselves.

We think that if we can only be tough enough, if we can only off the pig enough, we'll have become revolutionaries; as though we could become revolutionaries by individual or small-group action. But what is a revolution if it is not a mammoth and dynamic relationship between people? Revolutionaries cannot make themselves—even by throwing themselves into the most desperate situations. Revolutionaries are made by working within and shaping the struggle to make a mass revolution.

A revolution that can be made by isolated groups of fighters is not a revolution; it is a coup. It is certainly necessary for most of us to become tougher and more able to fight. The way we do this is by building things we will want to fight for, and by working with people different from us who know how to fight already (like Viet vets, for instance) and who will teach us.

Another way people have gone to extremes recently (in relation to the goal of building a mass movement) is an exclusive emphasis on inner change, head change, and the quality of personal relationships within a narrow movement friendship circle. Obviously personal relationships are important. It has been the unique historical contribution of the women's liberation movement to make their importance real in political terms. But this is not to say that they are the *only* important thing for revolutionaries to concentrate on. Yet people say it.

It is our doubts about our own legitimacy that makes us carry every conclusion to its extreme; and our sense of isolation and impotence that makes us go from one extreme to another. That, and our persistent feeling that there must be *one* right strategy somewhere. Instead of perceiving and accepting the situation we have at this time—not one movement but many separate movements of different kinds of people with different needs —we tend to view it as a situation of competing strategies, in which one must be right for everyone. Yet how could a program to organize housewives in Somerville be right for street kids in Lynn? Couldn't both be equally right for what they're doing? Don't they at any rate need to be evaluated separately?

Consider the impact of Weatherman on the Movement last year. At the time Weatherman was a tendency that had committed itself to working with street kids. It was good and necessary to do that work. Weatherman tried hard to convert other movement people to do that work; and consequently many of us felt threatened, rather than pleased, at the advent of Weatherman because they seemed to be saying that if you did anything less "heavy" you were being finky—or rather, "wimpy." A lot of us felt that if we didn't want to organize street kids, we weren't revolutionaries.

We were wrong to feel that way; at the same time, any strategy for organizing one group that poses as the work everyone should be doing is probably wrong. First, because we need movement that reaches out to lots of different kinds of people in lots of ways. Second, because any one strategy is bound to be wrong as work for a lot of *us,* as individuals. Not all of us are likely to do a very good job organizing street kids, to say the least. Failure to recognize this has been very destructive to lots of people. For some it meant temporary withdrawal from any political work; for others it meant pushing themselves in self-destructive ways to do work that they found very alienating and that they weren't good at.

It is good for extremes to exist as dynamic parts of a whole movement. The Movement should continually be forced to synthesize new ways of acting and being. But a movement that is made up only of extremes is not one that can grow. As long as we are caught in the competitive cycle of being "more left than thou." we will keep getting further out and more unable to communicate with most Americans. For people who live at the extremes are those most alienated from American life, and thus least able to communicate with people still trapped in the old ways.

We have to develop a sense of dialectic in our Movement, of interchange between extremes, and between extremes and the middle. Clearly inner change and political outreach should feed into each other. But that never seems to happen. We never seem able to learn from anything we do. We rush from one extreme to the other, never synthesizing, never consciously thinking back to what we have learned that we take with us. We adopt some tactic or style as the one perfect answer to all our problems; and when it fails, as it always does, we reject it totally, instead of using what we can from it and going on. So we are doomed to endless repetition of the same scenario.

This is terrible for the growth of a revolutionary movement. We cannot afford to go on like this, from one total strategy to another every six months or so. It is also terrible for our souls. We have to find a better balance between struggling to change ourselves and accepting our limitations.

Faced with an endless series of political freak-outs on the one hand, and the inhumanity of movement life on the other, people drop out. This is our greatest loss. A life span in the Movement is so short. People talk of copping out or selling out as great problems, but they are exaggerating; our real problem is that people get burnt out. They just can't take the frustration anymore. They run for their lives. Think of all the women who were exploited and shat on first in the Civil Rights movement and then in SDS, until they just couldn't take it any more; they were emotionally exhausted. And now they're gone, just when we most need them.

Many of us who don't drop out find ourselves, for these same reasons, running from one organizing project to another. This is terrible for us and worse for the people we're organizing. Most of these people, whom we work with in shops, schools or communities, are there because they live there—that's their *life*. We come, we organize for a month or two, maybe six; we may even get our local friends some unfriendly attention from the cops and their neighbors. Then, for personal reasons, because we've changed, or because we feel so alienated, we split. They can't. Many of them will be in the same community for the rest of their lives. They're left holding the bag.

We have to find ways to make long-lasting commitments in such places. Which means we have to give ourselves the kind of support we need to be able to stand it. It's *crazy* to move to a place where we know no one, leaving all our closest friends behind, to live with a few other movement people we don't know well, and to do work the nature of which is undefind and unsupported. How can we expect to be happy and do productive work in projects that start like that? We have to find better ways of organizing ourselves, so we can stick it out, not desert the people we've made friends with in our organizing, and give ourselves the support we need to stay human.

We have to create a movement that people can *live* in, that won't drive them crazy with its impossible goals and standards of purity, with its rapid alterations of line and its inhumanity. If we can't keep people in the movement, we've lost all possibility of continuity and learning from our past. We need all the human resources we have or have ever had, because without them we will not have enough to win our fight, or the experience to deal with the even greater battle, the real revolution that will begin only when we win.

Because we don't really do much consistent outreach, and spend a lot of time with other people in the Movement, we are very conscious of the need to be purely revolutionary. Many people express this need mainly in language; unless every sentence they say has either the word "imperialist" or the word "capitalism" in it, they are afraid they will be accused of insufficient zeal. Most movement people are most afraid of doing something that anyone else in the movement could call reformist. This limits their scope of action to militant events, since any program which has any actual effect on anyone's life is bound to be called reformist by someone in the movement. This dynamic leads to a spiral of revolutionary purism which takes us farther and farther from reaching anyone but ourselves.

Linda: We need to worry less about talking like revolutionaries and more about acting like them. Which means:

We need to talk about the things we care about in a language people can understand, instead of our own peculiar jargon. If we use words like "imperialism" we should explain what they mean, too; and we should never use them more often than we use more ordinary words that mean the same thing.

And which means:

If we are acting like revolutionaries, we won't need to show off by talking big. No one who is doing things that are dangerous should talk about them at all. People who are doing solid organizing from day to day will find it useless to talk about how "heavy" they are.[4]

There was a sorrow and anguish in the *Old Mole* statement that went deeper than the pains of political or personal defeat. The emotions, lying just beneath the analysis, were much like those of many 1930's Communists. Not those who had bandaged themselves with the American flag and gone on to merchandize their anti-Communism, but the others, who had made the party repository of all their ideals, and who

afterwards had become the hollowest of men, unable or unwilling even to mouth other slogans, knowing secretly, that after all and despite all, those years in the party had been their best years. The *Old Mole* collective were not ex-radicals but they too had mortgaged themselves to certain political ideas, not to an ideology but to a moral absolutism that demanded that they go further, become purer, more revolutionary, their politics turning them in narrow, more perfect circles, until they stood alone, spinning among the radius of themselves.

In late 1970 and early 1971, many underground editors and Movement people were going through similar crises. The Weatherman "New Morning—Changing Weather" statement, received at LNS, the *Liberated Guardian,* and several other underground papers in the middle of December 1970 admitted frankly, "This tendency to consider only bombings or picking up the gun as revolutionary, with the glorification of the heavier and the better, we've called the military error. . . . We became aware that a group of outlaws who are isolated from the youth communities do not have a sense of what is going on, cannot develop strategies that grow to include large numbers of people, have become 'us' and 'them.' " LNS decided that it would have to develop a broader journalism, and the *Berkeley Tribe* seemed to muffle its rhetoric and actively sought to involve the community in the paper. Other papers were changing as well, and it seemed that the underground press might spawn a third generation that would synthesize the Movement at its richest and most complex.

LOS ANGELES FREE PRESS

Newspaper

35¢

Beginning a new legal column
25th anniversary of the Bomb
A revealing look at Art Linkletter

190 places to go this week — see page 32

In two parts: Part One
Copyright 1970
The Los Angeles Free Press, Inc.

Volume 7, No. 29 (Issue 313) $6.00 per year   Phone: YES-1970   July 17—23, 1970

JURY COMMITS CRIME IN CONVICTING FREEP

U.S. Constitution found guilty

ART KUNKIN

The jury had been out for six days, days in which we had been sitting in the Mexican restaurant next to the courthouse drinking endless cups of coffee and feeling part of a Kafkaesque nightmare called "The Wait," when the buzzer rang; the jury had a verdict.

And I must confess (because all of us have a certain lesson to learn in this) that I sat there for the next minutes like a stupid fool, certain, despite all that I intellectually know about the prejudice of an American jury, that after hearing the

lack of evidence in the five week trial the jury could not possibly find former *Freep* reporter Jerry Applebaum, the *LA Free Press* Corporation, and myself guilty of the phony and absurd charge of receiving stolen property.

At the beginning of the trial, we defendants and our attorneys, Walter King and Mel Albaum, knew that the jury had been "purified" by the prosecution. There were very few blacks or young people to begin with in the panels we had to choose jurors from, and when the prosecution finished with their

challenges, there wasn't a young face or black face there.

All that was left in the jury box were middle-class, middle-aged suburbanite types; retired men and women; and some city employees; and a few nondescript unemployed types. The youngest person on the jury was a woman in her thirties who was a member of the District Attorney's Law Enforcement Advisory Council, and we left her on because she, at least, was a college graduate. There was no reason to have illusions about that jury and yet, as the trial ended, we were sure that reason would prevail.

Well, reason did not prevail, and, if our experience means anything, it is not likely that reason will prevail in an Amerikan courtroom. That is the lesson of the Chicago Conspiracy trial; that is the lesson of the Panther trials; that is the lesson of most of the student trials.

Yes, you go into a courtroom hoping that at least this time it will be different. You cut your hair (or maybe you don't). You put on a suit and tie (or maybe you don't). And you listen quietly to the evidence and you help your attorney cross examine the prosecution witnesses and you help with the gathering of defense witnesses and you wonder if the so-called liberals who are on the prosecution team of attorneys really mean what they say as they lie to the jury and twist the facts.

And it's worth fighting in the courts on their own terms because once in a while it *is* different. Once in a while a judge has the courage to dismiss an unwarranted prosecution despite his political considerations. Once in a while even a biased American jury can be swung over to the side of justice and common sense by a forceful defense. But how can justice be anything but occasional in the Amerikan courts, particularly when an underground newspaper catering to youth and dissenting intellectuals is involved, when fifty percent of the national population is under 25 and, as in the *Free Press* case, **not one juror was under 30?**

There should not have been a conviction in the *Free Press* case. Look at the two sides!

In their closing arguments Deputy District Attorney Alex Kahanowicz and Deputy Attorney General Ronald George charged that all of the elements involved in the crime of receiving stolen property were proven against the defendants. They said that there was property ("Look, we have some pieces of paper stapled together. What else are these but property?"); it was stolen ("Look, this clerk said he brought it to the *Free Press*"); it was received by the *Free Press* ("Look, there was a discussion about money and there

are fingerprints of the clerk, Applebaum and Kunkin"); there was knowledge that it was stolen property ("Look, Ma! They wrote articles saying the material was secret. How could they look at these particular documents and the hair style of the clerk without being put on notice that the documents were stolen?") .

On the other hand, in his closing argument, defense attorney Mel Albaum went over the same elements (*all of them must exist for a guilty*

(please turn to page 3)

'J'Accuse!' says Free Press publisher Art Kunkin   Photo by Allan Zak

LOS ANGELES FREE PRESS

25¢

Waters: There is an acid test
Youngblood: Television with balls
Ron Cobb: Philosophical Mandala

113 Places to go this week—see page 52

Volume 6, Issue #264 $5.00 PER YEAR   WE 7-1970   August 8-14, 1969

NARCOTIC AGENTS LISTED

There should be no secret police

The people should know the men who are policing their communities. Even the Black Panthers do not propose simply abolishing police departments. Even they recognize the need for peace officers-but their program for community control of police demands that the policeman openly lives in the community in which he works so abusive exercise of power can be controlled.

Secret police forces are a threat to democratic government. History demonstrates that the secret policeman invariably uses his anonymity to become unaccountable to the people over whom power is exercised.

Recently there have been published stories of abuse of power involving narcotics officers. Several officers of many years standing have even been discharged for faking evidence.

Many, if not most, narcotic cases are thrown out of court because the officers have violated the constitutional rights of the suspect in conducting illegal searches and seizure.

But the public at large does not ordinarily hear of the violations of law committed by these secret policemen who are attempting to enforce laws as unwise and unenforceable as the now-banished prohibition of liquor.

There should be no secret police! In this spirit we are publishing in this issue on page 5 the official personnel roster of agents in the California State Bureau of Narcotics for the cities of Los Angeles, San Francisco, Santa Ana, and San Diego. The list is current as of June 1969. Know your local narc!

Know your local Nark

See Page 5

9 Repression

olice boots in the night. Arbitrary arrests. Bone-chilling fears. A bland and shackled press. These are the clear and certain signs of repression. Thus, when most middle-class Americans hear the word "repression" used in describing the contemporary United States, they are irritated, even infuriated at such rhetorical excess. Their anger is misplaced. Enveloped in the soft cocoon that is the American middle class, they can't possibly see that blacks, radicals and youth culture are suffering from persistent and increasing harassment and that our civil liberties have steadily and inevitably declined after half a decade of war.

Underground papers have not only observed, they have also suffered from that repression. Editors have been arrested on trumped-up charges. Paper sellers have been pushed off the street. And printers have been warned not to take work from the underground press.

A thousandfold worse than such common and frequent harassments as these are other abuses that lie in that dark and growing area beyond the traditional boundaries of our civil liberties. Here are monstrous evils that some day may step over into conventional life to haunt us in ways we can scarcely imagine. Nowhere is this more true than with the historic case involving the *Los Angeles Free Press.* In July 1969, twenty-four-year-old Jerry Resnick, a slim young man with vaguely long hair and a wisp of a voice, came into the *Freep*'s office. He said he was a clerk at the state Attorney General's office. He told Jerry Applebaum, then a free-lance reporter for the paper, that he had something that might interest the paper. Resnick showed Applebaum a Xeroxed copy of a report that had been sent to Chief Deputy Attorney General Charles O'Brien by Richard Huffman of the D.A.'s Los Angeles office. It was a shocking document dealing with alleged misconduct on the part of members of the U.C.L.A. police department. The report went so far as to allege that one particular officer may have participated in a burglary of university property and may have committed forcible rape. No journalist could ignore such a document. After deleting the name of the accused officer, the *Free Press* placed an account of the report on the front page under the headline "Secret Report Probes Crimes of U.C.L.A. Cops"

Several days later Resnick returned, this time with a printed pamphlet that contained the names, addresses and phone numbers of eighty California narcotics agents, many of whom were involved in frequent undercover work. In its August 8–14 issue, the *Freep* listed the information on page five and ran this editorial on the front page:

There Should Be No Secret Police

The people should know the men who are policing their communities. Even the Black Panthers do not propose simply abolishing police departments. Even they recognize the need for peace officers— but their program for community control of police demands that the policeman openly lives in the community in which he works, so abusive exercise of power can be controlled.

Secret police forces are a threat to democratic government. History demonstrates that the secret policeman invariably uses his anonymity to become unaccountable to the people over whom power is exercised.

Recently there have been published stories of abuses of power involving narcotics officers. Several officers of many years standing have even been discharged for faking evidence.

Many, if not most, narcotics cases are thrown out of court because the officers have violated the constitutional rights of the suspects in conducting illegal searches and seizures. But the public at large does not ordinarily hear of the violations of law committed by these secret policemen who are attempting to enforce laws as unwise and unenforceable as the now-banished prohibition of liquor. There should be no secret police. In this spirit we are publishing in this issue on page 5 the official personnel roster of agents in the California State Bureau of Narcotics for the cities of Los Angeles, San Francisco, Santa Anna, and San Diego. The list is current as of June, 1969. Know your local narc!

The *Free Press* had justified its position with radical *élan,* flourish and libertarian absolutism, but it is nevertheless true that narcotics traffic is among the most lucrative and vicious areas of organized crime, directed by criminals who might very well kill an undercover police agent. To this, radicals argue that the government has shown absolutely no interest in sustaining a campaign against big-time pushers and operators. It is the hippie youth who is most likely to be arrested by the undercover agent. In any case, the eighty agents suffered only mild harassment, and within days their phone numbers had been changed.

At worst, the *Free Press* had been irresponsible in printing the list, but almost immediately the state of California set out to silence the paper. The state filed a ten-million-dollar obstruction-of-justice civil suit against the paper. Some of the agents also filed a fifteen-million-dollar class action on behalf of the agents, claiming invasion of privacy. That latter suit was filed before all the agents knew of it and was presented to the *Free Press* by men from the Attorney General's office, government officials who never before had served papers in a private lawsuit. Soon afterwards, the state charged Art Kunkin, the publisher, and Jerry Applebaum with receiving stolen property—a felony. The law dealing with this practice was aimed at the professional fences, who make the stealing of property a profitable business. Receiving stolen goods is considered a more serious offense than the actual theft (which can be a misdemeanor), and it is punishable by as much as ten years' imprisonment and a fine of ten thousand dollars. The state had to resort to such a farfetched charge, since at that time the act of publishing such "private" public documents was not illegal—an oversight that has been corrected in a new law rushed through the state legislature.

The act of publishing the documents, then, was theoretically not in question, and the state did not appear to have much of a case. Irresponsibility is not a crime. If the *Free Press* were convicted, then any editor who even looked at a proffered document, or a Xeroxed copy for that matter, could find himself charged with a criminal offense. As every reporter knows, investigative reporting is necessarily a nefarious craft. Often it is built out of the whispered tales of the bitter and the discontent

or of the frankly amoral cunning of the reporter. Seymour Hersh, who broke the story of the My Lai massacre, followed a trail constructed of bluffing and half-truths that led him from a Washington rumor to Lieutenant William L. Calley—subsequently convicted of murdering Vietnamese civilians—in Fort Benning, Georgia. At one crucial point, as Hersh himself admits, he got a private "to steal Calley's personal file," [1] not a Xeroxed copy or a printed pamphlet but the battalion information sheet itself. For these sins Hersh received the 1970 Pulitzer Prize in International Reporting, the highest honor in American journalism.

Disgruntled former employees of Senator Thomas Dodd secretly entered the Connecticut Senator's office, removed documents from his private files, Xeroxed them, and after replacing the originals gave the copies to Drew Pearson, the syndicated columnist. Although Pearson knew that the information had been stolen, he made the documents the basis for a major exposé. Senator Dodd filed a civil suit against Pearson, but the court ruled against the Senator; it said that

the question here is not whether appellee had a right to keep his files from prying eyes, but whether the information taken from these files falls under the protection of the law of property, enforceable by a suit for conversion. In our view, it does not. The information included the contents of letters to appellee from supplicants, and office records of other kinds, the nature of which is not fully revealed by the record. Insofar as we can tell, none of it amounts to literary property, to scientific invention, or to secret plans formulated by appellee for the conduct of commerce. Nor does it appear to be information held in any way for sale by appellee, analogous to the fresh news copy produced by a wire service.

The state's case against the *Free Press* rested on the prosecution's ability to block out First Amendment questions from the courtroom, to convince the jury that the information was stolen property and to make Kunkin and Applebaum out as common criminals. It was clear, too, that a jury of laymen would find it difficult to separate the act of receiving the documents from the more dramatic and morally ambiguous and legally irrelevant one of publishing the information. If the prosecution could smudge that crucial dividing line between receipt of the documents and their publication, it would be to the state's advantage. To argue their case, the state of California took the almost unprecedented step of having as prosecutors Deputy Attorney General Ronald George, a high official who specializes in appellate law and almost never argues cases in court, along with Alex Kahanowicz, a deputy district attorney.

Walter King and Mel Albaum, the defense attorneys, are high-strung, intense criminal lawyers, proud of their abilities to shave legal nuances. They were not Movement lawyers. By inclination and training they were prepared to argue the case with much the same restraint and care they would employ with their more typical cases, and only occasionally would they burst out of their traditional court demeanor and highlight by gesture, rhetoric and defense that this was a blatant and unprecedented political trial.

As for their clients, Applebaum is a wily, fidgety twenty-five-year-old radical with a receding hairline, a stringy beard, and an abrupt diffident manner calculated to offend many Americans. Kunkin is generally mild-mannered. He may have hair that falls down in a pageboy, but in court he wore a conservative suit and tie.

Nevertheless, Kunkin and Applebaum were not defendants with whom most juries would feel an instant affinity. On the jury in this case, the youngest member was a woman in her mid-thirties, a college graduate and a member of the District Attorney's Law Enforcement Advisory Council, and there were two aged retirees and a solid contingent of middle-aged suburbanites. In all it was a jury of such good, solid citizens as might be expected to view long hair with bewilderment and possibly contempt.

The judge was a different matter. Harold J. Ackerman is a heavy-jowled, highly respected veteran of the bench, with a reputation for sound opinions and, if anything, a liberal bias. Judge Ackerman treats the law as a subtle mechanism, more a product of physics than of the liberal arts. And thus he guided the *Free Press* trial along careful, classic lines, favoring challenges and objections as a gourmet would a particularly exotic buffet, and in the process refining out the political content.

This may have been all very well, but as to what the jury understood —whisked in and out of the courtroom, presented with days of complicated arguments—it was, of course, impossible to ascertain. At least the public could hear the full arguments, but few spectators, either friend or foe of the paper, ever visited the court. Except for a scattering of perennial court watchers—those sad, querulous types who gain their emotional subsistence feeding off the courtroom lives of others—the public seating area was empty. Almost no members of the press even looked in on this precedent-setting trial. A few blocks away, though, scores of journalists scrambled into the Manson trial to provide grist for the public rumor mill. The local media did not consider themselves the least bit derelict in their duties. "It's just an ordinary trial," Bill Thomas, city editor of the *Los Angeles Times,* told this writer in the midst of the proceedings. "It has nothing to do with freedom of the press. For what they did they got what was coming to them."

Deputy Attorney General George, a refined, well-dressed attorney in his mid-thirties, presented his case with care and great detail. In their closing arguments the prosecuting attorneys George and Kahanowicz tried to show that they had proved all elements of theft. First, the Xerox copy and the pamphlet were property. Second, since the clerk had taken them from the mailroom and brought them to the *Free Press* office, they were stolen. Resnick and Applebaum even discussed payment, although none had been authorized or made. Finally, the *Free Press* headline "Secret Report" above the story proved that they knew the documents had been stolen. What could be a clearer case of receiving stolen property?

In summation for the defense, Albaum argued that those three elements of theft, all of which must be present to warrant a guilty verdict, simply were not there. He pointed out that the materials in question were public documents bearing no indication that they were to be considered secret. Even if they had been marked "secret," newspapers still have a right to ferret out information which government agencies arbitrarily withhold. As for the material having been stolen, Albaum asserted that the prosecution had not offered firm evidence that the Xerox was made on government equipment; the narcotics roster, itself, was a printed document that circulated widely in the District Attorney's office and even was used by secretaries and others for Christmas-card lists. On the third point, whether Kunkin and Applebaum knew the documents were stolen, Albaum stated that the testimony of Jerry Resnick, the clerk, proved that Kunkin and Applebaum did not know. Resnick had testified that he had told Applebaum he had obtained the documents through his employment. Moreover, Resnick had told the court that he stated explicitly to Applebaum that he was only lending the documents to the *Free Press;* he definitely wanted them back.

After Albaum had worked his way through the evidence, arguing with much the same restraint, shrewdness and narrow logic that he would employ in any criminal case, he began his concluding remarks. Now his voice crescendoed and he spoke at a fever pitch:

When I sit and listen to the prosecution's tangential approach, when they say we are just dealing with the receiving of stolen property, I think that I've lost my mind. I sat on the beach on the Fourth of July with my children and all I could think about was "They are trying to destroy my country."

This prosecution is the most vicious, sneaky, pernicious back-door attack on a fundamental American freedom that I have ever seen or read. I think that it is more vicious than the attack on Pearl Harbor, because this country will never be destroyed by force or violence, from without or within. The way we will lose our freedom is to abdicate it through the back door, by taking away the freedom of the press while telling you they are prosecuting for receiving stolen property. That's the real purpose of the prosecution. It's been evident from the very first day of the trial: take away the freedom of the newspapers.

During the trial the thought crossed my mind that I had mishandled this case by muzzling my clients. But I believe in this system of justice. You will get the court's instructions that you must rely on the state of the evidence, and I told my clients, "There is no evidence here, you have committed no crime, absolutely no crime. Every scintilla of evidence points to innocence, and you may rely on the state of that evidence."

They want you, the jury, to destroy a newspaper and to destroy freedom of the press without ever telling you. That is their intention. And I say: Base your verdict on the evidence, and don't do it. Refuse to do it!

After six days of deliberation, the jury returned its verdict: Guilty. Late in August Judge Ackerman issued sentences so light that they could be construed only as a direct rebuke to the government and its case. The court fined Kunkin one thousand dollars and put him on three years' probation, Applebaum five thousand dollars with three years' probation, and the *Free Press* Corporation five hundred dollars (execution of sentence suspended) with no probation. Immediately, the *Free Press* appealed the case. By this time, the *Los Angeles Times,* the premier newspaper of southern California, had finally realized the implications of the case and now publicly supported the *Free Press* in its historic appeal. "Should this case stand and become a precedent," Gene Blake wrote in the September 20, 1970, issue, "the impact on the investigative efforts of the press to disclose wrongdoing in government could be devastating." The *Los Angeles Times* reprinted that article and mailed it to about a thousand publishers and journalism schools across the country.

The *Free Press* settled the ten-million-dollar "obstruction of justice" civil lawsuit out of court by agreeing to pay the State $10,000 in twenty monthly installments of $500. This smacked of compromise or even capitulation, and in the December 15, 1970, *Free Press* the paper carefully, almost legalistically, explained the decision:

". . . The law firm of King and Albaum felt that it would be difficult, if not impossible, to get a jury in the ten-million-dollar civil action which would be capable of looking behind the emotional issues of narcotics law enforcement to the substantial freedom-of-press issues in the case. Their judgment was that the case would ultimately have to be appealed and that it might cost as much as $40,000 for the *Free Press* to be vindicated. . . . Therefore, when the negotiations . . . showed that it was possible for the *Free Press* to get rid of the Attorney General's case out of court without admitting liability, much as two insurance adjusters might settle an automobile-accident claim out of court to avoid the expense of trial, the *Free Press* was forced by practical financial considerations to submit to the unfair settlement. . . . We felt it was better to do this than be forced out of operation; better to lose a battle and still preserve our ability to continue fighting for what we believe to be right."

Kunkin did not bother with so thorough an explanation when, four months later, he settled the fifteen-million-dollar civil suit with the California Narcotics Agents out of court for $43,000. This is to be paid in installments of $2,000 a month, beginning in February 1972. The settlement also obligated Kunkin to apologize to the wives and children of the agents in print, which he did on the front page of the *Free Press* in the April 23, 1971, issue ("I willingly agree to this apology and tender it here because, frankly, it had never entered my mind nor was it my intention that the publication of the list of Narcotics Bureau personnel would lead to harassment of the families of the agents"). The agreement was neatly and ironically summarized in the banner headline above the apology: NARCS 43,000 —FREEP 0.

Local authorities do not have to employ court cases to pressure underground papers out of existence. In many communities, papers are lucky to last six months. A couple of arrests for littering or soliciting without a license, a fine as small as two hundred dollars often can wipe out the entire staff and capital. Printers are another problem. The Jackson, Mississippi, *Kudzu* has to be printed in New Orleans; Austin's *Rag* in a city a hundred miles away; Atlanta's *Great Speckled Bird* in Montgomery, Alabama; New York's *Rat* in various cities along the Eastern seaboard.

One of the few printers who resisted intimidation was fifty-seven-year-old Bill Schanen, of Port Washington, Wisconsin. A soft-spoken man with the build of a drill sergeant, Schanen had published the weekly *Ozaukee Press* since 1940. During most of 1970 he also published *Kaleidoscope,* the Milwaukee underground that political radicals often criticize as "bourgeois." When the word got around that Schanen was involved with *Kaleidoscope,* the *Press* became the subject of a boycott led by a local right-wing industrialist and such organizations as the American Legion. In June 1970, the very week that the *Press* won first place in general excellence in the 1969 National Newspaper Association contest, twenty-five advertisers canceled. Many others followed. Stores refused to carry the paper. The F.B.I. paid a visit. In all, Schanen lost about $200,000 in 1970. He even had to sell two of his three papers. But he refused to stop printing *Kaleidoscope.* He was a stubborn man. He said he believed in freedom of the press. In February 1971 he died of a heart attack.

The harassment of underground papers pushes them relentlessly, inexorably away from the trust and openness that once was at the essence of the Movement. In San Diego, for instance, over half the twenty-member commune that put out the San Diego *Street Journal* live and work out of a grand old mansion once owned by a local aristocrat. Despite a dearth of solid furnishings, an assortment of beat-up cars drawn up outside, and a high raw-wood fence put up by the next-door neighbors, the house retains something of the elegant lassitude of old San Diego. So it is doubly incongruous—in relation both to the habits of this palm-tree-lined, middle-class neighborhood and to common journalistic practice —to learn that from 8 P.M. to 6 A.M. every night, the men and women of the "people's commune" take turns keeping shotgun watch on the front porch.

These underground journalists are by no means paranoiac, acting out someone else's fantasies of revolution. In late October 1969, the paper—then still known as the San Diego *Free Press*—published an exposé of the financial chicanery of C. Arnholt Smith, a leading citizen and multimillionaire. The piece, credited to one "M. Raker," was largely a rehash of a substantial exposé that had appeared in the *Wall Street Journal* in June 1969. It told how Smith had pyramided his fortune by having the U.S. National Bank and the Westgate-California Corporation, publicly owned firms on whose boards of directors he sits, buy Smith-family-owned companies at inflated prices. The message to *Wall Street Journal* readers was to steer away from Smith-controlled enterprises. The "people's commune" had a different message. Next to the muckraking article, the paper presented an elaborate power-structure chart depicting Smith as standing at the center of a small group of business leaders, all directors of either the U.S. National Bank or the Westgate-California Corp. Here, the paper suggested, is San Diego's power elite.

Unfortunately for the *Street Journal*, San Diego is run as a very taut ship. The city has the look and feel of the prewar Honolulu that James Jones depicted in *From Here to Eternity*. In this naval base, flag-waving patriotism is an obligation, a pastime and an economic necessity.

It is a corrupt city, with Mafia links documented in grand-jury reports, and a police force noted primarily for duplicity and graft. Nevertheless, San Diego's tiny business elite are unabashed boosters, terribly proud that their city may soon surpass San Francisco to become California's second-largest city. They have absolutely no use for those who fancy themselves radicals or revolutionaries.

In November the *Street Journal* began to suffer harassment that in the paper's eyes appeared intended to drive them out of town. On November 18, bullets from a 38-caliber weapon shot through the office window. On November 23, five patrol cars surrounded the offices, entered, and searched the premises without a search warrant. On November 29, the office's glass front door was smashed and 2,500 copies of the *Street Journal* were stolen—with little police investigation. In that November more than twenty street venders were arrested by the police for "obstructing the sidewalk," were handcuffed, searched and jailed, under an ordinance subsequently declared unconstitutional by the municipal court. On December 11, police without a search warrant entered the "people's commune" residence and arrested a guest on "suspicion of burglary," handcuffed him, and later let him go without taking him to jail. On Christmas Eve someone broke into the offices and destroyed over four thousand dollars' worth of typesetting equipment—with little police investigation. On January 3, a *Street Journal* car was firebombed, with little police investigation. On January 18 and 25, venders were arrested, handcuffed, searched, and booked for littering.

Any journalist worth his salt

Street Journal

& SAN DIEGO FREE PRESS   VOL. 2, NO. 10, ISSUE 35   JAN. 16 - 22

SAN DIEGO FREE DOOR ATTACKED

WHEN WILL WE STOP THIS TERRORISM?

Wednesday, January 14, the office of the San Diego Free Door was broken into and over $1000 worth of equipment was damaged or destroyed.

More shocking than this, several hundred names, phone numbers and addresses of local people were stolen from the Door's files. What these perverts intend to do with this information is frightening.

Meanwhile, several people remotely associated with the Street Journal have received death threats since a December 25 vandalism spree conducted on our office. Apparently, the intruders did more than destroy our machinery.

So what?

Did you know that every member of the extremist, right-wing Minutemen organization carries a card that bears the name of a person that the particular member is required to assassinate once the word is given?

Did you also know that San Diego and Orange counties are bastions of Minutemen stength? How many indictments and co convictions of such people have you seen in our county?

What happens when the Free Door asked to have an investigator take fingerprints? "We'll try to have someone come out on Friday or Monday."

The Street Journal has had a car fire-bombed, $4000 in machines destroyed and 2,500 copies of one issue stolen by "burglars", all while police maintain a 24-hour surveillance on us and our home. The police respond by: busting a cocktail party intended to raise funds for local projects, arresting our people on the street for insane charges, impounding our cars and taunting our street vendors.

The City responds by harassing us with housing, licensing and business codes so unenforced dust obliterates their type!

Likewise, a local Free School is virtually destroyed by Minutemen who leave a calling card. Bullet holes appear in the windows of local bookstores and liberal lawyers' offices by the same people. One lawyer's office was blasted by a home-made bomb several months ago.

What has been done? What is being done?

Local agencies manage to exterminate the local chapter of the Black Panther Party and their Free Breakfast Program. At the same time they know that the area headquarters of the Minutemen is located in an old DC-3 at the Ramona airport -- yet they don't act!

Where will the fascist perverts strike next?

Maybe against us. Maybe against you. Who will protect us -- the police??

It would be a precedent.

It is time to show our disgust that multi-millionaires can turn the city administration on and off like a cold water tap, that insane terrorists can rampage the county with impunity and local police, charged with protecting and serving the People, have nothing better to do than hassling longhairs, blacks and chicanos.

Now the names of many local citizens are in the hands of of maniacs. Is your name among those stolen?

We all can fight back by demanding a thorough investigation of local terrorists and their involvement with local law enforcement agencies.

We are the People, each one of us -- and our demands had better be answered!

There will be a mass demonstration to DEMAND ACTION!

Information will be circulated throughout the city regarding time, place and whatever.

DON'T SIT BACK WHILE AMERICA TURNS INTO A NAZI GERMANY AND SAN DIEGO INTO A DACHAU!!!

would have taken one look at the *Street Journal*'s troubles and known he had the makings of a great story. It was a story that involved journalistic freedom, and newspapers are terribly conscientious about protecting their own freedoms. Nevertheless, the Copley-owned *Union* and *Evening Tribune* exercised their news monopoly in San Diego by burying the story, further substantiating their reputation as two of the most biased right-wing papers in America. It wasn't until *Time* picked up on the *Street Journal*'s problem in March that San Diegans could read in an aboveground publication an account that presented the situation with a modicum of fairness and thoroughness.

Fed up with the banal pap served up twice daily by the Copley Press, many San Diegans began reading the *Street Journal*. By the end of 1969 the paper had become a major conversation piece, and the circulation of the year-and-a-half-old paper nudged above 8,000. The local fame —or notoriety, if you will—helped the "people's commune" in its investigative reporting. There were not a few residents with axes to grind. In the early months of 1970, the *Street Journal* featured exposés on the Copley Press empire; on Irvin J. Kahn, one of the country's largest subdividers and land speculators, and a major local figure; and on the manner in which local citizens were allegedly duped into paying for a Sports Arena.

The most extraordinary report was a solid seven-page article in a March issue on the activities of ███ ████████ a colleague of ███████████ █████, and one of San Diego's most influential citizens. The article reported on corruption at ████ ███

██ ████ race track in Tijuana, explaining how the track managed to set its percentage at more than twice that of U.S. tracks and how horses are "sponged," their nostrils stuffed with cotton wads to impede their breathing and slow their performance. One of the more intriguing accusations involved the track's gallery of big winners, a display in which Mexican faces predominate:

The reason for this is that most of the Mexican winners are frauds. In reality, they are track employees; in reality the money they've won is pocketed by ███ ███. From their angle, they are told by higher up track officials that they can make an extra $50–$100 bucks if they agree to "stand in" for an American winner who does not want to be photographed because "he does not want the publicity." The American who does not want the publicity is always a close associate of ███████████. For example, in the picture shown below, ████████████ is shown as the winner of $39,047.20. Actually, he works on the track in the capacity of groom and is not afraid, when asked properly, to say that he did not win that money at all, but that he stood in for an American who did not want the publicity; the American turns out to be none other than █████████ niece!

(Now listen, ████████████, don't get angry and fire that poor little ████████ ███ because he admitted to your fraudulent practises [sic]. I lied to him because I told him that I did not want to pay the U.S. Federal tax on it, and I was told that he could cash it for me and not pay the tax in return for a few bucks. But how could I trust him not to run off with all my bread once I gave him my ticket? Humbly but proudly he told me that he just wanted a few bucks and that he could prove his trustworthiness because he had posed for ███████████ neice [sic], and done the same thing for her. Don't fire him, nurture him: he is a good student and faithful person—he's probably got a lot of kids to feed.)

It was the sort of report that if it had been published in an establishment paper might have been considered for national journalism awards. It happened that on April 7, 1970, Alessio was indicted for income-tax evasion. The laurels the paper won from local liberals did not sit well on the heads of the people's commune. "To us muckraking is just public relations," says Lowell Bergman. "It's a hype. It creates attention." The *Street Journal* did not want the city to forget for a moment that they were attacking capitalism and not just a few bad guys.

By the autumn of 1970 the pressure on the *Street Journal* had let up, perhaps because the paper was seeking an injunction against the police, or because of national publicity, or because of that shotgun watch. The tension remained. The people's commune believed that in Mexico some of them had ten-thousand-dollar price tags on their heads as a result of the Caliente exposé.

In Houston, the front door of the *Space City!* office is double-locked and braced with plexiglass. At night the building is lighted up with floodlamps and watched over by a staff member who sleeps there, a loaded shotgun at his side. No one used to sleep in the office. Then at midnight in July 1969, not long after the paper began, two people tossed a bomb through the door, blowing up part of the front office and the glass-and-chicken-wire door.

Not long afterward someone broke into the office and stole a photo enlarger and papers. By then it was clear that one staffer would have to stay in the office at night. Sherwood Bishop, an earnest twenty-four-year-old former union lobbyist, volunteered. "I was afraid for a long, long time. I had only been there for about a week when two of them broke in. I was standing at the top of the staircase. I sprayed them with Mace. They ran out the door and jumped in a car with a girl. They were Ku Klux Klan. They had a NEVER license plate. Later I happened to see one of them downtown and I told him I was the one who had maced him. 'Yeah,' he said, 'Next time we'll blow your head off.' "

Since then, though, the paper has not been invaded. Instead the attackers have taken to slashing tires of *Space City!* cars. They attach a knife to a long pole and puncture the tires as they cruise slowly by. In April, the terrorists added a new weapon to their arsenal. It was the day Abbie Hoffman, the Yippie leader and Chicago conspiracy member, was scheduled to arrive in Houston. He had been asked to Houston by *Space City!*, and the invitation had been a subject for considerable local debate and numerous direct threats against the paper. The *Space City!* people have learned to take such threats seriously.

During the night two people kept watch, peering out of the upstairs front window, each with a shotgun in his lap. At 5:45 A.M. a car known to the commune as a K.K.K. vehicle pulled up. A passenger got out, cocked a crossbow and fired a heavy steel arrow through the plexiglass door. According to *Space City!* the police did not respond to their telephoned call for help. The police were unable to locate the assailants even though commune members had

20¢
in Dallas
25 cents Texas
30 cents out of state

DALLAS NOTES

October 15 – November 4, 1969   Volume III, Number 15

SPEED ISSUE

given the car's description and li-cense-plate numbers. Jack Miller, a Houston community-relations officer, pleads extenuating circumstances. "This is a situation that can't be helped," Officer Miller says. "We're understaffed and underpowered. We'd like to improve."

Farther north in *Dallas Notes* country Bret Steiner—or Stoney Burns, as he is commonly known—has had even more problems. *Dallas Notes* is an often outrageous pastiche of news, cartoons, exposés, a heavy meld of cultural articles, and an oc-casional nude, all put together with a gleeful, nothing-is-going-to-stop-us irreverence. This does not sit well with Dallas authorities. In October 1968, police converged on the paper's rambling old house with a search warrant allowing them to look for "pornographic materials." They car-ried over two tons of material out to their two waiting flat-bed trucks—back issues of *Notes* and other under-grounds, four typewriters, credit cards, costume jewelry, and two cans of spice—and left the office a sham-bles, strewn with papers, ripped-up letters, torn-out lamp wiring and refrigerator controls. Steiner stood calmly by, shaking his healthy mane of hair and reading from his little red book of *"Quotations from Chair-man Mao"* such observations as "The organs of the state must practice democratic centralism, they must rely on the masses, and their personnel must serve the people"—with that not terribly subtle irony and put-on obli-gatory for underground-press life in Dallas.

Police charged the *Dallas Notes* editor with "possession of pornog-raphy," a charge subsequently re-jected by federal courts. (The two tons of material were returned only after a suit against the police.) In November the police returned, this time to search for drugs. Finding none, they arrested Steiner for ob-scenity. This charge also was thrown out. The following January, un-known persons broke into the house and destroyed the typewriters. In May, two other typewriters were van-dalized, while everything else in the house was left untouched. Lieutenant Truman Snider, who led the first October raid, denies that the police have acted with less than professional acumen toward *Dallas Notes*. "We returned their material," he says. "Everything was in order. We aren't going to be guilty of tearing up anybody's property. They also claim that we are watching their house. Believe me, we have more to do than that."

When Doug Baker, who had founded *Dallas Notes* at South-ern Methodist University in 1967, returned to Dallas he was taken aback by the constant harassment. In a March 1970 issue, he cata-logued Steiner's woes: "Assault-mur-der threats—cop-pig raids—arrests—having his automobiles shot up, van-dalized and stolen—thousands of dol-lars of production equipment com-pletely destroyed; daily crank calls at all hours and the confiscation of everything from spices to the sub-scription list—hauled off in two po-lice/pig moving vans—have all been part of Stoney's daily existence here in Dallas. Not to mention corporate threats and anonymous letters that lie about our paper which all our advertisers received/receive."

Such attention can go to the head of a Dallas-bred Yippie peace freak. Steiner's hair has grown longer and longer into a magnificent crescent calculated to infuriate the matrons of Dallas. The paper, itself, if anything, tweaks the noses of local sacred cows with even greater bite and now with biweekly regularity to a paid readership that reaches 15,000.

Dallas Notes is nonetheless in no danger of being clasped to the bosom of the Establishment. On the second Sunday in April 1970, Steiner went to Lee Park to join two or three thousand others in the Sunday rock and good-vibes scene that is part of youth culture in practically every town and city across the United States. When police arrested several people swimming in Turtle Creek the crowd booed and whistled. Reinforcements soon arrived including one officer with a shotgun, and the groovy Sunday afternoon turned into a full-scale riot. The police arrested Steiner and charged him with instigating a riot, an offense that can bring from two to ten years in prison.

According to Jay Gaulding's story in *Dallas Notes* and the corroboration of several witnesses, that wasn't quite what happened. "Stoney and

longer into a magnificent crescent

I were standing about forty feet from the pigline on a grassy knoll sort of overlooking the confrontation," writes Gaulding. "One of the motherfuckers pointed directly at Stoney and yelled 'There's one we want, right there!' Four of them charged up the hill towards us. 'Run, goddamit,' one *Notes* staffer yelled, 'We've got an issue to put out this weekend.' 'No,' Stoney replied. 'They know where I live and would just come after me anyway. I've got bond money and I'll just go peacefully.' All he had time to do before the four cops jumped him was throw up both hands in the air and shout, 'I'll go peacefully!' They knocked him to the ground and beat the holy shit out of him. They dragged him down the hill to the concrete and then, joined by a fifth crony carried him to a nearby pigmobile."

Steiner has since left *Dallas Notes*. At his first trial, in February 1971, the arresting officer, A. M. Cessna, testified that Steiner had been a leader of the crowd. "I was somewhat confused and scared," the policeman told the court. "He [Steiner] walked towards me, pointed right at me and said, 'Kill that pig bastard.' Then my reaction was to grab him the best way I could and that's what I did. I was in fear of my life. I figured he might kill me but he was gonna have a pretty good fight." The first trial ended in a hung jury. At the second trial, during the summer of 1971, the jury found Steiner guilty and the judge sentenced the young activist to three years in jail, a sentence Steiner has been appealing. After the trial one of the jurors was quoted as saying that he and his colleagues had decided that "yelling and jumping up and down is not the way to

KUDZU 25¢

MAY 1970
VOL. II NO.6

JACKSON STATE
MASSACRE

protest and we actually agreed on the verdict because of the obscene 'fuck the pig bastards' statement and the raising of the 'revolutionary clenched fists.' " [2]

So much of the hatred of *Dallas Notes* is based on the idea that the paper is disgusting, degenerate, perverse, obscene filth. Charles Robert Poteet, a rotund family man, was so upset after purchasing a copy of the paper that he formed a League for Decent Dallas to stamp out such literature. "If we continue the way we are for the next ten years," Poteet told the Dallas City Council in June 1970, "people will be mating in the streets of Dallas." The Council members agreed, to the last man, that something would have to be done about *Dallas Notes*—this in a city with at least twenty "skin flicks," and as many sex-book stores. What offends people like Poteet is not the limited sexual content of *Dallas Notes* but its context. The sexual content is not carefully delineated as permissible vice but is blatantly set out as part of a youth-peace-sex-dope-love convulsion that seems poised to swamp all the desperately cherished beliefs and folkways of middle America.

In Jackson, the capital of Mississippi, and a city of 230 churches, the *Kudzu,* the local underground, is viewed as an anti-Christ, the malignant carrier of the germs of degeneracy and anti-Americanism. Here again, it is not the political radicalism and the mild attempts at investigative reporting that so infuriates the citizenry. "The last issue shocked a lot of people," says Charles Smith, city editor of the *Clarion Ledger,* about the May 1970 *Kudzu.* "It was all those four-letter words. People just don't understand why they put those four-letter words in. It shakes people up so."

The cover of that issue displayed a full-page photo of a bullet-riddled dormitory under the large black headline, JACKSON STATE MASSACRE. "We were at first reluctant to use the word 'massacre' in referring to the Jackson State killings," the *Kudzu* editorialized, "but the dictionary definition of a massacre is: the killing of a number of human beings under circumstances of atrocity or cruelty. The Mississippi State Highway Patrol perpetrated a massacre at Jackson State." The lead story detailed in restrained, almost legal language, the events leading up to the shooting deaths of two students, the steady cadence of facts and details building up to a terrible condemnation of Mississippi, racism and police brutality.

This story did not faze white Jackson in the least. It was those two small cartoons, lost among display ads, on the last two inside pages of the *Kudzu* that so upset them and set them to talking. They weren't even cartoons, really—just two panels from underground comic features, one showing a group of people saying, "Aw fuck it," the other a longhair giving a policeman the finger and saying, "Cops eat shit." They simply made no *sense.* Thrown into the paper to add graphic interest, they confounded the logic of Jackson. They simply had to have some hidden meaning, some reason for being there.

The *Kudzu* takes its name from a thickly foliaged vine that grows almost uncontrollably through the deep South, its tentacle-like extensions wrapping around trees, fences, tele-

phone poles and even houses. The cover of that first September 1968 issue showed the familiar kudzu vines clutched around Mississippi, the state peopled by an improbable combination of symbols—a black and a white hand shaking, a burning cross, a hangman's noose, a peace symbol, a hookah and a mushroom. As one might expect the *Kudzu* staff had little time for ideological disputes. Founded by David Doggett on money he had saved while on subsistence wages as an organizer for the S.S.O.C. (Southern Student Organizing Committee), the *Kudzu* is a slapdash, irregular affair, heavy in Southern and hip-cultural coverage, and full of tales of the paper's latest run-in with the local vice squad, accounts complete with names and descriptions of the offending officers.

Those steeped in post-Reconstruction history might suggest that the most amazing thing of all is that here, in the cradle of the Confederacy, the *Kudzu* can exist at all. The paper is able to publish primarily because of those two maligned and tired survivors of the Southern integration movement—civil-rights lawyers and the United States Constitution. "If it weren't for the lawyers, the *Kudzu* would be out of business and the staff in jail," says Armand Derfner, Jackson counsel for the Lawyers Constitutional Defense Committee (L.C.D.C.) of the A.C.L.U.

The life of the *Kudzu* staff has not been a bed of magnolias. They have been harassed to such an extent that in less than two years the paper has gone through at least four turnovers in staff. Doggett alone remains, a guiding force and resident historian.

"At the beginning there were so many hassles. Four people selling the paper were arrested for obstructing traffic and resisting arrest. The next day fifteen of us went out and everybody was thrown into jail and charged with vagrancy and some with resisting arrest. That's not so bad now, but there's all that petty shit of getting evicted from apartments, getting parking tickets, and stuff like that. Last year someone loosened the wheel bolts on our Volkswagen bus. I was driving and luckily I felt the car wobbling. Twice this year I've been slugged. The first time happened when a high-school student pulled my peace leaflets away from me and knocked me to the ground. The other time was at Millsap College at the football stadium. I was coming on campus when a drunk leaving a game started swearing at me. I gave him the bird and he rushed up and started swinging."

Until recently the *Kudzu* people lived in a rickety old two-story house, the slate-gray paint chipping so badly that it seemed the building was shedding its skin, the front porch sagging menacingly, and the bathroom resplendent with a hole in the floor. Here all the local long-hairs and white malcontents would congregate to sit in the tiny living room listening to the Stones, the Beatles, Airplane, and Santana, ignoring the dull clunking of the air conditioner and the ever-present possibility of a police drug bust.

The drug bust is a familiar scene on underground papers. Drug laws represent another of those dark areas beyond the traditional framework of civil liberties. "They got Al Capone for income-tax evasion not for bootlegging," says Bret Steiner, editor of *Dallas Notes.* "That's the hardest thing to get people to realize. If they had gotten us for dope during the police raids on our office, the A.C.L.U. wouldn't even have taken the case." In comparing himself to the Chicago gangster Steiner has perhaps not chosen the aptest of metaphors. He is correct though, for even among that minority of lawyers concerned about abridgment of our freedom, it is a rare man who gets upset over arrests for bonafide narcotics violations.

This lack of concern might be acceptable if there weren't such a selective enforcement of drug laws. Who among the estimated twenty million Americans who have smoked marijuana is most likely to be arrested? The hip radical. He is the one whose very appearance categorizes him as a suspicious character. He is the one whose car is likely to be stopped. Scores of underground press people have been arrested. And since marijuana is as ubiquitous in the underground as crab grass in suburbia, underground press people live with the pesky fear that today may be the day of the big bust. To all this one might well argue, "Aren't the police only doing their duty?" Imagine, though, if police posed as waiters and bartenders while others hid outside elite drinking places, in order to enforce laws regarding drunken driv-

ers, the horrors of our weekend highways. That kind of duty would end promptly.

Discrimination does not end once the arrest is made. A first offense in one state can bring a lengthy prison term, whereas somewhere else it means almost automatic probation. The sentence often depends on the whim and wisdom of the individual judge, the wits of one's lawyer, and the wealth of one's family. Almost inevitably, too, a radical is going to receive a much stiffer sentence than anyone else. In Texas, in August 1968, Lee Otis Johnson, a former S.N.C.C. organizer, was sentenced to a maximum of thirty years in federal prison for handing a marijuana cigarette to an undercover police agent. In provincial towns like Jackson, drugs often take on an overwhelming importance in hip culture. For a long-hair what else is there? No music concerts. No groovy scenes. No hip area. Nothing. In the last two years marijuana, LSD, even Methedrine have found their way into the colleges and high schools of the area. The *Kudzu,* like many underground papers, prints a "consumers report" on available drugs, and understandably the police have gotten the impression that the *Kudzu* people are involved in the drug traffic.

Experimenters in the Jackson area have injoyed [sic] a wide ranging variety of hallucinogenics and a very stable market of hashish. Although weed has been pretty scarce overall some very fine Mexican and Vietnamese grass has been available for between $15 to $20 a lid . . . Jackson during the last few months has enjoyed a host of good hash in dependable amounts. Lebanese Red, Black Turkish (opiated), and Black Afghanistan (opiated) were here and enjoyed by everyone who smoked them. The price of hash has ranged between $1 and $5 for singles and from $1 to $2.50 for quantity. . . . As yet heroin, morphine, cocaine, etc., have found no substantial place on the overall Jackson market.

—Stone

The vice squad's logic told them that anyone who takes drugs over any length of time almost inevitably ends up dealing—and it is true that some underground papers have made ends meet by selling a little marijuana here and there. This didn't happen to be the case with the *Kudzu,* although the paper's provocative, baiting articles on the drug scene and police antidrug activities drove some younger Jackson officers to near distraction. It wasn't just the articles. It was the way the *Kudzu* people talked, and dressed, and even walked, that taunted the police so terribly. It was Peggy Stone and Sharon Gordy, two local women with the looks and upbringing that should have made them fawned-over, much courted Southern women ("If you're not what they think a Southern woman is, they go crazy.") whose very existence mocked the police, whose short skirts, profanity and mannerisms mocked them as no one else in Jackson dared to.

In the spring of 1970, then, the *Kudzu* house became hot, very hot indeed. On several occasions the vice squad entered the building, usually in the predawn hours, sometimes with and sometimes without a warrant. On one such visit the police found marijuana seeds beneath the house but they made no arrests. The pressure was such that two *Kudzu* people, Doggett and Bill Rusk, found a house elsewhere, although other staff members stayed on.

In early June the vice squad rented a house directly behind the *Kudzu* residence to provide constant day-by-day, hour-by-hour surveillance. The police could drive up to their quarters through driveways on either side of the *Kudzu* house, but whenever a car belonging to the *Kudzu* people or to one of their friends was parked in one driveway, the police would choose that side and force those inside to come out and move their cars. On the morning of June 12, the police agreed to use whichever driveway was vacant. That evening, however, the *Kudzu* people heard a police car honking, and Bill Rusk went out to talk to the officers.

"I reminded them of our intentions to be neighborly," says Bill Rusk, a wiry, soft-spoken conscientious objector, "and I ended up saying 'Now you motherfuckers come and do this.' Twenty minutes later the car I was driving was stopped and I was arrested on warrants for abusive language. I was immediately handcuffed behind my back. While being frisked at the side of the car, I was lifted off my feet. As I came down the officer said that my elbow touched him and that was assaulting a police officer. Saying that, he hit me below the right eye with the butt of his flashlight.

"Inside the patrol car the officer said that I was four-eyed and hardheaded and that he would take care of me. Then he took my glasses off saying that otherwise they'd get broken. At the police station basement I got out in a circle of five policemen. Each hit me with openhanded, roundhouse blows around the head. Then I was dragged across the floor twenty or thirty feet. At the elevator I was picked up and my head was rammed against the cement wall. I fell down and I was told no sitting's going to be allowed, and was yanked up by my hair. I found out standing wasn't allowed either. They knocked me up and down several more times. Inside the elevator two other officers got in their licks. One jammed his elbow in my stomach."

Upstairs Rusk was charged with resisting arrest, abusive language, assaulting an officer and failure to yield to an emergency vehicle. After paying $162 bail he was released. Eventually, all the charges except abusive language were dropped. On that latter charge Rusk paid a small fine. As for Rusk's story of having been beaten up, police spokesmen say it is a complete fabrication. The surveillance of the *Kudzu* house is no longer an issue, since everyone has moved out.

Even selling the *Kudzu* is a challenge not intended for the fainthearted. In March 1970, several staff members were thrown off the campus of Mississippi College, in nearby Clinton for peddling papers without a license. This set off a controversy among student-body leaders. Both the *Jackson Daily News* and the *Clarion Ledger*—papers that Pat Watters, the Southern writer, considers "likely to be among the worst newspapers in the world"—are sold on campus. Why not the *Kudzu?* The official reason, according to the Mississippi College *Collegian,* is that the owners of the two Jackson dailies "had given such financial assistance . . . However . . . *Kudzu* had not contributed to the college."

Two months later, three *Kudzu* people drove out to Clinton in Bill Rusk's rusty hulk of a car to try to sell the paper on the sidewalk outside the campus. Rusk, who rolls his own cigarettes and has flaxen hair and fine features and works with the Delta Ministry as well as with the *Kudzu,* fully expected to be arrested. After a brief consultation the three set themselves up just outside the college gates, in front of the neat geometric pattern of red brick buildings and lawns and paths laid out with military precision. Sales could not have been better. Over a third of the passing students bought the *Kudzu* for a quarter, these white, pressed, polished and starched young men and women buying more out of curiosity than out of conviction on a campus where dancing and partying are prohibited.

After being reinforced by Clinton police, Billy J. Gilmore, the head campus security officer, approached and told the *Kudzu* people that the sidewalk was college property. They would have to move out in the street. The *Kudzu* staffers went along with the request, and Officer Gilmore proceeded to take pictures of the venders, anyone buying the paper, and students standing around watching or even sitting on the nearby grass. The husky security officer jumped out from the bushes, and peeked out from behind statues and columns and managed to photograph everyone in the immediate area. In the process, he thoroughly intimidated several undergraduate couples who chanced to be sitting on the front lawn. "Why is that guy taking my picture!" Now, they conjectured, their names would be added to some list of dangerous elements.

Through all this the Clinton police stood by and talked among themselves, and the *Kudzu* people kept right on selling the paper with a highly studied nonchalance. Suddenly, the police charged up to Rusk, pinioned his arms behind his back, handcuffed him, and pushed him into the back seat of a white patrol car. Rusk had dropped a cigarette butt in the gutter.

At the police station, while the local authorities decided whether to charge Rusk with littering, the other *Kudzu* people asked Charles G. Glass, Clinton's mayor, why they couldn't sell the paper.

"You need a license," Mayor Glass answered.

"Can we apply now?"

"Sure you can apply," the Mayor said savoring the sound of each word, "but I don't have much idea you're going to get it. I believe in the Constitution. I don't believe in the filth you're passing out."

Eventually, the police decided to let Rusk go, and the three *Kudzu* staff members left, trailed to their car by football players threatening "to beat the shit out of them," with everyone leaving unsaid the inevitable decision to return once again in the fall.

The summer passed uneventfully. The *Kudzu* people devoted much of their time to raising funds and interest in a youth center to be called "Edge City." In October, another official element, the F.B.I., became involved with the *Kudzu*. On several occasions F.B.I. agents showed up at the house ostensibly to look for fugitive radicals like Mark Rudd. "They barged in at all hours of the night," says Doggett. On October 26, at 6 P.M., eight local uniformed police officers arrived at the house with a search warrant and drawn guns. According to Doggett, the police threw files on the floor, took several guns

and poured liquid solder into them, destroyed negatives and other small objects. After one officer came out of the bedroom with a bag of marijuana in his hand—a bag the *Kudzu* people say must have been planted there—police took them to jail. Eventually, the charges against the *Kudzu* people were dropped for lack of evidence.

In New Orleans, the *Nola Express* has had a range of problems far surpassing those of the *Kudzu*. Bob Head and Darlene Fife, the co-owners and editors, are deeply private people. They work behind shuttered doors in a French Quarter row house. Their paper is an anomaly in the underground, with roots deep in the Beat Fifties and concerns that are self-consciously literary. A typical issue contains the gritty, proudly perverse prose of Charles Bukowski, the prince of the old hard-nosed Beats; poetry by Head or Fife or others; pictures of undercover police agents or tales of police excesses; bitter exposés of the local power structure, politicians, and businesses, articles that taunt and bait the New Orleans Establishment; stories and graphics, as often as not of a sexual nature, and inevitably frightfully weird. In recent months other people have gotten involved in putting out the paper and *Nola Express* often has the spaced out prose and layout of one of the older drug papers. It remains, however, a personal paper, printing only what Fife and Head truly care about, and its literary quality is such that over half of its two thousand subscriptions are mailed to New York and San Francisco; the other six thousand or so copies are peddled primarily to tourists in the French Quarter.

The stubborn iconoclasm of the

Nola Express fits perfectly into the French Quarter, or Vieux Carré. For well over half a century, Bohemians have made their home in the Vieux Carré, and today hippies share the streets with aging Beats of the 1950's, grizzled survivors of the thirties and forties, elderly gentry in linen suits, shills for the dozens of go-go and strip joints, homosexuals in bright plumage, and thousands and thousands of vacation visitors. The French Quarter lives off these tourists and like an aging harlot preserves its historic qualities with passionate self-interest.

As a hip center the French Quarter is unique. It is the one major Bohemian area in the United States that did not grow out of a slum, a substandard section, or a university-surrounding youth ghetto. The traditional tourist area and the hip "tourist" area are practically the same, and this may have led to the *Nola Express'* many woes. Almost from the moment *Nola Express* began publishing, the paper has suffered persistent harassment. Venders have been arrested for peddling without a license —although the charge was patently unconstitutional. Sellers have been so hassled by police that at one point Head and Fife could find almost no one who dared vend *Nola Express.*

The New Orleans Police Department pleads innocent. "The problem with the *Nola Express* arises," says Sergeant William Nolan, information officer, "when people selling the paper come to the attention of the police by quasi-legal or illegal acts. Originally, one of the alleged offenses was that they were harassing people by pushing papers in their faces." There is a certain irony to this charge. All along Bourbon Street stand gruff-voiced touts, half blocking the narrow sidewalks, loudly enticing tourists into a score of chintzy strip joints and go-go bars. The hippie newspaper venders, in their turn, have assumed the languorous nonchalance that is the mark of the New Orleans native, and for the most part they either sit on stoops or shuffle along, selling *Nola Express* with downright indifference.

"This is a very acquiescent community," says Kendall Vick, general counsel for the Louisiana A.C.L.U. "Personal idiosyncrasies are sometimes winked at. The good life has been part of the way of life for centuries. It's a conformist sort of good life. Now when you drop out and start attacking the Establishment, people here become increasingly insecure. They consider it deviant behavior, and they can't explain it. Take Bob Head. His father's a prominent local psychiatrist. Here's an Establishment kid thumbing his nose at them, going out of his way to see how far he can push them. Now the fact is that from the word go, the Establishment started pushing back."

The blatant harassment reached its peak in the summer of 1969. Venders scarcely dared even stand on Bourbon Street. Finally Patrolmen David C. Huber and Louis DeCastro allegedly approached Joel Max Fowler and Sharon Brunos, street sellers of another short-lived underground, *Arcane Logos,* and warned the two young hippies that they had better not be seen vending papers while the two officers were present. The next evening, Fowler says he was approached by the two policemen and told that "long-haired" types were not wanted in New Orleans. DeCastro allegedly said, "If you don't like the way we run our city, then get the hell out."

Several hours later the two policemen arrested Fowler for vagrancy while he was peddling *Arcane Logos* on Bourbon Street. According to Fowler's statement, he was seized from behind without warning by Patrolman DeCastro and pushed across Bourbon Street while constantly being kneed and poked on the back, ribs and head. Fowler attempted to run from the police officers and was tripped and struck repeatedly by DeCastro's nightstick. During the beating, as the sworn affidavit of a bystander attests, Fowler offered no resistance. At this point DeCastro drew his gun and for the first time told Fowler he was under arrest. At the police station Fowler was charged with aggravated assault, aggravated escape, battery on the police and vagrancy. He spent nine days in jail on bonds up to $25,000.

Later that night the two patrolmen tracked down Rita Santangelo and Phil Brigdon, witnesses to the arrest and beating, and arrested them for vagrancy. A few days later DeCastro and Huber chanced upon Fowler on Bourbon Street and reportedly told him "to stay off the street lest he get himself into a bigger mess."

The A.C.L.U. immediately took the case, viewing it not only as a blatant instance of abuse of police power, but also as a vehicle for carrying to the federal courts the broader issue of harassment of the underground press. Thus Bob Head and Darlene Fife and the *Nola Express* added their names to the affirmative suit to enjoin the harassment of the street venders and the underground press in general. Although

Fowler had left New Orleans by the late-November court hearing, the A.C.L.U. still had a strong case and a remarkable array of witnesses. Judge Herbert W. Christenberry of the United States District Court became visibly upset by the mass of evidence that unfolded during a long day in court. At one point he came close to threatening to put the New Orleans police, municipal court judges, and city attorney in jail if they continued to harass newspaper venders. Judge Christenberry concluded that "the evidence . . . overwhelmingly established a policy of the police to arrest persons selling underground papers under the guise that they were impeding pedestrian traffic."

At the end of the hearing Judge Christenberry issued a temporary restraining order against the city of New Orleans. Two weeks later he issued a preliminary injunction. The injunction could not have been much broader. It enjoined the city to refrain from threatening anyone engaged in the production and distribution of newspapers with prosecution under the Louisiana vagrancy statutes or the state obscenity statutes "unless a prior judgment and decree of 'obscenity' of a particular publication or issue thereof has been made by a court of competent jurisdiction." The order also provides that the defendants are "to refrain from any and all interference, harrassment, intimidation or any and all other efforts which deter plaintiffs, intervenors, or other persons from the public sale or distribution of published materials of any nature at any place within the jurisdiction of the court."

Less than six months later, on the

NOLA EXPRESS

20 ¢

NEW ORLEANS Mar 20 – April 2, '70 / No. 51 /UPS / Second Class postage paid at New Orleans LA / 20¢ New Orleans / 25¢ National

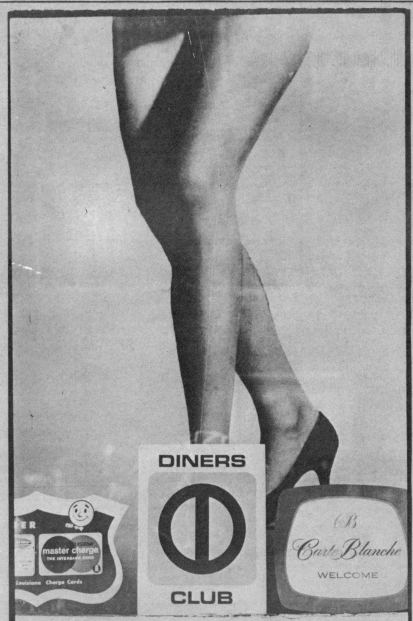

Cover Photo / Murph Dowouis

evening of April 6, 1970, Bill Henke, a young hippie, was selling the *Nola Express* on Bourbon Street at his favorite location. On several occasions, Patrolmen Huber and Foster had told Henke that he would be arrested if he continued to sell papers at that spot, but Henke figured the injunction was protection enough. He had just finished selling his last paper when the two patrolmen approached and without warning arrested him for "failure to move on." Patrolman Huber was brought before Judge Christenberry once again, this time for contempt of court. "If this man had the slightest understanding of people's Constitutional rights, he wouldn't be here," the judge said, "but he made himself the boss of Bourbon Street." Christenberry fined Huber $100 and suspended imposition of a jail sentence pending Huber's future conduct. (The judge later rescinded the fine.)

These events made Huber something of a hero to many New Orleans residents, a good cop just doing his duty, and the Bourbon Street patrolmen continue their cavalier attitude toward anyone whose hair is a little long. In subtle ways the police have continued to try to circumvent the injunction as well. They have attempted to get Head and Fife to provide a list of *Nola Express* venders. Of course, the request is absurd. Anyone can vend the paper by going to one of several distribution centers and leaving a small deposit or an item of value. There are scores and scores of venders, since selling papers is usually the only way a new hippie arrival to the Quarter can earn enough money for bread and lodging. Obviously, then, the only way to provide such a list would be on

an hour-to-hour basis.

All this has been petty stuff in comparison to the federal grand jury indictment for mailing obscene material that was returned against Head and Fife in January 1970—making the *Nola Express* the first underground paper indicted under federal obscenity statutes. If convicted, the two editors could have been sentenced to as much as five years in prison and fined ten thousand dollars. The issue in question was the November 21, 1969, one, specifically page 16, which the indictment characterized as "obscene, lewd, indecent, filthy, and vile matter." Page 16 was a parody of one of those *Playboy* house ads that tout the magazine as the bible of swinging, affluent young Americans. The *Playboy* ad, as it originally appeared in *The New York Times,* showed a clean-cut college man helping a pretty girl out of a sports car. "What sort of a man reads *Playboy*," the copy read, "He's on his way. He's young, active, affluent. A hard man to get through to." *Pterodactyl,* an Iowa underground, satirized the ad by printing the same copy but picturing a nude male masturbating before four *Playboy* centerfold nudes. *Nola Express* reprinted the item.

The picture incensed the local United States Attorney's office. "The court has before it issue no. 43 of the *Nola Express,*" the first government memo states, "a cheap and unorganized tabloid consisting of trashy editorials, letters from its readers, classified ads, cartoons, and on page 16, an obscence [sic] and filthy picture of an ugly naked man with his hand wrapped tightly around his erect penis masturbating to a climax in front of four pictures of

Playboy Magazine." The memo overstated the case. To many minds the *Nola Express* is no more a cheap and unorganized tabloid consisting of trashy editorials, classified ads and cartoons than are the *Times-Picayune* and *States-Item,* New Orlean's two notoriously mediocre daily papers. The naked man is far from ugly, and it is problematic whether he is masturbating to climax. Curiously enough, for all its detailed description of the satire, the memo failed to mention that the four pictures from *Playboy* were themselves *nudes* —ebullient, air-brushed nymphs posing in the coy manner that has helped make Hugh Hefner a millionaire.

Curious, too, was the timing of the government's indictment. It came well over a month after publication of the November 21 issue. George Strickler, a young civil-rights lawyer for the Lawyers Constitutional Defense Committee of the A.C.L.U. and one of three lawyers who handled the defense, offers his explanation: "I think the real reason is that the police made a deal with the United States Attorney's office to put this before the grand jury." Kendall Vick shares this opinion. "I don't think there is any doubt but that the city got the feds and the postal inspectors involved. First, the city moved to vacate and modify the *Nola Express* injunction. The hearing was supposed to be held on December 31st, but the judge said 'I'm not going to hear any motions on New Year's Eve.' So the motion was carried over. The motion said that the city wanted the injunction removed so that they could prosecute Head and Fife and/ or *to have the United States Attorney indict them.* Then on January

6th, *pow,* Head and Fife got it."

What remained clear, though, was that an erection had always been the *sine qua non* of legal obscenity. Even the defense attorneys admitted that they had been unable to discover a picture of an erection that had not been declared obscene. Of course, that was frightfully mechanistic. Those who produce pornographic materials are able to avoid such technical "obscenity" and yet sell pictures with the most crude and chilling displays of sado-masochism and an almost infinite variety of couplings and perversity.

On September 1, 1970, Judge Rubin of the United States District Court at New Orleans, issued his judgment on the case, a ruling that deserves to be quoted at some length.

Contrary to the government's assertions, it [*Nola Express*] is remarkably uniform in its approach to its general subject— the assumed foibles of the way of life generally accepted in this country today. Because it is a newspaper, it is comprised of discrete articles, but it is more thematically integrated than most magazines or newspapers of general circulation and, in this regard, it adopts a single point of view of life, much like a novel or a film.

Critics of the established order have frequently found it necessary to use language that shocked their audiences— neither Ezekiel nor Martin Luther spoke in bland terms. The defendants in this case were engaged in another kind of social and political criticism: they were attempting to expose what they consider hypocritical and venal in everyday life. They used emphatic, shocking and disturbing language and techniques of communication in their paper both to express their own depth of indignation and to arouse their audience. While their editorial format may be experimental, their objective is serious. Another section of this court has held that the First Amendment protects defendants and their street venders from arrest and harassment by street authorities. The United States is at least equally constrained by the Constitution. . . .

The picture [on page 16] is indeed shocking and repellent; it seeks precisely to arouse shock and disgust at *Playboy* and at the social outlook that magazine represents. It is fair to say that it would be patently offensive to any general audience. But offensiveness alone does not constitute obscenity in the constitutional sense. The first requisite is that the dominant theme be appeal to prurient interest, and the commentary accompanying the picture demonstrates that its intent was not to arouse lustful instincts but to ridicule other publications that do attempt such an appeal. . . .

As literary matter, *Nola Express* does not belong on the same library shelf as *Ulysses* or *Lady Chatterley's Lover*. But it is newsprint, evidently intended for social commentary rather than artistic achievement. It represents a relatively new medium of political and social discussion in this country, sometimes called the underground press. In their newspapers, defendants urge a radical departure from the generally accepted way of life, and they use a new and radical means of expressing their point of view. . . .

For these reasons I hold that the material that defendants are charged with mailing was constitutionally protected, and that therefore the indictment must be dismissed.

Despite this verdict, Head and Fife seem destined to remain at the center of controversy. The *Nola Express* is the one place in New Orleans where the hip community can have its say. Thus these two resolutely private persons—quietly addicted to poetry, beat rhythms and beer—have become spokesmen for the hip community. Their paper is the one certain means for hippies to earn money, and if the city is to rid itself of young Bohemians it must somehow break this alliance of convenience and economic good sense. This is more than mere mimicry of hippie paranoia. In New Orleans a pattern of municipal behavior has developed that is increasingly seen across the United States and spells enormous troubles for Bohemians and the underground press.

On Bourbon Street there is an invisible dividing line where the exuberant imbibers of Singapore slings, Jax Beer and gin fizzes give way to the quietly stoned legions of the hippie community. Business is bad in the strip palaces, hotels and bars, thanks to the recession and perhaps also to the very different preoccupations of a new generation, but the owners blame it all on the hippies. In May 1970 some fifty French Quarter business establishments banded together as the Vieux Carré Association "to preserve and strengthen the unity of the French Quarter as a unique place in which to live and engage in business." The most pressing problem, according to Arshag Casbarian, hotelier and Association president, is "the influx of young vagrants." The real enemy, however, is the entire hip community. Originally the association's membership was to be open to any French Quarter business, but when the perfectly legitimate hip boutiques and head shops of Burbon Street attempted to join, the entrance requirements were changed so as to exclude them. During the summer of 1970 the city tried to clean out its "undesirables." Police made some seven hundred arrests, including a girl who chanced to be wearing "clothes of the opposite sex" (jeans with a zipper in the front).

The police did not affect neutrality. The cover of the June 1970 issue of the newspaper, *The New Orleans Police Department Speaks!* headlined THE QUARTER'S UNDESIRABLES above a picture collage of young people standing on the street and in one instance sleeping on the floor of an apartment. None of this is one bit illegal. "It is not intended or implied that any or all of the persons depicted here are classified as undesirables—several posed for the police camera," the police admit beneath the collage. "All photographs were made prior to the . . . Police Department's major campaign to eliminate undesirable persons from the French Quarter." Inside the newspaper are excerpts from an official police report of Bourbon Street activity. The document is a private, privileged communication, and yet there it is spread out before the eyes of middle-class New Orleans, complete with initials of individuals mentioned and the name of the *Nola Express* and several hip boutiques.

Even officers used to presenting the official police view are not the least bit restrained in placing blame. "By hippies I guess you mean those long-hairs, those dirty permissive types lounging around leading useless lives," says Sergeant Nolan, information officer. "As a by-product they have long hair, but they're just bums! We've had bums for years. These are just that. They're just dressed differently. Now, of course, some of these others, college types, for instance, they're good people who just grow their hair long."

Officer Nolan's distinction between the good and the bad long-hairs is a crucial one. The police have no particular quarrel with the middle-class Bohemians of style. To the law the dangerous element is the full-fledged hippie, and such people have good reason to say that society considers them "the new niggers." What has happened since Haight-Ashbury's short summer of 1967 is that the hippie movement has lost its middle-class glow. These New Orleans hippies and street people are predominantly lower class. They are neither terribly photogenic nor articulate, and most of them exhibit little of that sweet-tempered generosity of their San Francisco progenitors. Worse yet, their presence certainly does increase drug abuse and possibly petty crime. Yet they will not go away. They have few alternatives. By early 1971 the city and its new mayor had called a halt to blatant harassment, and there were those—particularly among the liberal establishment—who believed that New Orleans hips and straights might yet live in harmony.

Atlanta, the South's self-proclaimed center of enlightenment, has also found it expedient to clamp down on its growing hip area, a center that has emitted a siren call to hip youth across Dixie. This New Jerusalem of Southern hippiedom called "the strip" is on the east side of Peachtree Street between Tenth and Eleventh. The strip consists of half a dozen hip boutiques—Cops and Robbers, Merry-go-Round, Atlantis Rising, Asterisk, Sexy Sadie, and Fahrenheit—two cooperative stores, the General Store, a shoddy, barren place stocked with posters, crudely made crafts and drug paraphernalia, and the Laundromat, filled with finely crafted leather goods and dresses; a gay bar; a "skin flick" movie house; a fish-and-chips shop; and several cheap restaurants.

It is not stag films, food or fashion that draws people here, but the opportunity "to let one's freak flag fly" and very often to buy drugs. In the spring of 1970 drugs were sold on the strip with an openness found nowhere else in the South. Some dared smoke marijuana on the street and anyone whose hair even nudged his ear lobes was bound to be asked to purchase "grass" or "acid." In the evenings the sidewalks were jammed with milling clusters of long-hairs, high-school students digging the scene, tattooed bikers, college kids buzzed on grass or beer, and hippie panhandlers every bit as professional as their Calcutta counterparts. At traffic lights youths stood selling *The Great Speckled Bird* with that brisk aggressiveness endemic in the capital of the New South to an endless parade of Atlantans out to capture snapshot images of the hippie life. Blocks back the traffic was still bumper to bumper cutting into legitimate businesses and according to one local restaurateur, Salvatore Padillo, improving an illegitimate one —prostitutes seeking out customers in the stalled cars.

During the spring of 1970 the word supposedly went out to hip youths across America: this is the summer to come to Atlanta. No one in Atlanta could quite say why or how they know, but there was no end of authoritative reports that twenty, fifty, or even a hundred thousand long-hairs would soon be descending on Georgia's capital, an invasion some compared in size and threat to that of the Union Army a century before.

Early in June Atlanta's Mayor Sam Massell went on television to talk about the Peachtree situation. "I ask every parent and every teenager to take time this very night to sit down as a family unit to share opinions of the hippies' life style, including but not limited to the problem of drug abuse . . ." he told his audience. "Now because of the increase of street congestion in the 10th Street area, and because of the universal reports which anticipate the migration of thousands of additional young people to the city at this season, and because of the acknowledged presence of an increased traffic in hard drugs in this section . . . I am, at this hour, declaring this neighborhood as an Intensive Care Section."

The role of the "Intensive Care Section" was hardly medicinal. Massell sent sixty-four policemen into the Peachtree area to form Atlanta's first and only precinct in modern times—notwithstanding the fact that the city has America's highest murder rate, a galloping crime problem, and a police force raked by persistent reports of corruption. The Mayor specifically asked Atlanta's "flower children" to stay away from the strip "so if arrests are made, those who may be seeking trouble will be isolated from the innocent."

Less than two weeks later Mayor Massell sent the following ad out to a dozen underground papers:

To All Travelers:

The city of Atlanta, Georgia, faces a severe shortage of jobs, housing, and space this summer. . . .

Unless you have bread and a pad, please find your thing somewhere else, or face a bad scene. City laws prohibiting drugs and loitering are being strictly enforced.

We love our city and have a good thing going. Please help us keep it that way by starting your own action where you are. If your pigs or straights need guidance, let us know.

> Sam Massell
> Mayor
> The City of Atlanta

The very language of the ad patronized young hips, demeaning them and their argot. The message itself had been a familiar one in America's immigrant past ("No Irish need apply"). If Massell had placed such an ad to discourage, say, the migration of poor Southern blacks to the city, there would have been an immediate and outraged reaction from liberals and those men of professional conscience, the editorial writers. As it was, few people thought the ad in poor taste—except for the hips and *The Great Speckled Bird*. *The Bird* asked other underground papers either not to run the ad or to run next to it *The Bird's* rebuttal, which said, in part:

> The Mayor's ad is a hoax. While the city spends thousands of dollars trying to attract white middle-class "straights" to Atlanta, it is deliberately attempting to drive members of the growing Woodstock Nation from the city with a policy of harassment and repression. Now Massell threatens longhairs across Amerika with arrest if they come to Atlanta. . . . Atlanta's hip community does have most of the same problems of other communities of longhairs—including most importantly a repressive government. But we are together in our determination to fight repression. We welcome freaks to Atlanta. Help us create the new nation here.

To the amazement of Atlanta's hips and straights alike, the hippie hordes never materialized. But over the summer the police greatly increased drug arrests, ended the open use and sale of narcotics, and used local loitering ordinance as a catchall against difficult hippies and street people. By the end of the summer the constant police attention had severed most of the hippies from their firm belief in peace and good vibes, and patrolmen themselves were being harassed when they tried to make arrests.

On October 10 a policeman tried to arrest two girls at the corner of Peachtree and 11th for allegedly violating the state narcotics laws, aiding and abetting the escape of another girl, and creating a turmoil. Immediately, a noisy and belligerent crowd surged around the policeman and his two captives, a crowd of long-hairs who by now had lost all faith in the good will and fairness of the police and their "intensive care." When another officer arrived these children of the children of Haight-Ashbury ripped at his uniform and tore his badge off. Soon a full-scale riot erupted on the streets in front of the boutiques, skin flick, snack shops and bars. Youths heaved rocks at the police, and shattered store windows and cars with their missiles. Some witnesses say pistol shots were exchanged. Since then the tempo of the community has grown erratic—pulsing to the tempos of common violence and fear—firebombings, robberies, murders (mostly attributed to several packs of Bikers), extortion. The police may not have been the sole carrier of this malignancy, but at very least they were the harbingers of violence, the catalyst that ended up destroying more than it protected.

Even Berkeley, the city Tom Hayden and others are wont to call a "liberated zone," instituted its own program to get rid of wandering hips. During the summer of 1970 Berkeley police stopped youths on street corners and stoops, checked rooftops, even raided apartments and crash pads. Outsiders over eighteen were allegedly often driven to the city limits and told not to return. Most of the more than five hundred out-of-town youths under eighteen nabbed by the police were abruptly shipped home. No matter that over half the teen-agers had specific parental permission for their travels.

In defense of their actions, police cited Sections 600 and 601 of the California Welfare and Institutional Code, which prohibit those under eighteen from traveling without direct adult supervision. According to many legal experts—including the federally funded Youth Law Center in San Francisco—the purpose of that legislation was clearly intended to stop runaways, and the police action was "at best a misreading and at worst a malicious misuse of statutes." Many Berkeley residents considered this legal jibber-jabber. The code was a godsend. A group of mothers even carried mops and brooms down to City Hall to dramatize their call "to sweep clear the city of Berkeley."

Then those liberated streets of Berkeley aren't necessarily that much safer for hip youth than the tourist-clogged ones of New Orleans. In both cities and across the United States this youth culture is growing to such proportions that it seems to threaten the folkways and institutions of the "American way of life." It is the most seductive of subcultures, by its mere presence weaning youth away from the more conventional form of existence.

Unfortunately, the traditional mechanisms for protecting civil liberties are shoddy instruments for guarding the rights of the citizens of Woodstock Nation. Lawyers, journalists, and others most capable by position and sentiment to stand in the forefront of the constant vigil to protect our civil liberties are barely able to see that rights are being violated. As specifically regards the underground press, the mélange of politics and youth culture found in most papers is simply too much for many of those concerned with civil liberties. Why, rubbing up against a power structure exposé is a collage of naked bodies! Within a lengthy exposé of city government, the writer spatters four-letter obscenities and insults. An article details the half-truths and deceptions of United States policy in Vietnam and then concludes with a histrionic tirade against American imperialism. How can one consider such papers worthy of high regard or protection? They are not *serious!*

One unfortunate result of this particular generation gap is that the aboveground media have almost completely ignored the problems of the underground press. When Attorney General John Mitchell issued guidelines to limit the subpoena of newsmen and their information, and the Justice Department pointedly refused to say whether the underground press was included, there was no outcry. No professional organization of journalists objected after realizing that some aboveground papers might next be excluded from the administration's definition of "press"; since then part of the liberal Establishment press—the *Washington Post, The New York Times,* and the *Baltimore Sun*—have had their reporters excluded from at least one Presidential briefing.

An indication of the general government attitude toward the underground press came in August 1970, when the Milwaukee, Wisconsin, *Kaleidoscope* ran a statement from a group calling itself the "New Year's Gang." In it the group took credit for the bombings of the physics lab at the University of Wisconsin. Almost immediately, a grand jury subpoenaed Mark Knops, *Kaleidoscope*'s editor. When the twenty-seven-year-old underground editor refused to say how he had gotten the story, a judge sentenced him to six months in jail. There was no outcry, no protest, no awareness on the part of Establishment journalists that the underground press stands in the foreground of everyone's First Amendment freedom. This is not mere metaphor. The government's attempt to suppress the *Pentagon Papers* and the harassment of CBS News over the prize-winning documentary "The Selling of the Pentagon" suggest just how perishable freedom of the press really is and how stupid and naive Establishment journalists have been to ignore the plight of the underground press. Indeed, *The New York Times* publication of the *Pentagon Papers* almost exactly paralleled the *Los Angeles Free Press'* publication of the California narcotics agent roster. In both cases, the documents were government property (although only the *Pentagon Papers* were clearly and unquestionably secret documents). In both cases, the documents were Xeroxed by an employee and brought unsolicited to the publication in question. Of course, the government doesn't pretend for a moment that *The New York Times* is no better than some seedy fence, and the Justice Department directed its initial indictments against Daniel Ellsberg. One doesn't need a particularly lurid imagination to imagine what would have happened if an underground paper had first published the *Pentagon Papers:* the people involved would have been immediately indicted; of that there can be little doubt.

On the rare occasion when Establishment journalists do talk of the underground press, it is usually with snobbish contempt. This is true even when newsmen are talking among themselves. "The typical underground journal, the *Rat*s and the *Screw*s that give it special flavor and odor, is self-righteously, frenziedly vulgar; serious only as hysterics are serious about their fantasy world," writes Eugene Lyons of the *Reader's Digest* in *Dateline,* the magazine of the Overseas Press Club. "The 'underground' press, of course, isn't—except in the sense that gutters and cesspools are below ground." [3]

This is the kind of banal stupidity that masquerades as wisdom and good taste. Those who accept it might easily stand by if our laws became a great treasure trove to be searched through to find measures to put down radical youths and the underground press. In such a situation the Constitution would soon become an antiquarian document protecting the half-forgotten liberties of another epoch.

...AND BEST IN THE FIELD IT CREATED

SCREW

THE SEX REVIEW

NO.
62
OUT OF NYC 75¢
50¢

**SCREW INTERVIEWS
HENRY MILLER! P. 4**

THE TASTE OF SPERM P. 6

HOOVER HUM JOB P. 14

10
The Cosmetic Bohemians

In this time, in this place, brothers and sisters, we gotta get our shit together! we gotta write together, paint together, sleep together, have children together, study together, build together . . . say YES YES YES together! we gotta, we gotta, we gotta! the time is ripe and the fate of everybody hangs in the balance.

— RAYMOND MUNGO, *Famous Long Ago*

Revolution is not what you believe, what organization you belong to, or who you vote for, it's what you do all day long, how you live.

— JERRY RUBIN, *Do It!*

A revolution of the spirit. Grooving together is revolution. Making love is revolution. Having a street party is revolution. Building together is revolution. Smoking dope is revolution. A revolution of the spirit.

A revolution of the spirit. Attending a pop festival is revolution. Wearing a groovy leather vest is revolution. Buying records is revolution. Drinking Coke is revolution. A revolution of the spirit.

Thus cultural radicalism is easily defused, packaged and merchandized to a youthful generation. The myth-making of Mungo or Rubin is readily transformed into advertising, furthering the prototypal American myth that consumption is the high road to happiness. This is the most subtle enemy of the underground press and radical-youth culture, for it is the perverse genius of the American system to be able to take any phenomenon, idea or value, no matter how radical or ethereal, and transform it into a product or a way of selling a product.

The one field outside specific youth-culture enterprises where hip men and women frequently reach executive positions before the age of twenty-five is advertising. "Talk in New York is that today at thirty-three or thirty-four, a member of an agency creative department is beginning to get a little senior," notes

Youth Report,[1] a confidential newsletter to business, and other leaders involved with youth. "Early twenties is preferred to late twenties."

Thanks to these hippie-looking, dope-smoking executives, increasingly one is able to identify with the Movement simply by buying a product. Time-Life sold over a million copies of the "Woodstock" special edition of *Life* at $1.25 apiece. Coca-Cola's "The Real Thing" advertising campaign is prophetic. "Over the years I've admired Coca-Cola," says Lester Rand, head of Youth Research Inc. "The Real Thing campaign is particularly good. The words don't matter. The pictures show all kinds of young people—long-hairs, Negroes with afros—and in all this there's a discreet criticism and a feeling of unity. They are quite cleverly tying in with the youth demand for telling it like it is."

Only three years ago most record companies had a lone, long-haired "house freak." "I think Billy James was the first company freak at Columbia," says Danny Fields, an early "house freak" himself. "I went to see him in Hollywood after he'd left Columbia and had been propped up by Elektra in their plush little suite in the Sunset Vine Tower, and it was fantastic—what a set-up. It was my first sight of a company freak, this charming, barefoot dynamo, running around the office, sitting on the floor, putting his feet up on the walls."[2] Now most record companies have staffs heavy with the most incredible collection of far-out heads.

With presumed benevolence and obvious self-interest, such hip entrepreneurs and well-paid underlings are invading the once sacrosanct and ignored territory of cultural radicalism. An "alternative media conference" at Vermont's Goddard College in June 1970 was even partly financed by the record companies. Young freaky executives dominated many of the sessions rapping endlessly and passing out free dope to bewildered radicals.

What is happening is that cultural radicalism is being transformed into a mass Bohemianism of style—a cosmetic Bohemianism that has now become the popular American culture. This is not all that unprecedented. The American middle class has never been fully at home within the confines of European bourgeois culture, and it has long hearkened to the call of *la vie bohème*—as long as it has been defused of its radical implications. Such an ersatz Bohemianism made its first appearance in 1894 upon publication of Du Maurier's *Trilby,* the sentimental saga of a poor young girl model set upon by that evil Svengali. The book set off an immense national fad. At first came the popular literary manifestations in cities across America—melodramas, a series of "Scenes and Songs from Trilby," literary debates, over a dozen magazines with "Bohemian" in their title —that stripped Bohemianism of its radical political and cultural meaning and turned it into emotional fodder. Soon New Yorkers could be seen parading down the city's élite avenues dressed in authentic Latin Quarter fashions and mimicking artistic mannerisms. Then inevitably came the crude hucksterism—Trilby ice cream, Trilby shoes, Trilby sausages, Trilby scarf pins, a Trilby cocktail, Trilby bathing suits, even a small Florida town which, when it was renamed Trilby, became a thriving tourist center.

Trilby, Florida, soon sank into well-deserved obscurity, and by 1910 the United States and in particular Greenwich Village had a vibrant, indigenous radical culture of its own. There in those few years before World War I, the Bohemian life style meshed with aesthetic experimentation, Socialist-anarchist politics, and tough, literate social criticism. Bohemianism alone had not been enough. The "puny, artificial, sex-conscious simmering in perpetual puberty of the gray-haired Bacchantes of Greenwich Village" were worthless, said Max Eastman, editor of the *Masses.* "The substitution of this personal revolt, and this practical communication of qualities, for the practical scientific work of mind or hand that the revolution demands of every free man in its desperate hour—it is that which is to be condemned." [3]

This prewar Greenwich Village "stood for the cafés and red lights of Europe, orange candles, batik, but also for a genuine community of feeling with the common man," [4] wrote John Dos Passos. The Great War wreaked havoc on such humane feelings but not on the real estate and the "orange lights and batik." By 1918 the Village had begun to fill up with Purple Pup tearooms, uptowners looking for apartments and good times, clubs, voyeurs, and the area was well on its way to becoming the undeclared capital of the Bohemians of style.

During the 1920's the stylishly and prosperously alienated prowled the artistic haunts of San Francisco; traveled to Taos, New Mexico, where middle-class dropouts worshiped at the altar of native American culture and cavorted in Indian dress as their grandchildren, the hippies, would forty years later; and lived in the famous art colony at Carmel, California, which by the late 1920's had become a place where "the newcomer found too many *nouveau riches* living noisily in their newly built, tasteless stucco houses; too many shrill voices discussing fashionable topics of *belles lettres,* psychoanalysis and sex abnormalities; too many modish lectures, dance schools, art schools, ritzy Hollywood-looking cars . . . too much attention (for an intellectual settlement) to the first nudist group in Carmel; too conscious an attempt to have colored pavements." [5]

It would take the bountiful, almost obscene affluence of the contemporary American middle class, however, to create the mass Bohemianism of style that is developing today and that by 1955 already had its own paper, *The Village Voice.* In its first anniversary issue, the *Voice* editorialized, "We assumed a year ago, and we know now that Greenwich Village is both a community and a concept. As a concept, the Village embraces a range of interests as wide and diverse as the world. We have tried to give form to those interests." In doing so the paper achieved a paid circulation of 140,000 —the highest of all weekly newspapers in the United States. In 1970, when a controlling interest in the *Voice* was bought by Carter Burden, the liberal socialite politician, the paper reportedly was worth $7,000,-000.

No wonder, then, that Dan Wolf, the editor—whose paper has 50,000 subscribers outside the Village, some as far away as Peru or Tanzania— has grown fond of saying, "The Village is a state of mind." The state of mind is that bewhiskered or side-burned cosmetic Bohemianism. According to the *Voice*'s own market survey, the average reader is a 32.4-year-old "trend maker" with a median family income of $12,206, who serves and uses alcohol in his home. Sixty percent read *The New York Times;* 52.4 percent are professionals; .5 percent are unemployed; 28.3 percent are over 40; 57.3 percent are over 30. The readership has grown immensely, but the interests of the individual reader have not changed that much. Early ads in the *Village Voice* were a meld of Navajo Squaw boots, hairstyling, French pastry, Middle Eastern cuisine, Indian spiritual teachers, liberal churches, leotards, folk albums, interior decorators, and art galleries. Fifteen years later there are more books, rock instead of folk music, computer-dating ads (although the *Voice* still rejects personal sex ads), except now the paper is 80 pages thick with 65 percent advertising, not 20 pages thick and 20 percent ads. And then as now when *Voice* readers said they bought the paper more for the ads than for the editorial content, they were offering an unintended insight into themselves and the *Voice* itself.

The *Voice* does not speak specifically to the under-thirty youth culture, and it was inevitable that a spate of hip capitalist publications should emerge to serve this New Adult. The first person to realize fully the journalistic possibilities of this was twenty-one-year-old Jann Wenner, who late in 1967 founded *Rolling Stone*, an offset-printed newspaper-magazine devoted to rock music. This was no modest trade magazine. Rock stands at the center of youth culture. During and even

after Haight-Ashbury's short Summer of Love it seemed that rock was not only the pied piper and national anthem but the motive force and invincible weaponry of the counter culture. Anyone who danced at San Francisco's rock ballrooms to the Jefferson Airplane, the Grateful Dead, or a score of other bands while great bursts of colored light played across the room and marijuana perfumed the air, sensed—in fact, *knew*—that music would lead youth into the promised land. It was the most mind-blowing, revolutionary culture this or any other society had ever seen. Or so it seemed.

In San Francisco *Rolling Stone* took these visions, ideals and aspirations and packaged them in a commercially palatable form. No one had ever reviewed rock with such vigor and honesty before or covered the music world with such dogged reporting, and soon *Rolling Stone* became an indispensable part of the music scene. From the beginning the magazine was terribly traditional, especially for a child of the postlinear age. The graphics are nicely composed journalistic photos. The layout is simple, even vaguely elegant, perfectly suited to display the articles that are the primary feature of the magazine. Be it a piece on Kent State or on the Beatles, the form of the journalism is the same—a loose, intimate prose lightly touched with slang and profanity, coupled to the detailed narrative structure of the news magazines. The stories are written for *us,* affecting intimacy the way other magazines affect distance. It has proven a brilliantly successful format. Now in towns and cities across the United States, youths devour each biweekly *Rolling Stone.*

They take from it their clothing styles, tastes, language and ideas, and they have helped the magazine to grow to a circulation of 250,000.

Nineteen hundred sixty-seven is gone, though, and *Rolling Stone* is selling cosmetic Bohemianism pure and simple. Although Wenner once worked for *Ramparts,* the radical monthly, his magazine pooh-poohs political activism. "You might say that my politics are the promotion of good vibes," Wenner told one writer recently.

What *Rolling Stone* does is to identify with the Movement, while subtly and insidiously putting down political activism. "Jann is much more politically sophisticated than most people would imagine," says Greil Marcus, *Rolling Stone*'s former associate editor. "His basic attitude is that violence is abhorrent but that any kind of resistance—not only violent resistance but resistance even in print—is ridiculous, because we're going to win. We're younger and we're going to take over. *Rolling Stone* covers things from that angle. You know, the Establishment has committed a hideous atrocity, but the Black Panthers, or whoever, were acting stupidly or foolishly. The message of the article is that it's too bad, but they got what they deserved."

For a while, particularly in early 1970, *Rolling Stone* did become more political. Wenner commissioned Gene Marine, the long-time Movement journalist, to write a lengthy article on the Chicago conspiracy trial. The piece, entitled "Chicago: The Trial of the New Culture," was heralded in full-page ads in several newspapers across the United States. It was by far the best reporting on the trial to appear in any paper, aboveground or underground. Indeed, that entire issue—including Allen Ginsberg's testimony in Chicago, a provocative political essay by Greil Marcus, a story about the commercialization of FM radio, as well as the magazine's typical first-rate music coverage—suggested that *Rolling Stone* might be able to fuse youth culture and politics. Most impressively the various writers had come to their political concerns with enormous hesitation. This charged the articles with poignancy and tension. There was no patronizing contempt for the "false consciousness" of others, no moralizing about the failure of liberalism. This was the most reluctant radicalism. Gene Marine concluded:

You can be as revolutionary as you like, or as disillusioned. You can know all there is to know about pigs from Oakland to Chicago, which is all there is to know about pigs, because those are the places where they really earn the title. You can be as convinced as you like that the system will never, ever, really allow the individual loving human being to be free. You can know that the capitalist thing has got to go, you can get your head into the ecological conscience, you can see all the present messes and the possible poetries.

But if you grew up in America, then somewhere, down deep inside, there's a crazy irrational piece of you that really believes it will somehow come out all right in the Supreme Court, that even though the executive and legislative branches were corrupt years ago, the judicial branch—the Supreme Court—will be fair and honest.

You can't help it. It's in there—especially if you're young enough to have paid attention only since Earl Warren's been up there, when the court, as courts go, has been pretty good about people who want to dissent. The trial of the

35¢

THE CRAWDADDY!

MAGAZINE

OF ROCK 'N' ROLL

**REVOLVER
REVIEWED**

BYRDS / TEMPTATIONS

ANIMALS / REMAINS

November 1970/40 cents
U.K. 4/9 (25p)

Rags

THE
HARDHATS
ARE
WATCHING

Work Clothes:
THE
UNIVERSAL
WARDROBE

Pop Tops / A Rags Road Test / The Great Pampero

Chicago Seven ends, or maybe you're even in the streets, but you find yourself saying—or maybe you found yourself saying it all the time as the trial went along—"Oh, they can't stand for *that!* Oh, *that* will be reversed, it's too much!"

They *can't.* They just can't.

I feel that way too. They just can't.

But suppose . . .

Shouldn't we at least be asking ourselves, a little more often and a little more insistently, what kind of country can do this thing, and what we can do about it, and isn't it time to get started? And can you—long-haired and freaky-clothed—can you handle, gently and without it letting it turn you into just another kind of pig, the fact that it's you that America is afraid of? * 6

That issue, with a picture of an aging-looking Abbie Hoffman on the cover, was a disaster for *Rolling Stone*. Despite the unprecedented national ads, thousands and thousands of unsold copies were returned. Several months later at the time of the Cambodian invasion and the Kent and Jackson State deaths, the editors prepared another special political issue: "A Pitiful Helpless Giant." It, too, sold miserably, and it was obvious that *Rolling Stone*'s foray into politics might prove a costly one.

Since then Wenner and his magazine have retreated back into their Bohemianism of style. This includes proselytizing for the use of mild drugs. In article after article rock stars and youth heroes are shown smoking dope and even sniffing cocaine. The magazine has offered new subscribers "roach holders" for smoking the last ends of marijuana ciga-

---

rettes. And *Rolling Stone* has its own "Dope Pages," which give the latest drug information, arrests, et cetera. In all of this the inference is that dope is a mandatory part of the groovy counter culture.

This is not so radical as it might appear. While some authorities still warn that marijuana weans youth away from the traditional American culture, others are beginning to realize that drugs can be used as a means of social control. In Portland during the summer of 1970, Oregon's Governor Tom McCall ended the threat of mass protest rallies at the American Legion convention by simply providing a free music festival outside the city, a hip oasis where drugs could be bought, sold and used, with no danger of arrest. The Portland underground press even claims that at a crucial moment the state provided a truckload of free marijuana.

Rolling Stone, itself, has a simply uncanny ability to smooth off the rough radical edges of any youth phenomenon to make it manageable and neutral. At least one would think the magazine could not possibly appropriate the underground photo journalism of the *Berkeley Tribe* and other papers that picture radicals clenching guns and staring militantly into the future. After all, how can a businessman peddle violent revolution in a nonlethal and profitable way? In the October 1, 1970, issue of *Rolling Stone* is the answer: a wonderfully lyrical picture showing five slim, bare-chested, long-haired young men wearing bell-bottoms and bandoleers and carrying rifles. They are members of Love's Army, a Mexican rock group. The picture is a publicity shot.

Ironically, or really not that

ironically, *Rolling Stone's* greatest success came at a time when many of those young hip intellectuals most committed to rock as the prime mover are growing disillusioned, nauseated by the shameless hype of the record companies, bored by the sheer banality of the rock scene, and dubious as to whether youth culture can fundamentally alter society. To them it seems sad, even shameful, that hip youth should identify so completely with such a limited and ultimately unradical thing as a rock magazine, especially one with a traditional hierarchical structure and unashamed plans to make it big. Richard Goldstein, one of the earliest rock critics and a perceptive and subtle writer at that, had this to say about *Rolling Stone* in an interview with Michael March in *Fusion,* another youth-culture publication:

"One of the basic myths of hip culture was that when we took over we would do things substantially differently from the way our parents did them. What has actually happened is that when we took over . . . we do things stylistically differently but essentially in the same way that our parents did. . . . It may be that under the surface there was actually a great deal more communication of attitudes between our parents and us than we are willing or able to believe. Because, despite the vast difference in the look of a publication like *Rolling Stone,* it can effectively be compared with *Time* in its early days. Even in its vitality and energy and its ability to restructure the world in terms of its own image and lingo —to protect certain myths for its audience." [7]

Even more suspect than *Rolling Stone* are the other rock or youth-culture publications. *Crawdaddy, Fusion, Big Fat, Zygote, Earth.* For a time their number grew weekly and appeared to threaten to crowd underground papers off the newsstands. For all the presumed richness and originality of youth culture, most of these magazines are bald imitations of *Rolling Stone*—similar in layout; published on newspaper stock, *de rigueur* for the stylized frugality of the Bohemians of style; offering their readers carelessly conceived combinations of rock and cultural materials. There was even *Rags,* a magazine that in the literal sense was about cosmetic Bohemianism. A monthly publication, *Rags* featured hip clothing, the wearer-designed fashions that consist of equal parts boutique, Salvation Army and ingenuity. This is poverty of style, taking the mandatory artifacts of the underclasses— brocaded old dresses, beaded bags, run-down shoes, just-so-tacky furs, pea jackets—and turning them into hip chic. Among the cosmetic Bohemians there is an almost indecent need to set off their very real afflu-

ence against their very affected poverty—a thousand-dollar stereo in an apartment with a mattress on the floor; a fifty-dollar peasant blouse, a contradiction by itself; rock stars in Rolls-Royces and tattered jeans.

The central intellectual personage of the rock-culture magazines and of commercialized counter culture is the male rock critic—the interpreter, the noncreator. He sits in darkened theaters or trails along behind his favorite band, a male groupie, spinning theories out of such thin stuff as lyrics and crowd reaction and nonverbal signs and symbols. He is the high prince of the alienated, for this youth-oriented cosmetic Bohemianism is a spiritual community of the alienated. "The alienated value most those moments when the barriers to perception crumble, when the walls between themselves and the world fall away and they are 'in contact' with nature, other people, or themselves," writes Kenneth Keniston. "These times of

breakthrough are relatively rare, for much of their lives seem to them dull, depressed, and ordinary. But when such moments come, the alienated describe them in mystical terms, emphasizing the loss of distinction between self and object, the revelation of the meaning of everything in an apparently insignificant detail, the ineffability of the experience, the inherent difficulty in describing a moment which transcends ordinary categories of language." [8] This is exactly what youth-culture publications are all about. They record the minutiae of those times when these alienated youth legions do "get it on" —at rock festivals, concerts, gatherings, and other short-lived meetings of the counter culture. They breed passivity. They provide an easy identity. They feed youth chauvinism. And, of course, they sell records.

These new publications have taken away much of the national advertising that once helped sustain the underground press. *Rolling Stone*

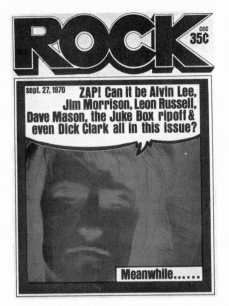

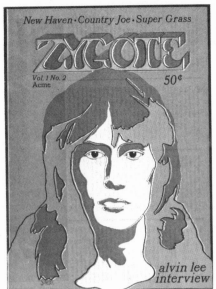

once charged $2,500 a page, and it is very much the proper etiquette of the record industry to introduce new rock LP's with at least a half-page ad. This is usually coupled with spot advertising on FM rock stations.

"Underground" FM rock stations are a crucial element in this mass Bohemianism of style. For years FM had been the poor cousin of commercial radio, relegated largely to playing classical music and programing public affairs. Precisely because of this, FM proved the perfect medium for progressive rock and youth culture. There was freedom, because no one really cared. "Underground" stations could feature disk jockeys who identified freely with the antiwar movement, play protest songs, talk long and freely about whatever happened to be on their minds, and not worry if a rock selection ran for ten minutes.

"The proposition has always been that the greatest freedom of speech is reserved for the media with the least potential influence," says Nicholas Johnson, the F.C.C. commissioner. "A whole lot of people have discovered music as an important medium, so now the pressure is on the music as well as the station." [9] Youth culture has grown beyond belief, and in the past two years "underground" radio has been neatly lobotomized. Now there are an estimated 350 to 400 FM stations presenting rock music in one form or another, and most cities have at least one "underground" station where disk jockeys rap in low, intimate tones, possibly even making occasional arcane references to dope or the war in Vietnam. They play lengthy selections from rock LP's that even may mention narcotics, protest United States policy, or be sufficiently raunchy so as not to be played on AM radio. The music is broken occasionally to advertise youth-oriented products, such as movies, rock concerts, records, hip clothing, soft drinks and skin cream, all sold as if they were mandatory accouterments for participation in youth culture. In essence, the stations have made themselves a very nebulous part of what seems to be the Movement, and by the very act of listening one can believe he has done something to change the world.

Such a segmented audience is irresistible to record companies and other advertisers. ABC radio wrote potential advertisers about its FM rock concept: "Like any successful business, we invest in new products, too. One of our latest is called LOVE . . . it communicates to a new kind of audience . . . the audience that thinks, feels and buys in the same way. . . . And LOVE is the only concept on radio that's effectively reaching them. . . ." [10]

Once money is spent on rock papers and FM stations, advertisers have little left for the highly political underground press. Even rock-culture publications that dare to veer away from strict music coverage may lose advertising. "We find that those papers that focus on music do best for us," says Linda Barton, a young account executive at Wunderman, Ricotta and Kline, the advertising agency that handles the Columbia Records account. "If they don't have much music, they have to prove themselves." Len Sutton, the twenty-eight-year-old publisher of *Zygote*, a new rock-culture publication, says that during the week his publication first came out he received phone calls from four advertising agencies and record companies warning him not to make *Zygote* any more political.

Nevertheless, hip capitalists are perfectly aware that the nucleus of their market is the Movement at its broadest point. The cast of *Hair*, the "Tribal Rock Musical" that neatly defuses political issues by existing externally in the never-never land of hippiedom 1967, are fixtures at mass protests presumably because the producers *care*. At the New York Moratorium demonstration in November at the United Nations, there they were singing with gusto and *élan*. At the Philadelphia Earth Day parade there the Philadelphia company was perched on a hay wagon singing for all they were worth. For *Hair*'s second birthday in April 1970, there they were belting out "I Got Life" and "Let the Sunshine In" before ten thousand people in Central Park's mall while radical youths snaked their way through the audience passing out pamphlets asking: "With all the green power *Hair* promoters have taken in, has any of it come back to the people?"

Hair has earned well over two million dollars' profit, none of which has helped foster the hippie culture the musical so effectively propagates. That extravaganza in the park may have cost eight thousand dollars, but the media covered the event as news, not advertising, and the show gained publicity untainted by the onus of advertising, the kind of publicity *Hair* has consistently garnered, and that has been fundamental in turning the musical into the theatrical institution par excellence of cosmetic Bohemianism.

This same sort of thing was evident at the April 15, 1970, Moratorium, when demonstrators trudged up Manhattan's Sixth Avenue beneath banners heralding everything from "Gay Liberation" to "Get Out Now." That rare togetherness of other marches, other years—when Joan Baez's voice seemed a moral incantation and acts of witness like

Vol. 1 No. 1

ACME

50¢

JOE COCKER:INT.
Grass Growers Guide
The Grateful Dead
Winter's End (21 pages)

sit-ins and draft resistance, invincible weaponry—was gone, and the young marchers chanted the familiar peace slogans automatically, with no more fervor than a sixth-grade class reciting the Pledge of Allegiance. Suddenly, though, hundreds of marchers left the march, bolted under police barricades and in a swirling, milling mass reached out toward a half dozen men who stood on a stoop passing out old copies of *Crawdaddy, the Rock Culture Newspaper.*

It was Marvin Grafton, president and major stockholder of New Crawdaddy Productions, who decided to give *Crawdaddy* away to "his" people. (Bundles of returned copies of the first issue sat on the floor of New Crawdaddy Production's basement office.) The twenty-seven-year-old Grafton typifies these hip capitalists who, by deed, if not by word, seek to revitalize capitalism, infusing business with some of the devil-may-care derring-do of the nineteenth-century entrepreneur. "Because a cat's got money, he's not a fucking pig," says Grafton in his tense, supercharged voice. "I believe in evolutionary change, and evolutionary change means that cats like me get more power. People will just have to get hip to that."

Some New York businessmen have gotten hip and it can be an unsettling experience to observe plump businessmen in coat and tie standing deferential, even cowed, before Grafton, who wears shaped suits of rakish cut, a golden medallion around his neck, a golden ring in his left ear, and whose mustache, bearded chin, long hair, and indolent features bear a close resemblance to daguerreotypes of the young Napoleon III. These businessmen realize perfectly well that they are in the presence of a colleague, a tough and shrewd entrepreneur who quite possibly has the drive and know-how to turn New Crawdaddy Productions into a major conglomerate of magazines, rock production, concerts, and other youth-culture enterprises.

Grafton's personal office is little more than a cubbyhole knocked together from white wallboard and decorated with half a dozen pop posters. Such posters are a perfect product of hip capitalism. In the affluent youth market the rational buyer of classic economic theory is a rare being and very often the "value added" by the hip entrepreneur is a short-lived hipness that has little to do with intrinsic worth. Thus posters produced for a few cents can be retailed for several dollars; cheaply made pipes for dope smoking go for $3.95; first-run tickets for *Woodstock,* essentially a low-budget documentary feature, cost as much as $5. The hip market has not yet been fully rationalized into the mass economy, and so a traditional entrepreneur such as Grafton can amass a fortune in a short time.

Grafton's six posters manage to cover the main symbols of the merchandized counter culture. Of course, there is the famous poster that originally was an ad for the Woodstock Peace and Music Festival and the inevitable picture from "Easy Rider," the first and best of the hip youth-cult films. Grafton's astrological sign, Scorpio, hangs on the wall too, exemplary of how dubious fads are quickly turned into books, articles, T-shirts, computer read-outs, and what-have-you. There are two sexual posters as well, a picture of a girl with her legs spread leaning on a weight-lifting machine and a cartoon of a husky fellow with an erect penis. And, finally, there is a modernesque rendering of stock market figures inscribed "Wall Street."

The classic example of hip capitalists extracting an element of an underground paper and refining it into a lucrative product deserves a detailed retelling. In the summer of 1968, Al Goldstein, a husky thirty-five-year-old New Yorker, whose career had ranged from photo journalism at the *Daily Mirror,* to writing "true stories" for the *National Mirror,* a shoddy sex-and-violence tabloid, walked into the West Side offices of the *New York Free Press,* a now defunct underground. He handed Jim Buckley, the managing editor, a story about his experience as a company spy against a union at Bendix, and the two became fast friends.

Theirs appeared the most incongruous of amities. Buckley is boyishly good-looking with page-boy hair, sultry features, and casual hippie manners while Goldstein is a chubby man with the vaguely cherubic face often seen on Manhattan cabbies, a mustache and goatee, who greets strangers with the boisterous, instant intimacy so common among native New Yorkers. Not long after that first meeting, Buckley suggested that the two of them put out a sexy paper. "I jumped at it," says Goldstein. "The *East Village Other* was carrying pages and pages of 'body ads,' making a mint. I knew that I bought *EVO* not for the politics or anything like that, but for the occasionally shocking sex ad. I knew that it was time for somebody to put the interests up front."

Here, then, was the historic marriage of the underground press to commercial sex journalism. Buckley brought with him as his dowry from the underground press a casual, intimate journalistic style; an identification with the New Left; and a far-out concept of layout. Goldstein contributed the crude irreverence of the sex tabloids, an almost pathological craving to best the older sex papers, and a big, boisterous personality that would rush headlong into turning out the most shocking paper in America.

Buckley and Goldstein took their initial $350 bank roll and after peeling $217 off to pay for the printing of 7,000 copies, counted out $75 for an ad in *EVO.* On November 29, 1968, the first issue of *Screw* appeared.

You are on the virgin trip of the first magazine-newspaper that gives sex a break and makes no bones about it . . . we will uncover the entire world of sex. We will be the Consumer's Report of Sex, testing new products such as dildoes, rubbers, and artificial vaginas. We'll review some of the movies which you never expected to get reviewed. We'll try to dignify the search for the hottest books and films by helping you get your money's worth.

Screw took the wet dreams of America and sold them for half a dollar. Interviews with pimps, prostitutes, movie stars, rock musicians. Product testing of flavored douches, dildoes, electric vibrators, penis enlargers. Reviews of sex books, films, plays. A column for homosexuals. Do-it-yourself articles on masturbation. Stories on personal sex experiences in a prose that coupled early *Popular Mechanics* to late Olympia Press. At first *Screw* did not have the pretensions of publications directed at the Bohemians of style, but it certainly did serve an audience at least partly alienated from American

SCREW

New!! Complete Sex Guide, Pg.19

Cunnilingus: A Symposium, Pg.8   The Selling of Sex, Pg.4

NUMBER 138

THE SEX REVIEW

50 CENTS

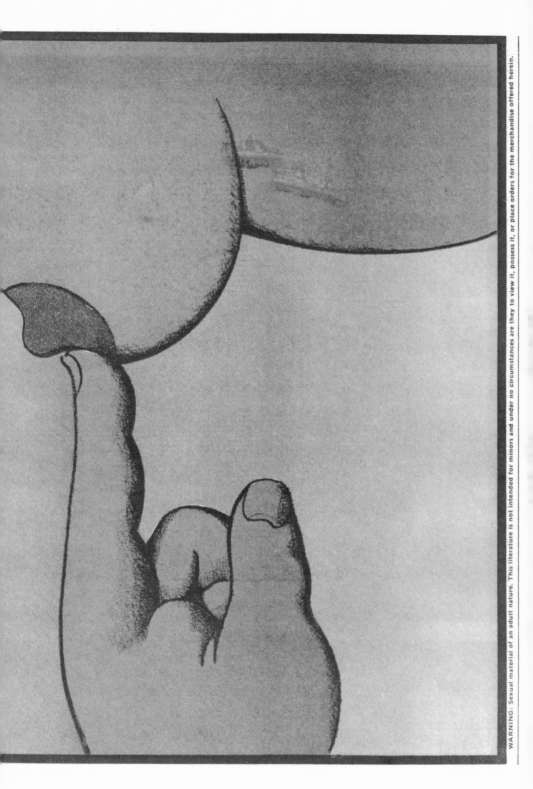

mores. True, it may have been "dildo journalism," as Jules Feiffer called it "basically narcissistic, antiwomen, and about as prosex as the clap," yet it allowed these self-conscious seekers of cellophane-wrapped *sex*— be they businessmen, students or tourists—to become legitimate consumers buying their papers on newsstands all over New York.

Screw was raunchy and crude and antiliterary, and it served a function no one had ever dared attempt to serve before. No longer would the lonely have to send away for sexual products that never arrived or were fake. No longer would men—and it was very much a paper for men— have to be conned into paying five dollars to see a sex film ("We dare to show it all") and then sit slumped in a grubby theater watching a washed-out 16mm print of veiled sex acts. *Screw* specifically evaluated films as to their sexual content:

I PETER-METER *MAN AND WIFE* WITH THE HIGHEST RATING IN SCREW HISTORY FOR ANY FILM EITHER DOMESTIC OR FOREIGN FILM ANY PLAY, SHOW OR ENTERTAINMENT OF ANY KIND. ITS PERCENTILE RATING IS 95%.

Possible	*Actual*
Sexuality—40%	40%
Interest—50%	49%
Technical—10%	6%

In rooming houses, hotels, efficiency apartments, and family houses as well, there are men who identify with *Screw* the way hip youths once identified with *EVO*. It is *their* paper and they empathize with Buckley and Goldstein, who are very much the main characters in *Screw,* bumbling, horny fellows who never quite manage to have sexual relations, and who gallivant around talking with prostitutes on the East Side, nude models in Copenhagen, Joe Namath in his dressing room, and John and Yoko Lennon in bed.

Screw, the paper of the "liberated" post-Puritans, is not politically radical. Even in their second issue Buckley and Goldstein felt compelled to editorialize, "We've learned that the left is as fucked up as the right when it comes to sex." And as *Screw's* weekly press run grew to 100,000 the paper became even less enchanted with the Movement. "Where is the New Left today?" says Goldstein. "If you read *Screw,* you can hate it."

The New York underground papers scarcely knew what had hit them. In a few weeks after *Screw* won general newsstand distribution, *EVO's* circulation plunged from a claimed high of 65,000 to disastrous depths the staff does not like to talk about. *Rat* suffered. The *New York Free Press* lost out as well. And John Wilcock discovered that when he put a nude girl on the cover of his personal underground, *Other Scenes,* he sold out 10,000 copies. When he did not, he would have at least 5,000 returns. Disgusted, unwilling to drape his paper with naked flesh every issue, and financially unable to take the wild fluctuations in circulation, Wilcock withdrew *Other Scenes* from the newsstands.

It was time for the underground press to go through the most critical and serious of re-evaluations, for of what puerile and sad stuff could this early counter culture, this new radical journalism be made, if it built its fortunes on the secret desires of anonymous American males. There was no time or desire or room for such self-criticism, however, and with a mixture of desperation and the entrepreneurial initiative that is sometimes referred to as greed, several underground figures began publishing their own sex papers—or "pornzines," as they are called. Marvin Grafton, who had been a founder and business manager of *Rat*, started *Pleasure,* the raunchiest of the new genre, featuring little but openly posed nudes, crude filler, and the cover notation: "This is the newspaper you can read with one hand." The paper was so successful that soon Grafton left *Rat* to start his own business and eventually to begin *Crawdaddy, the Rock Culture Newspaper.*

The *New York Free Press* published the *New York Review of Sex,* the most elegant of the pornzines and the earliest casualty, and *EVO* weighed in with *Kiss.* "Because the sexually liberated people of this country deserve more and better erotic literature and pictures to enjoy . . . to counter the righteous hypercritical groundswell of sexual repression presently growing in this country . . . To assert the constitutional rights of our artists and writers to print and peddle any form of artistic and literary gruel that they wish . . . To make a bundle . . . Mainly to make a bundle. We have decided to inaugurate yet another New York pornzine."

Unfortunately for *EVO,* there were already almost a dozen other pornzines on the New York newsstands. But the fall of 1969, when the pornzine craze peaked, *Pleasure* alone was the equal of *Screw*—with a circulation of well over 100,000. Since then *Pleasure* has remained as crude as ever, but *Screw* has developed a more sophisticated editorial concept that eventually might win

the paper a broader audience. *Screw* has had special issues on motorcycle cults, women's liberation, homosexuality, and the San Francisco sex scene.

The commercial sex scene in New York City has liberalized, so that *Screw* has had to retire its original "Peter Meter" for a new one with more rigorous standards of eroticism. Buckley and Goldstein have become almost respectable. Their movie reviews are quoted in advertisements in legitimate newspapers. Now they also publish a rather staid homosexual paper as well—*Gay*—and they soon will be putting out a travel magazine edited by John Wilcock. For the moment they have shelved plans for a daily news and sex paper.

The competition over the audience for everything from sex papers to FM radio to rock papers has become so fierce that the laws of the market place are taking their toll. For a while, *Crawdaddy,* the most crudely exploitative of the commercial rock papers, stopped publishing. Even Jann Wenner has had to pull in his horns. Not only has Wenner had to lower *Rolling Stone*'s ad rate from $3000 to $2400 a page and pare his staff down, but he has had to run from one big advertiser to another, soliciting ads and trumpeting the virtues of *Rolling Stone.*

Wenner has broadened *Rolling Stone*'s concept to include more coverage of political and social matters. Documents liberated from *Rolling Stone*'s New York office by the Rock Liberation Front suggest what is behind this editorial change. "There were letters from Jann Wenner with such gems as 'When we get enough ads we can tell everybody to go fuck themselves,'" the UPS news bulletin noted. "There was a statement that *RS* wants to branch out into non-

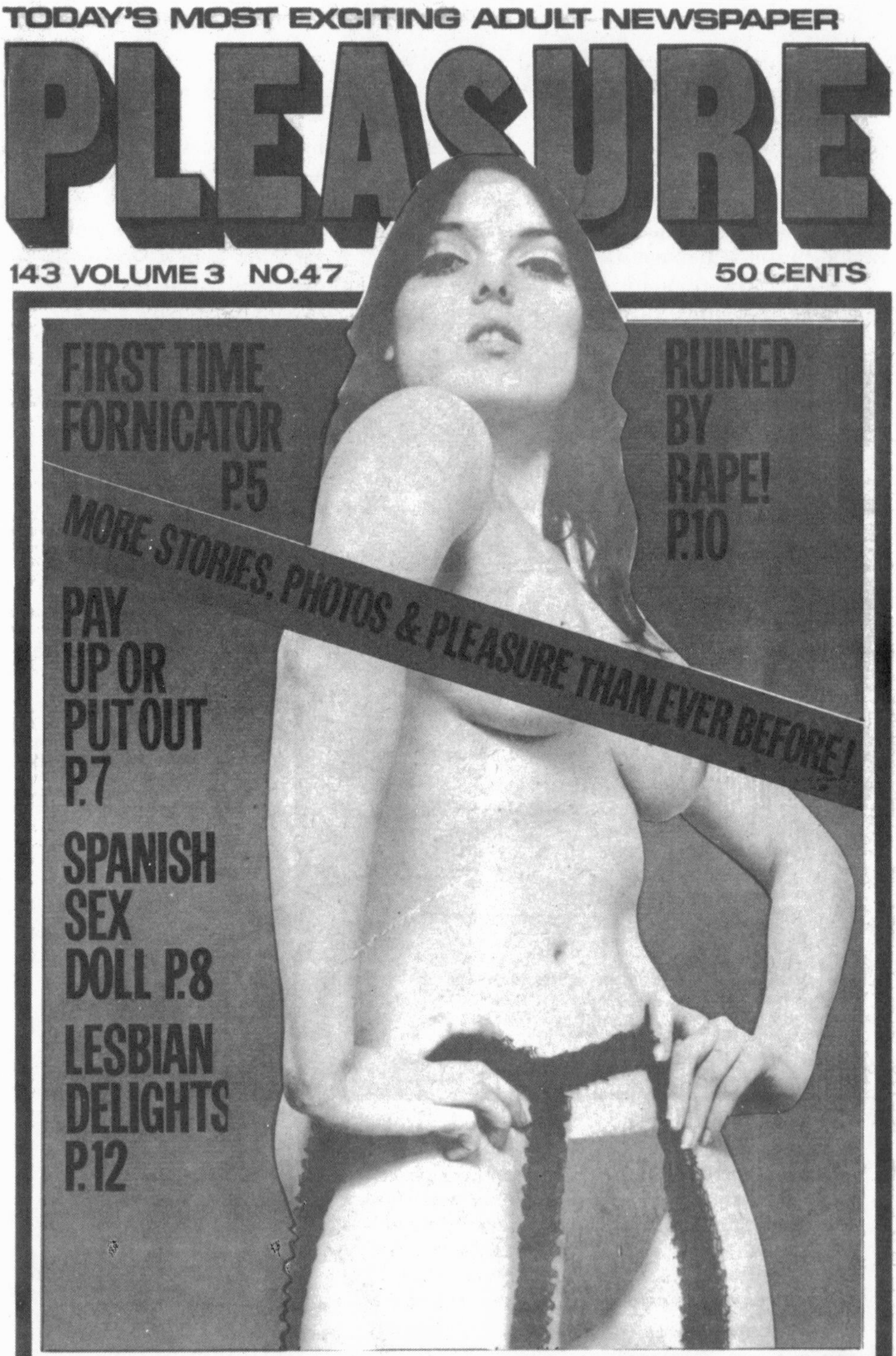

TODAY'S MOST EXCITING ADULT NEWSPAPER

PLEASURE

143 VOLUME 3 NO.47

50 CENTS

FIRST TIME FORNICATOR P.5

RUINED BY RAPE! P.10

MORE STORIES, PHOTOS & PLEASURE THAN EVER BEFORE!

PAY UP OR PUT OUT P.7

SPANISH SEX DOLL P.8

LESBIAN DELIGHTS P.12

WARNING: Sexual material of an adult nature. This literature is not intended for minors and under no circumstances are they to view it, possess it, or place orders for the merchandise offered herein.

rock culture to become a sort of hip *Playboy*."

This thunderous and unquenchable surge of protest and anger has also been neatly tapped by book publishers, magazines and movies to provide a renewed vitality to their products. For the first time in history publishing leftist literature and making anti-Establishment movies is highly lucrative. High-quality paperback lines such as Random House's extremely profitable Vintage Books are largely New Left and protest literature. Eldridge Cleaver's *Soul on Ice* has sold well over a million copies in the $1.95 paperback edition; reportedly McGraw-Hill, hardly a bunch of fellow travelers, has paid Cleaver $430,000 as an advance on his next book. Movies such as *Strawberry Statement* and *Getting Straight* turn the most serious of events into hip soap opera.

For radicals this is an ambiguous development. Their groups need money and publicity, and many editors and movie makers do honestly and fully identify with the Movement. What happens very often, though, is that movements become creatures of the media, plucked up and exposed to the mass audience before they have had a chance to develop organically. Black Power, Ecology, Women's Liberation—each has its brief day in the spotlight. Soon the public can no longer be titillated, and the media, a creature of no man, moves on, leaving in its wake a stunted and twisted political movement that has grown addicted to such publicity.

It is all enough to make Phil Bonosky, cultural editor of the Communist *Daily World*, downgrade the New Left as "largely a literary phenomenon." And we must wonder what would have happened to twentieth-century history if the *Communist Manifesto* had made the 1848 best-seller list and Karl Marx had been lionized on television talk shows as a brilliant social critic? One must wonder, too, what Marx would have made of Bob Dylan, the Rolling Stones, dope, acid, beads, love-ins, peace signs and rock festivals. Would he have agreed with Irwin Silber, cultural editor of the *Guardian,* who writes that "while the 'new' ideology seems to be attacking the long-established ethos of the capitalist rationale, it is actually generating the very schemes and styles which will serve as a corrective balance within the framework of the profit system." [11] Or would Marx have felt that a radical movement can never ignore the natural wellsprings of discontent— no matter how tainted they may be.

The brilliant mind-boggling effect of cultural radicalism is, of course, gone—dissipated into posters, pop art, television, magazines and advertising. No wonder then, that some young radicals, sickened by city streets filled with cosmetic Bohemians and by a society that has usurped everything about cultural radicalism except the essence, have retreated into the perfect purity of dropout radicalism or an equally pure and narrow political radicalism. They may be perfectly justified, but it does seem that any movement that gives up on these growing millions of alienated middle-class Americans is dooming itself. However, most of the radical youth propagandists have by no means gone quiet and they continue to walk that vague and constantly moving line between selling radicalism and selling out.

"All the News
That's Fit to Print"

The New York Times

LATE CITY EDITION

Weather: Partly sunny, cool today; cloudy and cool tonight, tomorrow. Temp. range: today 58-72; Monday 62-74. Temp.-Hum. Index yesterday 69. Full U.S. report on Page 85.

VOL. CXX...No. 41,415

NEW YORK, TUESDAY, JUNE 15, 1971

15 CENTS

MITCHELL SEEKS TO HALT SERIES ON VIETNAM BUT TIMES REFUSES

COURT STEP LIKELY

Return of Documents Asked in Telegram To Publisher

By MAX FRANKEL

Special to The New York Times

WASHINGTON, June 14—Attorney General John N. Mitchell asked The New York Times this evening to refrain from further publication of documents drawn from a Pentagon study of the Vietnam war on the ground that such disclosures would cause "irreparable injury to the defense interests of the United States."

If the paper refused, another Justice Department official said, the Government would try to forbid further publication by court action tomorrow. The Times refused to halt publication voluntarily.

The Justice Department's request and intention to seek a court enjoinder were conveyed by Robert C. Mardian, Assistant Attorney General in charge of the internal security division, to Harding F. Bancroft, executive vice president of The Times.

Spoke by Telephone

They spoke by telephone at about 7:30 P.M., which was some two hours before tomorrow's first edition of the paper was scheduled to go to press with the third installment of the articles about the Pentagon study.

An hour later, a telegram from Mr. Mitchell asked that The Times halt further publication of the material and return the documents to the Pentagon.

The Times then issued the following statement:

"We have received the telegram from the Attorney General asking The Times to cease further publication of the Pentagon's Vietnam study.

"The Times must respectfully decline the request of the Attorney General, believing that it is in the interest of the people of this country to be informed of the material contained in this series of articles.

"We have also been informed of the Attorney General's intention to seek an injunction against further publication. We believe that it is properly a matter for the courts to decide. The Times will oppose any request for an injunction for the same reason that led us to publish the articles in the first place. We will of course abide by the final decision of the court."

Telegram From Mitchell

The telegram from Attorney General Mitchell, addressed to Arthur Ochs Sulzberger, president and publisher of The Times, said:

"I have been advised by the Secretary of Defense that the material published in The New York Times on June 13, 14, 1971, captioned 'Key Texts From Pentagon's Vietnam Study' contains information relating to the national defense of the United States and bears a top secret classification.

"As such, publication of this information is directly prohibit-

Continued on Page 18, Column 4

Vietnam Archive: Study Tells How Johnson Secretly Opened Way to Ground Combat

By NEIL SHEEHAN

President Johnson decided on April 1, 1965, to use American ground troops for offensive action in South Vietnam because the Administration had discovered that its long-planned bombing of North Vietnam—which had just begun—was not going to stave off collapse in the South, the Pentagon's study of the Vietnam war discloses. He ordered that the decision be kept secret.

"The fact that this departure from a long-held policy had momentous implications was well recognized by the Administration leadership," the Pentagon analyst writes, alluding to the policy axiom since the Korean conflict that another land war in Asia should be avoided.

Although the President's decision was a "pivotal" change, the study declares, "Mr. Johnson was greatly concerned that the step be given as little prominence as possible."

The decision was embodied in National Security Action Memorandum 328, on April 6, which included the following paragraphs:

"5. The President approved an 18-20,000 man increase in U.S. military support forces to fill out existing units and supply needed logistic personnel.

"6. The President approved the deployment of two additional Marine Battalions and one Marine Air Squadron and associated headquarters and support elements.

"7. The President approved a change of mission for all Marine Battalions deployed to Vietnam to permit their more active use under conditions to be established and approved by the Secretary of Defense in consultation with the Secretary of State."

The paragraph stating the President's concern about publicity gave stringent orders in writing to members of the National Security Council:

"11. The President desires that with respect to the actions in paragraphs 5 through 7, premature publicity be avoided by all possible precautions. The actions themselves should be taken as rapidly as practicable, but in ways that should minimize any appearance of sudden changes in policy, and official statements on these troop movements will be made only with the direct approval of the Secretary of Defense, in consultation with the Secretary of State. The President's desire is that these movements and changes should be understood as being gradual and wholly consistent with existing policy." [See text, action memorandum on change of mission, April 6, 1965, Page 21.]

The period of increasing ground-combat involvement is shown in the Pentagon papers to be the third major phase of President Johnson's commitment to South Vietnam. This period forms another section of the presentation of those papers by The New York Times.

The papers, prepared by a large team of authors in 1967-68 as an official study of how the United States went to war in Indochina, consist of 3,000 pages of analysis and 4,000 pages of supporting documents. The study covers nearly three decades of American policy toward Southeast Asia. Thus far The Times's reports on the study, with presentation of key documents, have covered the

Continued on Page 22, Col. 1

This is the third in a series of articles on a secret study, made in the Pentagon, of American participation in the Vietnam war. The study was obtained from other sources by The New York Times through the investigative reporting of Mr. Sheehan. The series was researched and written over three months by Mr. Sheehan and other staff members. Three pages of documentary material begin on Page 19.

MAYOR'S BUDGET OF $8.8-BILLIONS AVOIDS LAYOFFS

ATTRITION ON JOBS

Losses Put at 14,320 And 5,013 Vacancies Due to Go Unfilled

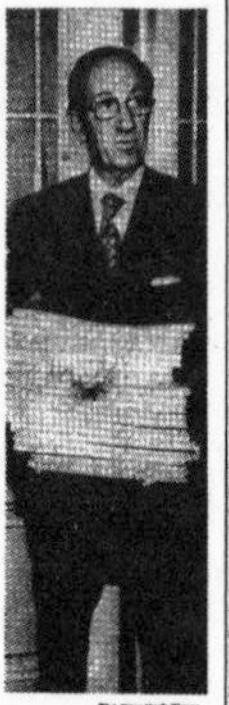

The New York Times

Thomas J. Cuite, City Council majority leader, with new budget papers.

By MARTIN TOLCHIN

Mayor Lindsay reduced his proposed expense budget by $377.2-million yesterday — mostly by postponing payments rather than reducing services—and presented an $8.8-billion budget that called for no layoffs of city employes.

"We're right at the hairline where it's possible for us to avoid layoffs," Edward K. Hamilton, the city's Budget Director, said at a City Hall briefing.

Mayor Lindsay said that the proposed budget "would allow New York City to maintain at minimally adequate levels the basic services which our citizens rely upon." The Mayor had described his previously submitted $9.1-billion budget as a "survival" budget.

$5-Billion for Employes

More than $5-billion of the proposed budget for the fiscal year beginning July 1 is earmarked for wages, pensions and fringe benefits for the city's 381,000 employes.

The budget submitted for action by the City Council and the Board of Estimate called for the loss of 14,320 Civil Service jobs through attrition — deaths, retirements and resignations.

The proposed attritions include 1,300 policemen, 360 firemen, 960 sanitationmen (but 40 sanitation management engineers" will be hired), 4,580 teachers and 1,000 social workers.

Moreover, 5,013 jobs currently unfilled will be eliminated, for a total reduction of 19,333 positions. In addition, 25 jobs in executive management also will be eliminated, Mr. Hamilton said, conceding that "I don't know how many are actually filled, but I would suspect that more are filled than are vacant."

But despite the city's announcement that there would be no layoffs, Murry Bergtraum, president of the Board of Education, said yesterday that the city's school system might have to lay off as many as 1,000 employes.

Warnings Are Recalled

The budget message capped two months of unceasing warnings from City Hall that up to 60,000 city employes would lose their jobs, and 30,000 more jobs would be left unfilled, unless the city obtained the fiscal package it sought from the Legislature in Albany.

The warnings were met with widespread skepticism. Many City Hall observers believed that the Lindsay administration was attempting to enlist in its fight for more funds from Albany not only eight million New Yorkers threatened with loss of services, but also 400,000 civil servants.

Mayor Lindsay, asked last April why the warnings of layoffs and cutback of services were more genuine than those of previous years when no reductions were implemented, cited the recession, inflation and mid-year cuts and said, "The problem is entirely different this year, much worse than it's ever been before, it's of substantial dimensions."

The Mayor and the Democratic leaders agreed on June 5 that there would be only "minimal" layoffs of city em-

Continued on Page 28, Column 6

COURT SAYS CITIES MAY CLOSE POOLS TO BAR RACIAL MIX

5-4 Ruling Backs Shutdown of Recreational Facilities to Blacks and Whites

By FRED P. GRAHAM

Special to The New York Times

WASHINGTON, June 14—The Supreme Court ruled 5 to 4 today that communities may close their publicly owned recreational facilities rather than comply with court orders to desegregate them.

The dissenters protested that such closings expressed an official policy that "Negroes are unfit to associate with whites," but the majority held that Jackson, Miss., acted constitutionally when it closed its swimming pools rather than operate them on an integrated basis.

Because the city closed all pools to whites and blacks alike, its action did not deny Negroes the equal protection of the laws, the Court held.

Warning by Black

Justice Hugo L. Black, who wrote the majority opinion, went beyond the written decision in his statement from the bench to declare that the ruling was not an invitation to Southern communities to avoid school integration by closing schools.

"Any subterfuge used or utilized" to avoid school desegregation "will not be allowed," he said. He promised that "we will look through" any schemes by which public schools are closed and publicly supported segregated schools take their place.

The Court majority was composed of Justice Black plus President Nixon's two nominees, Chief Justice Warren E. Burger and Justice Harry A. Blackmun, and Justices Potter Stewart and John M. Harlan. The dissenters were Justices William J. Brennan Jr., William O. Douglas, Thurgood Marshall and Byron R. White.

Five Pools Closed

The crux of the decision, according to Justice Black, was that when the Federal courts ordered Jackson to integrate its four white pools and one Negro pool in 1963 the city ceased operation of all five. The reasons given by the Mayor were that the mixing of whites and blacks at pools might touch off violence and the pools would operate at a loss.

Justice Black said that although racial prejudice might have been the motive for closing the pools the Court could not overturn such an action unless the effect was discriminatory. This action was not, he said, because both whites and blacks were left without public pools.

Chief Justice Burger added in a concurring statement that to hold that a public facility could not be closed, once it was opened, "would plainly dis-

Continued on Page 26, Column 4

JERSEY APPROVES AIRPORT RAIL LINK

Bistate Action Completed by Legislature—Cahill Signs Bill for Easier Divorce

By RONALD SULLIVAN

Special to The New York Times

TRENTON, June 14 — The New Jersey Legislature completed today bistate approval of a measure authorizing the Port of New York Authority to finance and build high-speed rail connections between midtown Manhattan and Kennedy International and Newark Airports.

In another major development, Gov. William T. Cahill signed into law a liberalization of New Jersey's 64-year-old divorce statutes. The new law eliminates the requirement, in many cases, of placing blame to dissolve marriages and includes an 18-month voluntary separation period after which divorce can be granted by mutual consent.

At the same time, the Senate gave final legislative approval to a one-year moratorium on local cable television franchise awards. The actions took place during a special session of the Legislature originally called for

Continued on Page 29, Column 1

FACTORY OUTPUT CLIMBED IN MAY

0.7% Rise, Biggest Since January, Called Recovery Sign by Treasury Official

By The Associated Press

WASHINGTON, June 14—The Federal Reserve Board reported today that industrial production showed a sharp gain in May, adding new evidence that the nation's economy was picking up momentum.

The board said the key indicator of how industry was producing advanced by seven-tenths of 1 per cent last month, up from a moderate gain of three-tenths of 1 per cent in April.

[The prime interest rate on business loans was raised on Monday to 5¾ from 5½ per cent by the First Pennsylvania Banking and Trust Company, Philadelphia's largest bank. Details on Page 61.]

The May rise in the industrial production index was its sharpest upward movement since January, when it climbed by the same percentage as output of automobiles resumed after the settlement of the strike at the General Motors Corporation.

"It looks good," said Assist-

Continued on Page 67, Column 3

Italian Neo-Fascists Make Gains in Regional Voting

By MARVINE HOWE

Special to The New York Times

ROME, Tuesday, June 15—The province of Rome, the island of Sicily and major towns in southern Italy swung to the right yesterday with the neo-Fascist Italian Social Movement making important electoral gains at the expense of the dominant Christian Democrats.

In local elections involving one-fifth of the national electorate, the neo-Fascists made substantial advances almost everywhere, late but incomplete results show.

Final results from Rome Province, announced early today, showed the neo-Fascists with 15.6 per cent of the votes against 10.7 per cent in last year's regional elections. The Christian Democrats polled only 27.2 per cent of the votes as compared with 30.9 per cent in 1970.

Complete returns from Bari in the south gave the neo-Fascists 13.7 per cent of the vote or 2.5 per cent more than last year. Even in the predominantly left-wing city of Genoa, the neo-Fascists won 5.5 per cent of the vote, 1 per cent more than last year.

The Communist party, the leading party in Genoa, held its own with 33.8 per cent of the vote. In Bari, however, the Communists suffered a setback. The 15.9 per cent of the vote they won was 4.7 per cent lower than last year.

In Rome Province, the Communists held last year's position

Continued on Page 11, Column 1

Vittoriano Rastelli

Neo-Fascist party symbol and slogan "With us new order" on building wall.

U.S. SUES SUBURB ON HOUSING BIAS

Blackjack, Mo., Is Charged With Blocking a Project—Romney States Policy

By JACK ROSENTHAL

Special to The New York Times

WASHINGTON, June 14 — After months of study, the Nixon Administration sued Blackjack, Mo., today, charging the St. Louis suburb with illegally blocking an integrated housing development.

Filing of the suit in St. Louis was announced here by Attorney General John N. Mitchell 35 minutes after the Administration disclosed another initiative in the politically volatile field of suburban housing integration.

George Romney, Secretary of Housing and Urban Development, issued proposed guidelines that would limit Federal grants for community development to those communities that agree to plan for low-income and moderate-income housing.

Last Friday President Nixon issued a detailed policy statement on the subject. He called for strong legal action against racial discrimination but said he would not compel suburbs to undergo economic integration.

Filing of the Blackjack suit, first recommended six months ago, was in accord with Mr. Nixon's policy. And Mr. Mitchell, at a joint news conference with Mr. Romney, said the Department of Justice would soon file eight other housing discrimination cases around the country.

Mr. Romney, praising the

Continued on Page 33, Column 1

Soviet Says U.S. Fleet Harassed Grechko Ship

By BERNARD GWERTZMAN

Special to The New York Times

MOSCOW, June 14—The Soviet cruiser carrying Defense Minister Andrei A. Grechko on his visit last weekend to the Soviet naval squadron in the Mediterranean Sea was constantly followed and harassed by United States ships and aircraft, a Soviet newspaper said today.

Izvestia, the Government paper, in a report from its correspondent Valentin Gortsev aboard the cruiser Dzerzhinsky, said the tracking was so close that at one point the Soviet commander flashed a semaphore message to the American destroyer escort Ricketts:

"Sir, this is not Broadway. Find a safer place for your promenades."

The surveillance was apparently routine for the Mediterranean, where ships and planes from both the Sixth Fleet and the Soviet squadron regularly track each other. It is not known whether the Americans knew that Marshal Grechko was aboard. Izvestia said the cruiser had been flying the Defense Minister's flag.

Marshal Grechko, accompanied by Adm. Sergei G. Gorshkov, commander in chief of the navy, and Gen. Aleksei A. Yepishev, the chief political officer of the armed forces, visited the Mediterranean squadron yesterday and Saturday.

Tass, the Soviet press agency, made public a brief report on

Continued on Page 4, Column 3

Navy to Scuttle That Old Sailor Suit

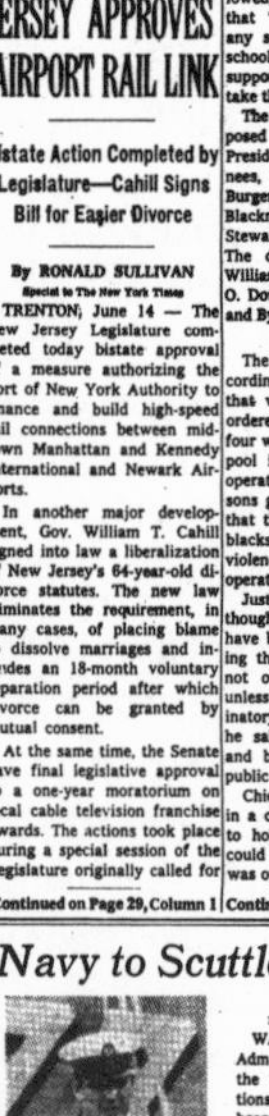

The New York Times

The new Navy dress blue

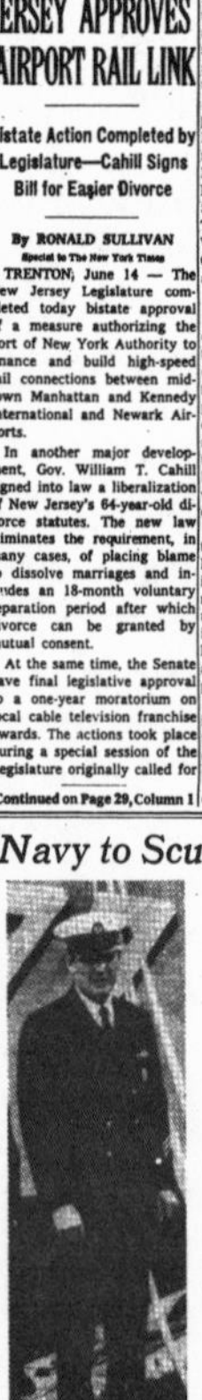

By United Press International

WASHINGTON, June 14—Adm. Elmo R. Zumwalt Jr., the Chief of Naval Operations who brought beer and beards to the "mod" Navy, announced today that bell bottoms and sailors' round hats were being abolished in the most sweeping uniform change in United States naval history.

The enlisted man's entire dress blue uniform—with its jumper, neckerchief, flap at the back of the neck and wide bottom trousers—will be replaced. All seamen, instead, will wear the uniform long used by commissioned officers and chief petty officers—the dark blue double-breasted suit, white shirt, black tie and white military hat with peak.

The change will cost the Government about $3-million, Navy officers said, with stocks of old uniforms to be used up first. The new uniforms will go into use July 1, 1977, and for two years after that the old uniform will still be allowed. The action brings the dress code of all services into line.

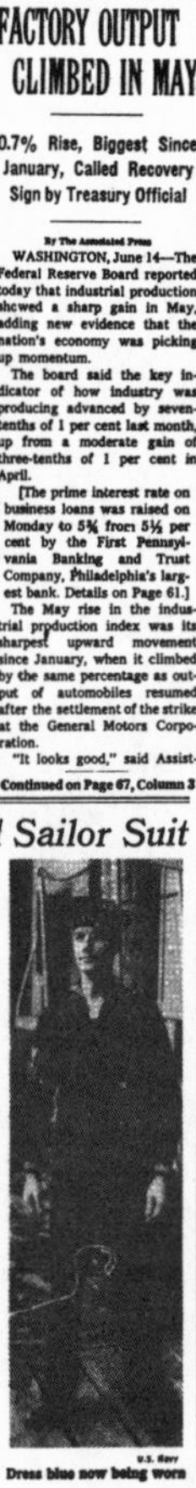

U.S. Navy

Dress blue now being worn

7 Slain in Detroit; Drug Link Suspected

By AGIS SALPUKAS

Special to The New York Times

DETROIT, June 14—Three young men and four young women suspected by the police of involvement in heroin traffic were found shot to death early this morning in a house near the area where the 1967 Detroit riot began.

The police said that all seven had been shot in the head at close range. Three of the women had been tied with rubber surgical cord.

An eighth victim, Robert Gardner, 28 years old, of Highland Park, was shot twice in the chest and is in critical condition.

James Bannon, district inspector in the Detroit homicide bureau who is heading the investigation, said in an interview: "There's no question of an execution-type slaying. But we don't know what the motive was."

He said one possibility was that it was one of a series of robberies of narcotics dens that have occurred in the city this year. "They're ideal victims," he said. "They have money and narcotics and they don't complain to the police."

However, Inspector Bannon said that about $600 had been found on Mr. Gardner and small amounts of money on the other victims, casting doubt that robbery was the motive.

The other possibility, he said, is that it was a fight among narcotics rings over territory. He said that the narcotics trade in Detroit was fragmented now and that a struggle could be going on among various factions. The seven slain today were all Negroes.

This year, about 25 persons have died in killings that were related to the narcotics trade.

Inspector Bannon gave the following account of what happened today:

Policemen in the 10th Precinct received a call from neighbors on Hazelwood between 12th and 14th streets that they heard shots at about 4:30 A.M. coming from a three-level brick house at 1790 Hazelwood.

The police also received a call from the wife of the wounded man, saying she had entered the house, found her husband shot and had taken

Continued on Page 34, Column 1

NEWS INDEX

	Page		Page
Books	41	Obituaries	46
Bridge	40	Op-Ed	43
Business	61, 71	Society	53
Crossword	41	Sports	55-57
Editorials	42	Theaters	48-51
Financial	58-71	Transportation	85
Letters	42	TV and Radio	87
Man in the News	5	Wash. Record	36
Movies	48-51	Weather	85
Music	48-51	Women's News	52

News Summary and Index, Page 45

11
The Mass Media and the Underground Press

This is an age of political and cultural insurgency, and the underground press is the impassioned voice and prose poet of that revolt. The papers are an alternative communications network, and in the end they may prove as important a journalistic innovation as the popular press of the 1880's. Already, the papers have popularized the use of marijuana and other drugs, taken ecology and women's liberation and other ideas and carried them into the consciousness of the mass media, brought thousands to Chicago in 1968 and to other demonstrations across the country, and helped forge a mass radical-youth culture.

In half a decade the underground press has shown enormous vertical growth, in the size of its audience, but much less horizontal growth, in the scope of its interests. The underground press is just not an "alternative medium," story by story, analysis by analysis, seeking to match the coverage of the aboveground press. Sometimes the underground press may totally ignore what the Establishment press would consider an important story, while on other occasions they will give certain events inordinate attention. In New York City, for instance, the mass media covered the bombing conspiracy trial of the Black Panthers irregularly and cursorily; however, a reporter for the *East Village Other* attended all the sessions, writing about it as a blatantly political trial, and *EVO* played the story up every week in a manner that would confound "rational" news judgment. When the jury found the defendants not guilty most New Yorkers had reason to be surprised, although not those who read *EVO*. Indeed, writing in the

Nation, one of the jurors cited *EVO* as an example of one of the few places where the trial was covered fairly.

Throughout the underground press, the deaths of Jimi Hendrix and Janis Joplin were treated the way the deaths of heads of state are handled in the Establishment media. Events that have radical implications are given prime importance. "What might be the first Tupamaro-style revolutionary rip-off in the U. S. has been unravelling over the past two weeks. On Sunday, Sept. 20, the National Guard Armory in Newburyport, Mass., was robbed." [1] Issues are explored in the broadest political implications, and alternatives and actions are openly suggested in news stories. ("Most of us are becoming aware of the intensity of the environmental pollution foisted upon us by a vast and irresponsible industrial system . . . At present our range of possible responses is limited by our lack of knowledge. But . . . we suggest, as a starter, that the specific list of major polluters of Peachtree Creek basic be called and confronted." [2]) And demonstrations and protests are announced in news stories and free ads.

 ⌐ The astounding growth of the papers is partly due to the failures of the mass media to deal with issues that affect many Americans, and to give a fair hearing to the voices of protest⌡ This is an intolerable failing, for in a democratic society, as Carl Becker writes, "the sole method of arriving at the truth in the long run is by the free competition of opinion in the open market." The mass media, however, run a company store, and in the name of integrity, good

taste and profit, day after day they peddle the same bland product to a public that has never tasted the gritty, rich flavor of reality.

The Establishment press is so unmitigatedly bad in San Diego, Jackson, Dallas, and scores of other cities, that in these places, almost despite itself, the underground press has become an "alternative medium." In such cities aboveground papers simply refuse to print legitimate radical or liberal or even vaguely anti-Establishment news, and one has to go to the local underground to try to find out what's happening. In San Diego the Copley papers practically ignore the city's blacks and Chicanos who make up 30 percent of the population. They print almost no significant news of Movement and antiwar activity. Their columnists run the gamut from Ralph de Toledano to Max Rafferty. They print no advertisements, reviews or news of X-rated movies, including the Academy Award-winning *Midnight Cowboy.* The *Dallas Daily News* reports a world where protest movements are practically nonexistent and Texas antiwar activity the figment of some wild-eyed radical's imagination. Even the best American papers often have staffs so resolutely middle-class and Establishment-liberal that they can't begin to understand the fury and depth of the protest movements they cover. *The New York Times,* at least, has recognized the need for other voices to be heard in its pages and in the fall of 1970 established an "op-ed" page. Here the other Americans—of left, right, and center —would have their say. So far, though, the typical guest columnists have been prominent individuals such as

John Kenneth Galbraith and Gore Vidal, and only in recent months have little-known or unknown Americans begun to get their hearing.

Television has an even tighter grasp over *its* air time, *its* programs, *its* stations, and the networks are run almost like private principalities. For instance, in May 1969 three prominent journalists—Stewart Alsop, a *Newsweek* columnist; and Howard Felsher and Ira Skutch, television producers—went to Herbert Klein, President Nixon's director of communications, and set before him an idea for a weekly television program. Wouldn't it help bridge the generation gap, they suggested, to have a weekly series of discussions between individual members of the Nixon administration and young Americans —all on television.

"Put it all on paper," Klein told them, "and let me talk about it with a few people."

After five months of telephone conversations, letters and discussions, Klein called and said, "O.K., we'll try it. That is we'll try one, to see how it goes."

It would have been of incalculable value to have opened up the television medium to human dialogue; to have given young dissidents a hearing; and to have brought to the very top of the Nixon administration the voices of protest.

All three networks—NBC, CBS and ABC—turned down the program, for they have a policy never to allow outsiders to produce public affairs and news programing.

"This program was not the first to lose its chance for life because of 'policy'. . ." writes Howard Felsher in *TV Guide*. "Significantly, the net-works don't attempt such a policy in their entertainment programing. Many entertainment shows are created, owned and produced by non-network people. Radio, when it was as big and as important as television is today, had no such policy. Newspapers and magazines have no such policy. Television should find better reasons than it has to maintain this policy—or abandon it. How else can it operate fully in the 'public interest,' as it is bound to do by law?" [3]

The TV networks were not acting cavalierly or arrogantly. In their news coverage they and the other mass media are selling credibility. Surveys repeatedly show that the American public has much greater faith in television news than in newspapers or magazines. The public has this confidence because television's public-affairs programing is not obviously biased, while at the same time it is sleekly professional. This credibility is precious and unreplenishable, and the networks are not about to risk it by running programs produced by outsiders, programs that might prove opinionated or amateurish.

This is a credibility more of form than of content. One need only look at kinescopes of the best of early TV news programs to realize this. When Edward R. Murrow denounced Senator Joseph McCarthy on "See It Now" in March 1954, television journalism came of age. The effect of that program on viewers was electrifying. Yet a few years later that program appears so crude and amateurish in technique that we cannot possibly accept its reality. That half hour was crammed with content, but it is no longer "credible." We are conditioned to accept only an amazingly sophisticated medium.

The television journalism of the 1970's is one of the most brilliant technological achievements of our age. The communications satellites bring to world events an intimacy and an immediacy that are almost unbelievable. The filmed reports themselves are often as brilliantly conceived and edited as the best of Hollywood films. Yet with all these tools, contemporary television journalists are sad heirs to the tradition of Edward R. Murrow. The satellites, remote cameras, and the breathtaking professionalism of the filmed stories are used to create an overwhelming "reality" that can achieve credibility without content.

Television news is at its best when it is covering live events such as moonshots or election nights. Then television's "reality" comes close to reality, and we are enriched and ennobled by it. Television is at its worst in covering complicated, important events and issues when it only occasionally provides illumination and insight. This is not that important, though, since television can make the grossest banality appear rare wisdom. Television has taught the public to expect such exciting film and rapid-fire elucidation of complicated news stories that the average American probably couldn't even sit still to listen to current events handled in their true complexity. He is just too used to accepting the current-events drama of the seven-o'clock news. To get behind this "reality" one need only read a script for an evening network news program. It has the same relation to substantive journalism that stage directions have to a play.

The print media too attempt to create this credibility through the formulas of objectivity, and in some ways our newspapers and magazines are quite extraordinary. The sophistication in world view and common knowledge that one finds in even the worst American papers is amazing. News magazines too are immensely rich in information and breadth of knowledge. Unfortunately there are fewer and fewer stories that can sustain an "objective" treatment, and our print media create their own false credibility.

Here our example is from *Newsweek,* one of our best and most innovative magazines. In the October 12, 1970, issue the magazine ran a long interview article with an alleged radical terrorist. It probably was the most chilling and terrifying piece of writing about revolutionary bombers that had appeared in any magazine or newspaper anywhere. It was a major journalistic coup for *Newsweek* and for the reporter, Karl Fleming, who now, as a contributing editor, is one of the top two or three reporters on the magazine.

In a brief preface *Newsweek* explained that Fleming had placed an ad in an underground paper and had rendezvoused with a youth on a beach near Venice, California. "The conditions of the encounter precluded any direct checking of the young revolutionary's statements (though a number of details that went into his story did turn out to be independently verifiable). In all, he convinced a seasoned, normally skeptical correspondent that he was a chillingly authentic specimen of what he purported to be." Here are excerpts from that article:

"We'll blow up the whole f—— world if

it comes down to it. And if our people start getting hassled and busted, we'll shoot police cruisers full of holes and kill every pig on the street."

The hard words sounded incongruous coming from the diminutive, red-haired kid in blue jeans and mustard-colored windbreaker who had approached me across the sunny Venice beach, glancing furtively over his shoulder to make sure that "the pig" wasn't lurking nearby.

He said his name was Larry. Period. He had lustrous brown eyes and softly freckled cheeks, and he wore his hair short. The haircut, he says, is camouflage. He belongs to a 50-member, all-white, all-male revolutionary terrorist gang, he says, and the short hair keeps him and other members of his group from attracting the attention of "the pig."

Over the course of the next week, in a series of interviews that totaled perhaps 24 hours, "Larry" revealed himself to be politically naïve and a mere foot soldier in his bitter, rebellious band—a spear carrier not privy to political strategy and top-priority secrets. Nevertheless, the information he had absorbed provided a rare glimpse of the operations and violent schemes of what appears to be a widespread if haphazardly organized network of underground guerrilla bands. . . .

Larry is 19 and a high-school dropout, the son of a Midwest steelworker. During his year in Vietnam he mastered lessons that would be valuable when he turned revolutionary. In "Nam," Larry learned, for example, how to extract a pound of C4 plastic explosive from a Claymore mine and ship it back to the U. S., and how to construct a bomb and place it against a building so that the charge will do the most damage. And his opportunity to rebel came soon enough. Always a malcontent, Larry finally refused to fight any more after he had killed three Viet Cong. He recalled his feeling during our conversations: "Man, they've got VC who'll stand in a field and shoot at jets with rifles. They must believe strong in something.

I can't kill people like that. I had just as soon kill Americans."

He talked that way in Vietnam, too, and attracted the attention of a member of the White Panthers, a Stateside revolutionary group. The White Panther, Larry says, "asked me if I wanted to join a group when I got home and fight against the U. S. I said sure, I could dig it." The recruiter gave Larry some phone numbers in Arizona, California, Montana, Ohio, Kentucky and Tennessee. After getting his undesirable discharge, Larry says, he used the numbers to make contact with his Los Angeles group.

He was duly examined and accepted, though few applicants are. Blacks aren't: "Accepting discipline from a group like ours hurts their status with their own people, so it makes bad vibrations and causes hassles." Women aren't accepted either. "Chicks can't be depended on," Larry says. Even so, he says, women are now being trained in secret guerrilla camps in the California, Colorado and Montana mountains to shoot, to carry ammunitions cross-country, to administer first aid, even to plant bombs. . . .

Before joining the California group several months ago, Larry says he visited a secret guerrilla camp so high in the Colorado mountains that it is obscured most of the year by clouds. His tale of the camp plays like a vignette from one of Jean-Luc Godard's more imaginative revolutionary fantasies—but Larry insists it is all true.

He got in touch with the mountain guerrillas, he says, by using another telephone number given in Vietnam. After reaching a contact in Flagstaff, Arizona, he says, he was told to travel to a certain intersection, where he was met by a guide who emerged from a clump of trees. They hiked six hours before reaching the camp, a strung-out array of sleeping bags and tents pitched beneath pine trees. Larry estimates that there were fully 1,000 people in the camp—most of them, he says he was told, were college students there for summer training. The guerrillas, he says, practiced firing and demolition and even staged mock battles. Their rations included rabbit and venison cooked on skewers over open fires, fish and a few staples. Provisions were bought in several different towns, Larry says, to avoid arousing suspicion.

About 100 guerrillas stay all year, he reports, burying their firewood in snow banks, cooking surreptitiously, living sparely so as to escape detection. Whatever money they needed was brought in by student sympathizers. Most of the members of the permanent guerrilla group, Larry gathered, were wanted by the police.

He stayed, he says, only a day, although he was asked by the leader, "a Castro-looking dude smoking a cigar," to remain as a demolition teacher. But he couldn't stand the cold, and for that reason also passed up a similar camp in Montana and chose California instead. From talking to the mountain rebels, Larry says he concluded that there are as many as ten such camps at various spots around the country.

I told Larry that some people simply wouldn't believe him, so he grudgingly agreed to submit to a lie-detector test if I wanted it. To try to corroborate and flesh out the study, I asked him to arrange for me to meet other members of his group. But fearing identification, they refused. However, I did get Larry to carry a tape recorder to last week's meeting and to invite the unidentified leader to say anything he wished. Larry returned with this terse, harsh-voiced message on the tape:

"What we're doing, we're making things so f—— uncomfortable people can't brush us off like fleas. We want freedom and peace, not half-truths and bull——. Small group? Man, others are everywhere. Watch out, we're not f—— followers of some Communist organization. Man, you want a message for the people:

Do what you believe in, but don't believe in something you're going to hate. Freedom and peace shall follow."

Next day, Larry telephoned to say the organization was now fearful that he had become a security risk and had ordered him into temporary exile. He said he was splitting—he didn't say to where.

The article was absolutely convincing, and millions of Americans must have read it with mounting fear and anger. Anyone with any real knowledge of radical activities in the United States would have read with mounting fear and anger also—but for different reasons. This writer called Fleming in Los Angeles to discuss the article with him. He was perturbed over his experience with the underground press, in this case, the *Los Angeles Free Press*. When the *Free Press* received Fleming's classified ad trying to set up a meeting with a "revolutionary anarchist bomber group," they immediately called Fleming and said they could run the ad only if it included a cautionary note. The disclaimer was to say that reporters and their notes have been subpoenaed before and that although Mr. Fleming had a reputation as a good reporter, others have caved in under pressure.

"I don't think I've ever been so mad in my whole life," says Fleming. "I called the paper and I spoke to the publisher's aide-de-camp. I just blew my goddam top. I said to her, 'All you're doing is torpedoing this by insinuating that I'm dishonest and nobody better deal with me. You people go into business on the premise that the Establishment press is crooked and dishonest and here you turn around and commit an even worse sin than the worst Establishment newspaper or magazine I've ever heard of.' And she said they thought they had an obligation to protect their readers. And I said,

'Well, that's a very interesting journalistic approach. Most of us in journalism feel that we have a obligation to tell the truth, to report the facts, and not feel that we have to play daddy or protect the morals of somebody.'

"Just who the fuck do they think they are, playing God? They're worse than the right-wing and racist papers like the Jackson *Clarion-Ledger*. The Jackson *Clarion-Ledger* never made any pretense about nobility and being honest. They were just a fucking racist newspaper. But these people would have you believe that they are the bastion of defense and the receptacle of truth. They just absolutely refused to run the ad until I agreed to some sort of disclaimer!"

The *Free Press* had acted perfectly reasonably. The government has served subpoenas on many aboveground journalists to call them to testify about their knowledge of radical activities; on innumerable occasions police have even posed as reporters to gain access to leftist groups. (Such undercover "reporters" were the backbone of the prosecution's case at the Chicago conspiracy trial.) Nevertheless, most Establishment journalists think there is something sacred about their unfettered pursuit of news. They are one of the last relics of Social Darwinism, and Fleming, good Establishment reporter that he is, thinks that nothing should stand between him and a "good story."

The *Free Press* just could not understand this. In the underground-press sense of the word, the *Freep* was acting *ethically*—only they would have been more ethical to have refused the ad completely. The aboveground media have their own ethical code. An Establishment reporter believes that the greatest evidence of journalistic integrity would be for his paper to run on the editorial page a biting and uncompromising editorial condemning ecological disasters committed by oil companies, while two pages back an oil company has a full-page ad bragging about how much it is doing for ecology. The underground press believes that to be ethical one must meld that editorial content into news stories, refuse to run the oil company's ad, and accept only advertising that furthers the vision set forth in the paper.

Aboveground journalists have a very difficult time reporting about youth culture and radical politics. Because of fear over who they are and what they may do with the information, no one wants anything to do with them. And thus a reporter has to be very careful in evaluating what information he does get. He is always being approached by "jive artists" who love to put him on, and "speed freaks" and others full of incredible stories—stories as convincing as they are false. Intuitively, he must follow the basic anthropological axiom that whoever first approaches him in a situation is inevitably the local drunkard, ne'er-do-well, outcast or liar.

The story in *Newsweek* contained a number of facts that should have made any reporter dubious.* The

* *The White Panthers, now disbanded, were a culturally radical group which would be highly unlikely to have members recruiting in Vietnam at all. The White Panthers were not like the Black Panthers. They had a very specific program and a national newspaper,* Sundance. *They were one of the few radical*

most dramatic "news" in the article was Larry's allegation that he had visited a guerrilla camp where he had seen a thousand revolutionaries in training and that he knew of as many as ten other such camps. This was an extraordinary revelation, since the Justice Department itself estimates that there are only 4,500 "left extremists" in the United States. Peter Goldman, a *Newsweek* senior editor who writes regularly about the Left, thinks there are fewer than that, "I would be surprised," he says, "if there were more than a thousand people in the white groups and eight hundred in the Black Panthers." Furthermore, the idea of a thousand revolutionaries getting together without government knowledge is inconceivable. Radical groups of fifteen or twenty members have been infiltrated by the police, and terrorists have had to split up into small affinity groups of five to ten members. Fleming was asked about this, but he had never heard of affinity groups. "You're thinking in terms of some sensitivity groups meeting in a house or room or something," he said.

All of this would be tedious and rather vulgar nitpicking if *Newsweek* could produce some documentation

---

or revolutionary groups in which men and women managed to relate on a close, equal basis; they almost certainly would not have had an all-male chapter. Fleming says the article did not distinguish between Black Panthers and White Panthers because "we didn't have the room to say what the hell the Black Panthers were. It's sort of a code word. People have some vague idea of what the hell it means. And it means one thing in Oregon and another in Michigan. Nobody knows what White Panther means anyway—most of all the people who are in it."

for their story. Fleming says his only real proof is that tape. "But mostly," he admits, "the way I checked it out was by my personal observations of the guy over several days." Fleming is very proud that *Newsweek* went ahead and printed the story—"The magazine's willingness to stick out its neck on the say-so of just one guy seems to me the extreme kind of comment on freedom of the press. Here's a multimillion-dollar operation with a tremendous amount of prestige. And they're willing to lay it all on the line on the basis of my judgment. I just think this says a lot about this company."

It does, indeed. In printing the article, *Newsweek* committed exactly the same crime that Establishment journalists self-righteously accuse the underground press of committing. The magazine had turned rumor into journalism. If *Newsweek* insisted on running the story, since it was a "good story," then the magazine should at least have made it clear that the account wasn't necessarily accurate. *Newsweek*'s Peter Goldman says this is exactly what the magazine did. "We thought we made appropriate signals," says Goldman. "The article is very narrowly defined. It's preceded by the greatest caveat I've ever seen in the magazine."

This simply does not come across to the reader. *Newsweek* is so concerned with a credibility of form that it is not about to admit that one of its articles may be fallacious. Each week the magazine creates a compelling "reality." Here, spread across the pages, is the world condensed and neatly packaged in briskly written prose. If the readers ever realize even for a moment that the articles are being reported and written by men of normal fallibility, knowledge and wisdom, then that precious illusion would be gone.

Our example from *Newsweek* is by no means unusual, but there is no use rushing to a more honest or credible mass magazine. *Newsweek* happens to be one of the best, but it is part and parcel of the ersatz professionalism of contemporary journalism. No profession is more traditional. While young doctors reject the certain and easy deference medicine can give them and talk to their patients with candor and ease; while young lawyers have burst out of the traditional decorum of law and become forthright proponents of reform and change; Establishment journalists continue to deal with this contradictory, ambivalent and complex world in uncontradictory, unambivalent and uncomplex reporting forms. Even leaders of the "newsroom revolt" of young Establishment journalists don't for a moment dare to suggest that the media throw off the pretensions and formulas of "objective journalism."

To change requires a great deal more out of both the journalist and his audience. It is so reassuring to accept the professional—the white-coated omnipotence of the doctor, the weighty justice of the courts, or the comprehensible and undemanding journalism of the mass media. In the end, though, this kind of journalism degrades and debases us. Like a Hollywood movie set for a Western town, it is little but a row of false fronts, more real than reality, a street on which our common myths are played and played and played, over and over again, long after they have become crude and worthless caricatures of themselves.

Some press critics take one look at this contemporary journalism and conclude that there is just no such thing as objective journalism. To that view we owe those excesses that come from mistaking sloth in reporting for involvement, and for imagining that impressions are interchangeable with facts. There *is* objective journalism, but it is not a bag of techniques handed out at journalism schools. If anything, it is that tenuous and imperfect condition attained after one realizes there is no such thing as objectivity and then proceeds by trying to take into account his prejudices or to honestly admit them.

The false scientism of contemporary journalism—so mistakenly labeled "objective journalism"—was not developed as a means to bring a richer and more honest news coverage to the public. Originally, it was simply a technique invented by the early cooperative news-gathering associations, so that their services could be sold to the highly partisan papers of the day.[4] As advertising and circulation burgeoned, the papers themselves became "objective." They could not afford to offend any element of their readership, and they too assumed a stance of political and moral neutrality. No longer, then, do we find the whopping lies and conscious distortions that are so shocking in Upton Sinclair's *Brass Check* and so amusing and nostalgia-producing in Ben Hecht's accounts of his Chicago newspaper days.

Today's press is infinitely more subtle in its distortions. There are, first of all, the sins of omission. As the Southern Regional Council reported in a recent study (January 1971) of the Southern press, even the

Atlanta *Constitution* and *Journal,* two of the region's best papers, do not do "any hard and detailed investigation of corporate structures; nowhere in a city which is the headquarters of large public utility consorts is there any serious study of the background to rate adjustment requests or insurance profits . . . Georgia Power and Lockheed, to name only two, appear bathed in a perpetually roseate light." [5] No part of the contemporary news media is engaged in the kind of systematic, broad investigative reporting that the muckrakers carried on more than half a century ago; too often the primary role of the press seems to be to comfort the comfortable and afflict the afflicted.

The sins of commission are no less apparent. The Indochinese war is the most tragic example of this, for after over half a decade, millions of words, thousands of television hours, pages and pages of articles, the American public remains abysmally uninformed about even the basic geographic and political facts of the war. Day after day our papers take the government's self-serving statements, cut them down to a neat pithy size, and call the result "objective journalism." Night after night our television news programs show one- and two-minute films of yet another vague and nameless battle, as if the war were a ritual ground where TV correspondents went to prove their masculinity, as if the war didn't require a kind of social and political analysis of unprecedented sophistication and clarity. And the editorial writers, mercenaries of conscience, at best summon up enough irritation to scold the government in pale and gentle prose. Thomas Jefferson would be aghast. He believed that the press's role was to provide that check on government that no other institution could provide; however, it was not the people's surrogate but the people themselves who took to the streets and made hawkish Vietnam stances untenable—in word if not in deed.

Admittedly, *The New York Times* and the *Washington Post* deserve

𝕿𝖍𝖊 𝕹𝖊𝖜

VOL. CXX . . . No. 41,431   © 1971 The New York Times Company   *NEW YORK, T*

SUPREME COURT, 6-3,

ON PUBLICATION OF T

TIMES RESUMES ITS

considerable credit for having published the *Pentagon Papers,* especially when some of our most distinguished dovish senators did not have the courage to release the study to the public. The underground press, for its part, has written about the whole affair with unmitigated disdain. After all, for over half a decade radical papers have been publishing their own "Pentagon Papers," their own running history and analysis of our involvement. For the past two years, in fact, underground papers have been publishing less and less news about Vietnam; their readership didn't have to be told in every issue that the U.S. government was deceiving the public and that the army's tales of success were phony.

In the wake of the *Pentagon Papers,* Establishment journalists have been going through a curious penance. The more vicious of our columnists have picked their way through contemporary history, trying to prove that this or that paper was hawkish just a few years ago. And many younger journalists have been indulging in public self-flagellation. So far, though, there have been few attempts to go back and seriously study the press's role in forming and reinforcing Cold War liberalism. The one book-length study of this development, James Aronson's *The Press and the Cold War,* has been either ignored or summarily dismissed. Reviewers were quite obviously offended by Aronson's Marxist views and only rarely dealt with the book's substantial research. Presumably there will be further full-scale studies of our contemporary press, but if the aboveground media, and the Pulitzer Prize committee in particular, feel a need for immediate penance, they might resist the obvious temptation to give a prize to *The New York Times* for publishing the *Pentagon Papers* and give it to I. F. Stone's *Weekly* instead. Not only did the *Times* not have to do any investigative reporting to get the material in the *Pentagon Papers,* but the paper had a substantial role in fostering our involvement in the Vietnam War. I. F. Stone, on the other hand, is an indefatigable re-

ɔrk Times

weather: Chance of showers today, tonight. Partly sunny tomorrow. Temp. range: today 74-94; Wed. 72-91. Temp. Hum. Index yesterday 82. Full U.S. report on Page 94.

Y, JULY 1, 1971   *15 CENTS*

HOLDS NEWSPAPERS
E PENTAGON REPORT;
RIES, HALTED 15 DAYS

searcher who, by himself, year after year, has documented the duplicity of one administration after another; for two decades he has been a clear and steady voice warning where our foreign policy was leading us.

This is not for a moment to suggest that the press should charge into every political and social struggle. Jefferson, himself, suffered enormously at the rude hands of the viciously partisan press of his day. The "Dark Ages of American Journalism," one historian calls the period 1801–1833,[6] for it was a time when freedom of the press meant the license to say whatever one chose, true or false, in news columns and editorials alike. Certainly, the press has improved since then, although many committed radicals might disagree. Aronson, the former editor of the *National Guardian,* for one, considers the early nineteenth century a highpoint in American journalism. "Freedom was embraced with a kind of wild abandon in the first decades of the nineteenth century," he writes. "The quality of the papers varied enormously, but it was in essence a healthy time." [7]

During a century when propaganda and news have been freely mixed, often with volatile, even tragic results, "wild abandon" hardly seems a worthwhile goal. "Socialism has more to gain from a free, artistic literature reflecting life as it actually is, than from an attempt to stretch points in order to make facts fit the Socialist theory," the *Masses* wrote in 1911, and it is not really a bad guideline for the contemporary radical press. A hopelessly bourgeois concept? Perhaps, but then the audience of the underground press is hopelessly bourgeois. Ultimately, truth is the best propaganda, and when underground papers automatically attest to the innocence of every "political" prisoner, the validity of every radical strategy, the duplicity of every government move, they risk making skeptics of all but their most impassioned supporters.

There are not two sides to every issue, as the mass news media so mechanically suggest; often there are ten or fifteen, and sometimes there is only one. A truly objective journalism must let a hundred flowers bloom, and not pretend that a dull and narrow reality can be labeled truth. As it is, the individual Establishment journalist is harnessed to narrow, unbending forms like a dray horse.

"The reporter hangs in a powerless-power—his voice directly, or via the rewrite desk indirectly, reaches out to millions of readers," writes Norman Mailer. "The more readers he owns, the less he can say. He is forbidden by a hundred censors, most of them inside himself, to communicate notions which are not conformistically simple, simple like plastic, that is to say, monotonous. Therefore a reporter forms a habit equivalent to lacerating the flesh: he learns to write what he does not naturally believe. Since he did not start presumably with the desire to be a bad writer or a dishonest writer, he ends by bludgeoning his brains into believing that something which is half true is in fact—since he creates a face each time he puts something into a newspaper—nine-tenths true. A psyche is debauched—his own; a false fact is created. For which fact, sooner or later, inevitably, inexorably, the public will pay. A nation which forms detailed opinions on the basis of detailed fact which is askew from the subtle reality becomes a nation of citizens whose psyches are skewed, item by item, away from *any* reality." [8]

There are no debauched psyches in the underground press, because articles are written organically out of perceptions, experiences and biases, with no fear of advertisers or superiors. The underground press does not hide behind that veneer of old-fashioned "objective reporting." The reader knows the articles are written by human beings full of the most extraordinary biases. If one is skeptical he must read with care and caution. It is true, though, that ideology can shackle the mind of a writer in as rigid a way, and increasingly there is a tedious sameness to many of the political articles in the second-generation underground papers. Not only ideology but the arbitrary limits of youth culture have fenced the papers off from relating to people in a way that brings deep insights. "Accounts of movement events in the underground press have had a depressing similarity this past year," writes Jeff Shero in *Sundance*, the national White Panther paper that came out in the fall of 1970. "It's us versus Them. The good guys versus the pigs, complete with details of every confrontation, pig atrocity and people's victory. If it's a politico's account, inevitably connections are drawn to the international anti-imperialist struggle. If it's a hip or yip account, the basic tale is embellished with descriptions of the wondrous quality of the dope, plus mention of the delights of the dancing, fucking, and blowing the minds of the bourgeoisie."

The second-generation papers risk becoming as boring and stylized as most of the Establishment media. The older papers have largely sucked dry their particular ideals and forms, and once again the underground press seems ready to conceive new visions of the Movement across its pages.

The May Day demonstrations in the spring of 1971 did, in fact, help to revitalize many papers, infusing them with new energy. Late 1971 and early 1972 did, in fact, see the emergence of several new publications including New York's *Ace* and Los Angeles' *Staff* that had an energy and sophistication and excitement to them that suggested they might, just might, be the harbingers of a whole new generation of underground papers.

If we are seeing, then, a third generation of newspapers beginning to emerge in the first half of 1972, what we are seeing really is a new generation not only of papers but of people. The first generation of a new people. Now there are people in their late teens and early twenties who have grown up on youth culture starting to work on underground papers. To them the pursuits of the Movement—equalitarianism, radical political conceptions, youth culture, women's liberation—are not intellectual ideals but the very basis of their whole beings. It is curious, as if in America Freud had been turned on his head, and here adolescence, not the earliest years, becomes the formative part of one's life, as if only during adolescence is one's very nature determined. Many of the papers have grown less shrill recently, more natural, more self-confident, as if these new people knew that they would and could win and that it would be a long struggle.

12
And Tomorrow?

America our nation has been beaten by strangers who have turned our language inside out who have taken the clean words our fathers spoke and made them slimy and foul...

all right we are two nations

— JOHN DOS PASSOS,
writing about the execution of Sacco and Vanzetti

These days there are many soothsayers of doom predicting the imminent demise of the Movement and the underground press. What they forget is that time and time again the Movement has fallen into discouragement and despair—after the Berkeley Free Speech Movement in 1965, the March on the Pentagon in 1967, the excesses of the Weathermen in 1970—only to be reborn again with renewed energy and strength. The difference, today, however, is that we now have a mass movement, and journalists and academic pundits analyze every political proclamation, squabble, and defeat much as soothsayers of another age examined the entrails of their enemies.

If early in 1972 a person wanted to find positive signs, he certainly could find them. There is hardly an occupation or profession in America that does not have at least a coterie of women and men who identify with the Movement. Out of their social and intellectual energies an intrinsically American radical critique is emerging, a critique for the most part blessedly free of rhetoric and old ideologies. Entrepreneurs and manipulators have ripped off everything about youth culture except its essence, but in recent months there has been a rediscovery of that essence. When Bob Dylan stood in Madison Square Garden during the Bangladesh concert singing the songs of the early 1960's, "Blowing in the Wind," "A Hard Rain's a-Gonna Fall," and "Tambourine Man," he was reaffirming that essence. In December 1971 when John Lennon went to Ann Arbor, Michigan, to appear in a concert to free John Sinclair and told the 15,000 freaks,

195

teenyboppers, and students, "Apathy won't get us anywhere. So flower power failed, so what, let's start again," he was speaking for much of a generation.

There may still be a revolution coming. It will not be like revolutions of the past; for, conceived in the fat belly of America, it will be more the product of psychic and spiritual emptiness than of material deprivation. It will be a revolution in which the alienated young middle class provides not only leadership but most of the rank and file. It will be a revolution in which the possibility of violence cannot be ruled out, for the joyful apocalyptic anarchism of the early hippies and the profoundly decent moral witnessing of the young New Left are largely parts of history. It will be a revolution that very well may be successfully resisted—not primarily by overt violence, but by the society's ability to create antibodies, social forms that cloak themselves in the surface aspects of youth culture and that isolate and destroy the essence, and by the jailing of prominent dissidents after "democratic" show trials. It may be successfully resisted by society's ability to reform itself—through the radical liberalism of consumer groups, political coalitions or third parties. It may be successfully resisted, too, simply because the radical movement proves unable to conceive alternative forms and ideas that can claim the full allegiance of distressed and alienated Americans, and in the end the underground press may prove not the voice of a growing radical movement but only the chronicler of a sociological phenomenon.

The wedding of cultural and political radicalism that is radical youth culture is not the social substance out of which radical political change has usually grown. For a century and a half the bourgeois artist has stood apart from society; as his numbers have grown, as often as not, we find him living in Bohemian communities. By dropping out of society the alienated artist is acting radically, but such actions have only rarely changed society or been part of substantial political movements. In America the tradition of revulsion against middle-class values runs from Thoreau through Melville, the Lost Generation, and the beats, to the hippies. Previously only in that short brilliant period before World War I were daring artistic experimentation, an open-ended nonsectarian radicalism and a Bohemian life style forged together in an important political movement—most memorably in a journalistic and literary form in the *Masses*. This was preeminently a bourgeois radicalism, and as such it is a precursor to the contemporary radical-youth culture and underground press. Of course, there was no Dada, no youth cult, no Marxist internationalism in the decade from 1910. Bohemianism itself was a revolt only of artists and of those who aspired to art; indeed, up through the beat Bohemianism of the 1950's to have any status at all in a Bohemian community one had to be writing, painting, sculpting, dancing ("Against the ruin of the world, there is only one defense, the creative act"), or at least pretending to.

This massive contemporary Bohemianism is spawned on affluence.

To the hippies, life itself is art—a necessary democratization of Bohemianism as it assumed a size and significance that it had never known before. For its part, the political radicalism of the early New Left was a rich patchwork stitched together from elements of anarchism, direct democracy, non-sectarian socialism, non-violence, and reformist liberalism all carried with a feisty optimism. Today much of the political left is seriously revolutionary, striving to "get out of the middle class bag." Often this leads to a kind of stylized rhetoric that doesn't mean very much to most Americans, but it is true that by the fall of 1971 many highly political papers had begun to emphasize strong analytical pieces devoid of verbiage, and stories that involved actual reporting. The problem essentially is that the amount of analysis and rhetoric is often so heavy and the assumption of prior knowledge so large that the uninitiated really can't be turned on to the papers. A Manhattan secretary doesn't pick up *Rat* to learn about Women's Liberation; she buys *Cosmopolitan.* The *New York Daily News,* a conservative paper, is America's largest working class paper, largest because it does not talk down to its readers.

The political and cultural aspects of this modern radicalism ride together in uneasy tandem yanked this way and that by purists of both positions. The pure cultural radicalism of circa 1967 Haight-Ashbury has been neatly rationalized and codified in a best seller, Charles Reich's *The Greening of America,* while the narrowly political position is found in dozens of Movement journals. There is no simple resolution of the conflict for there is an inevitable tension between the two traditions, and the staffs of underground papers live with this schizophrenia inside their heads, their papers, their daily lives.

It is true, though, that living within youth culture a person gets a gigantic, jolting transfusion of life, and it can leave him near giddy with enthusiasm. A person can travel from coast to coast staying with his brothers and sisters, he can regain that sacred sense of community and fellowship. He can eat their food, and take their time, and smoke their dope, and they will feel enriched for it. High on his enthusiasms he can forget the Indo-China war; the monstrous, unmanageable economy that churns out guns and oleo and has no room for all who would work; the adolescent derelicts of youth culture who twist the argot and spirit of the Movement so that it will feed them and buy them dope; the repression of radicals; and he can *know,* literally *know,* that radical-youth culture will triumph, triumph simply because *it has to.*

The underground press knows, though, that personal and communal joys do not melt cannons or put food in the mouths of undernourished black babies, and these radical journalists are torn between developing what is efficient to bring them a rich personal life and what is efficient to sustain radical institutions and media. This conflict is never resolved, nor can it be, and if anything it will be even more difficult a problem in the future. Many papers are growing to a size that will require compromises in structure that will not please anyone. The underground press, itself, has reached a certain stability that calls for the birth of innumerable other alternative institutions, underground media, and outright organizing. There is no blueprint, no manifesto, no obvious scheme to tell them in which direction to go—

whether to build leather co-ops or grade schools or farm communes or breakfast programs or alternative universities; whether to create national magazines or daily papers or closed-circuit television or publishing houses or wall posters or FM radio; whether to organize poor whites or hips or the working class or suburban housewives or homosexuals or college students or young women. There is no blueprint, but what may happen is that the Movement will burst forth building all sorts of institutions, creating a rich range of media experiences, and organizing a great many kinds of people in ways that speak directly to them. What could happen, too, since the only predictability in any of this has been the total lack of predictability, is that the cultural side of the underground press might turn into itself, remaining in the narrow youth ghettos and dropout communities, to become the scribe of an aberrant community. The highly political papers, for their part, might cling to their revolutionary purity and end up tearing at the entrails of American life.

The underground press has always avoided sounding too preachy or self-consciously mature, believing not unreasonably that in this society "wisdom" is usually an old man's plaything, but the papers may have to learn to criticize their own culture and politics. If not, the underground press could split into rigidly cultural and rigidly political papers. If not, the scores of impressionistic voices of dissent may drown each other out.

If not, terrorists and other forms of impressionistic radicalism—forms as dubious as they are spectacular—might become the focal points of attention.

Regardless of how thoughtful the papers might become, repression may very well continue. There is no simple answer as to how the papers should react. Should they sandbag their offices and arm themselves in self-defense; should they act pacifically and try to ignore the harassments; or should they go fully underground and print surreptitiously? But whatever answer is found, the underground press must somehow, despite all odds, sustain that magnificent openness and trust that is the central flame of the contemporary Movement. And somehow, too, the government and the Establishment must be made to realize that radical-youth culture is a richly complex organism; by driving it into a corner and prodding it, the government only turns the Movement surly and mean, ready to lash out at any moment, with any means at its disposal.

Ultimately at question is the validity and spirit of that culture and Movement, and what aspects of it will become part of American life. To the third generation of underground papers, then, will go the task of proving how noble that spirit is, how rich that vision, how attainable that dream. There is nothing inevitable in the outcome—but for the underground press there is no looking back.

Notes

Chapter I

1. "Runaways: A Million Bad Trips," *Newsweek*, October 26, 1970, p. 67.
2. Quoted in Jack A. Nelson, "The Underground Press," *Freedom of Information Center Report No. 226*, School of Journalism, University of Missouri at Columbia, August 1969, p. 1.
3. John Dos Passos, "Grandfather and Grandson," *New Masses*, December 15, 1936, p. 19.
4. Frank Luther Mott, *A History of American Magazines*, Vol. 4, p. 176.
5. James Weinstein, *The Decline of Socialism in America 1912–1925*, p. 85.
6. *Call to Reason*, May 23, 1896, p. 1.
7. *New York Call*, May 30, 1908, p. 1.
8. Frederick J. Hoffman, Charles Allen, Carolyn F. Ulrich, *The Little Magazines*, p. 244.
9. Daniel Aaron, *Writers on the Left*, pp. 90–91.
10. Michael Gold, quoted in Introduction to *Proletarian Literature in the United States*, Granville Hicks *et al.*, eds. (New York: International Publishers, 1935).
11. Granville Hicks, *Where We Came Out*, p. 28.
12. Dwight MacDonald, *Memoirs of a Revolutionist*, p. 16.
13. Morris U. Schappes, *The Daily Worker, Heir to the Great Tradition*, p. 15.

Chapter II

1. Kirk Sale, "The Village Voice," *Evergreen Review*, November 1970.
2. Ann Charles, ed., *Scenes Along the Road* (Gotham Book Mart) quoted in *Rolling Stone*, January 7, 1971, p. 60.
3. Lawrence Lipton, *The Unholy Barbarians*, p. 20.
4. Francis J. Rigney and L. Douglas Smith, *The Real Bohemia*, p. 30.
5. Jacob Brackman, "The Underground Press," *Playboy*, August 1967, p. 151.
6. Daniel Wolf and Edwin Fancher, eds., *The Village Voice Reader* (Garden City, N.Y.: Doubleday, 1962), pp. 258–59.
7. George Orwell, "Politics and the English Language," in *Inside the Whale and Other Essays*, p. 153.

Chapter III

1. *Los Angeles Free Press*, January 8, 1971, p. 9.
2. John Wilcock, *Other Scenes*, April 1967, p. 2.
3. Thorne Dreyer and Victoria Smith, "The Movement and the New Media," *Orpheus*, Vol. 2, p. 12.

Chapter IV

1. Thorne Dreyer and Victoria Smith, "The Movement and the New Media," *Orpheus,* Vol. 2, p.12.
2. Thorne Dreyer, "The Rag," *Other Scenes,* April 1967, p. 3.
3. Raymond Mungo, *Famous Long Ago,* p. 19.
4. Thorne Dreyer and Victoria Smith, "The Movement and the New Media," *Orpheus,* Vol. 2, No. 2., p. 21.
5. Seymour Halleck, "The Toll Youth Pays for Freedom," *Think,* September–October, 1969, p. 21.
6. F. Engels (Jan.–Feb. 1873) *Almenacco Repubblicano* 1874, quoted Karl Marx and Friedrich Engels, *Selected Works,* Vol. 1 (London, 1950), quoted in James Joll, *The Anarchists,* p. 110.
7. Daniel Aaron, *Writers on the Left,* p. 217.
8. Jacob Brackman, "The Underground Press," *Playboy,* August 1967, p. 154.

Chapter V

1. John Burks, "The Underground Press," *Rolling Stone,* October 4, 1969, p. 26.

Chapter VI

1. Jeff Shero, interview "Bill Graham," *Rat,* October 18–31, 1968, p. 20.
2. Jeff Shero, "A Star is Born," *Rat,* August 23–September 5, 1968, p. 3.
3. Jeff Shero, "Blockade and Siege," *Rat,* May 13–16, 1968, pp. 3, 11.
4. Thomas Forcade, interview, "An Advertisement for Revolution," Free Range Intertribal News Service, March 16, 1970.

Chapter VII

1. Carl Oglesby, *The New Left Reader,* (New York: Grove Press, 1969), p. 14.
2. Sheila Ryan and George Cavalletto, "Palestinian Hijackings: The People's Story," Liberation News Service, September 26, 1970.
3. Dennis Fitzgerald, "Up Against the Wall Culture Vultures," *Space City!* July 4–17, 1970, pp. 3, 22.
4. Victoria Smith, "What Do We Do Now?" *Space City!* August 1–21, 1970, pp. 4–5.

Chapter VIII

1. Albert Maltz, "Bodies by Fisher" in *New Masses, An Anthology of the Rebel Thirties* (New York: International Publishers, 1969), p. 170.
2. Jack Newfield, *A Prophetic Minority,* p. 43.
3. Timothy Leary, "Free," *East Village Other,* October 20, 1970.
4. "Life in the Movement," Liberation News Service, December 5, 1970, pp. 6–8.

Chapter IX

1. Seymour Hersh, "How I Broke the Mylai 4 Story," *Saturday Review,* July 11, 1970, p. 48.
2. Mark Wilson, "Stoney Burns Convicted," *Space City!* July 6, 1971, p. 9.
3. Eugene Lyons, "A Few Kind Words About the Underground Press," *Dateline,* April 1969, p. 74.

Chapter X

1. *Youth Report, A Confidential Letter to Business, Religious, Social and Educational Leaders Engaged in Dealing with Youth,* November 1969, pp. 2–3.
2. Danny Fields, "Who Bridges the Gap Between the Record Executive and the Rock Musician," *New York Scenes,* July 1969, p. 35.
3. Daniel Aaron, *Writers on the Left,* p. 41.
4. John Dos Passos, "Grandfather and Grandson," *New Masses,* December 15, 1936, p. 19.
5. Albert Parry, *Garrets and Pretenders,* p. 248.
6. Gene Marine, *Rolling Stone,* April 2, 1970, p. 50.
7. Michael March, interview, *Fusion,* June 12, 1970, p. 14.
8. Kenneth Keniston, *The Uncommitted.*
9. Ben Fong-Torres, "FM Underground Radio: Love for Sale," *Rolling Stone,* April 2, 1970, p. 6.
10. *Ibid.,* p. 6.
11. Irwin Silber, "The Cultural Retreat," *Guardian,* December 6, 1969, p. 17.

Chapter XI

1. "Revolutionary Rip-off," *Berkeley Tribe,* October 9–16, 1970, p. 3.
2. "Peachtree Creek is Full of Shit," *The Great Speckled Bird,* February 23, 1970, p. 3.
3. Howard Felsher, "The President Was Willing," *TV Guide,* October 24–30, 1970, p. 10.
4. Fred S. Siebert, Theodore Peterson, Wilbur Schramm, *Four Theories of the Press,* p. 60.
5. Frank O'Neill, "Censorship: In the South the Means of Resisting Are Weak," *South Today,* January–Febuary 1971, p. 5.
6. Frank Luther Mott, *American Journalism: A History: 1690–1960,* 3d ed., p. 169.
7. James Aronson, *The Press and the Cold War,* p. 12.
8. Norman Mailer, "Ten Thousand Words a Minute," *The Presidential Papers of Norman Mailer,* p. 218.

Bibliography

Aaron, Daniel, *Writers on the Left.* New York: Harcourt, Brace & World, 1961.

Aronson, James, *The Press and the Cold War.* Indianapolis and New York: Bobbs-Merrill, 1970.

Churchill, Allen, *The Improper Bohemians.* New York: Dutton, 1959.

Draper, Theodore, *The Roots of American Communism.* New York: Viking Press, 1957.

Du Maurier, George, *Trilby.* New York: Harper, 1894.

Eastman, Max, *Journalism versus Art.* New York: Knopf, 1916.

Freeman, Joseph, *An American Testament.* New York: Farrar and Rinehart, 1936.

Gillet, Charles, *The Sound of the City.* New York: Outerbridge & Dienstfrey, 1970.

Glessing, Robert J., *The Underground Press in America.* Bloomington, Ind.: Indiana University Press, 1971.

Hicks, Granville, *Where We Came Out.* New York: Viking, 1954.

Hoffman, Abbie, *Revolution for the Hell of It.* New York: Dial, 1968.

———, *Woodstock Nation.* New York: Random House, 1969.

Hoffman, Frederick J., Allen, Charles, and Ulrich, Carolyn F., *The Little Magazines.* Princeton, N.J.: Princeton University Press, 1946.

Hofstadter, Richard, *The Age of Reform.* New York: Vintage Books, 1955.

———, *Anti-intellectualism in American Life.* New York: Knopf, 1963.

Hopkins, Jerry, *The Hippie Papers.* New York: New American Library, 1968.

Joll, James, *The Anarchists.* New York: Grosset & Dunlap, 1966.

Keniston, Kenneth, *The Uncommitted: Alienated Youth in American Society.* New York: Harcourt, Brace & World, 1965.

———, *Young Radicals.* New York: Harcourt, Brace & World, 1968.

Kornbluth, Jesse, *Notes from the New Underground.* New York: Ace Publishing, 1968.

Lipton, Lawrence, *The Holy Barbarians.* New York: Messner, 1959.

MacDonald, Dwight, *Memoirs of a Revolutionist.* New York: Farrar, Straus and Cudahy, 1957.

Mailer, Norman, *The Presidential Papers.* New York: Putnam's, 1963.

———, *The Presidential Papers of Norman Mailer.* New York: Bantam Books, 1964.

———, *The White Negro.* San Francisco: City Lights Books, 1964; originally published in *Dissent,* 1957.

McLuhan, Marshall, *Understanding Media.* New York: McGraw-Hill, 1964.

McNeill, Don, *Moving Through Here.* New York: Knopf, 1970.

Mosse, George L., *The Crisis of German Ideology.* New York: Grosset & Dunlap, 1964.

Mott, Frank Luther, *American Journalism: A History: 1690–1960,* 3rd ed. New York: Macmillan, 1962.

———, *A History of American Magazines 1885–1905,* Vol. IV. Cambridge, Mass.: Harvard University Press, 1957.

Mungo, Raymond, *Famous Long Ago.* Boston: Beacon Press, 1970.

Neville, Richard, *Play Power.* New York: Random House, 1970.

Newfield, Jack, *A Prophetic Minority*. New York: New American Library, 1967.

North, Joseph, ed., *New Masses*. New York: International Publishers, 1969.

Nuttall, Jeff, *Bomb Culture*. New York: Delacorte, 1968.

Oglesby, Carl, and Shaull, Richard, *Containment and Change*. London and Toronto: Macmillan, 1967.

Orwell, George, *Inside the Whale and Other Essays*. London: Penguin Books, 1957.

Parry, Albert, *Garrets and Pretenders, A History of Bohemianism in America*. New York: Covici-Friede, 1933.

Rigney, Francis J., and Smith, L. Douglas, *The Real Bohemia*. New York: Basic Books, 1961.

Romm, Ethel Grodzins, *The Open Conspiracy*. Harrisburg, Pa.: Stackpole, 1970.

Roszak, Theodore, *The Making of a Counter Culture*. Garden City, N.Y.: Doubleday, 1969.

Rubin, Jerry, *Do It!* New York: Simon and Schuster, 1970.

Schappes, Morris U., *The Daily Worker, Heir to the Great Tradition*. New York: Daily Worker, 1944.

Siebert, Fred S., Peterson, Theodore, and Schramm, Wilbur, *Four Theories of the Press*. Urbana, Ill.: University of Illinois Press, 1956.

Stewart, Kenneth, and Tebbel, John, *Makers of Modern Journalism*. New York: Prentice-Hall, 1952.

Teodori, Massimo, *The New Left: A Documentary History*. Indianapolis and New York: Bobbs-Merrill, 1969.

Watters, Pat, *The South and the Nation*. New York: Random House, 1969.

Weinstein, James, *The Decline of Socialism in America 1912–1925*, New York and London: Monthly Review Press, 1967.

UPS Member Papers

United States

AKWESASNE NOTES
c/o Mohawk Nation
Box 435
Rooseveltown, N.Y. 13683

ALL YOU CAN EAT
5 Railroad Plaza
New Brunswick, N.J. 08903

ALTERNATE FEATURES
  SERVICE
Box 2250
Berkeley, Cal. 94702

AMAZING GRACE
212 W. College Ave.
Tallahassee, Fla. 32301

AMERIKAN PRESS
  SYNDICATE
Box 5175
Beverly Hills, Cal. 90210

ANDROMEDA
Box 8
Stillwater, Okla. 74074

AQUARIAN WEEKLY
292 Main St.
Hackensack, N.J. 07601

ASTRAL PROJECTION
Box 4383
Albuquerque, N.M. 87106

AUGUR
207 Ransom Bldg.
115 E. 11th Ave.
Eugene, Ore. 97401

BERKELEY BARB
Box 1247
Berkeley, Calif. 94701

BERKELEY TRIBE
Box 9043
Berkeley, Cal. 94709

BETTER WORLD NEWS
Box 88
West Point, Calif. 95255

BIG MUDDY GAZETTE
Box 892
Carbondale, Ill. 62901

BOISE CITY HERALD &
  TRIBUNE
Box 953
Boise, Idaho 83702

BOTH SIDES NOW
10370 St. Augustine Rd.
Jacksonville, Fla. 32217

BUGLE AMERICAN
2909 N. Humboldt Ave.
Milwaukee, Wis. 53212

CANDLE
Box 3-163 ECB
Anchorage, Alaska 99501

CHINOOK
1458 Pennsylvania St.
Denver, Colo. 80203

COMMON SENSE
Box 1335
Bloomington, Ind. 47401

COUNTRY SENSES
Box 465
Minortown Rd.
Woodbury, Conn. 06798

CREEM
3729 Cass Ave.
Detroit, Mich. 48201

CRYSTAL CITY NEWS
Box 12, University Hall
Bowling Green State Univ.
Bowling Green, Ohio 43402

DAILY PLANET
Suite 2
3514 S. Dixie Highway
Coconut Grove, Fla. 33133

D.C. GAZETTE
109 8th St. NE
Washington, D.C. 20002

DOOR
Box 2022
San Diego, Cal. 92114

DRIFTWOOD NEWS
33 Church St.
White Plains, N.Y. 10602

DRUMMER
1609 Pine St.
2nd floor
Philadelphia, Pa. 19103

EAGLEBONE WHISTLE
832 W. Mistletoe Ave.
San Antonio, Tex. 78212

EAST VILLAGE OTHER
20 E. 12th St.
New York, N.Y. 10003

EDCENTRIC
2115 S St. NW
Washington, D.C. 20008

EVERYWOMAN
1043B W. Washington Blvd.
Venice, Cal. 90291

EYEWITNESS
23 Woodland Ave.
San Francisco, Cal. 94117

FAIR WITNESS
Box 7165
Oakland Sta.
Pittsburgh, Pa. 15213

FIFTH ESTATE
4403 2nd Blvd.
Detroit, Mich. 48201

FITS
4672 18th St.
San Francisco, Calif. 94114

205

FLORIDA UNDERGROUND
NEWS
1655 E. Forest City Rd.
Apopka, Fla. 32803

FLY BY NIGHT
3712 Military Rd. NW
Washington, D.C. 20015

FPS
2007 Washtenaw Ave.
Ann Arbor, Mich. 48104

FREEDOM NEWS
Box 1087
Richmond, Cal. 94801

FREE PRESS
Box 676
Coconut Grove, Fla. 33133

FREE RANGER TRIBE/UPS
Box 26
Village Sta.
New York, N.Y. 10014

FREEWAY
1705 W. 2nd Ave.
Duluth, Minn. 55806

FUSION
909 Beacon St.
Boston, Mass. 02215

GOOD NEWS-ACID
2936 Esplanade
New Orleans, La. 70119

GOOD TIMES
2377 Bush St.
San Francisco, Cal. 94115

THE GREAT SPECKLED
BIRD
Box 54495
Atlanta, Ga. 30308

GREAT SWAMP ERIE
DADA BOOM
14016 Orinoco
E. Cleveland, Ohio 44112

GUARDIAN
32 W. 22nd St.
New York, N.Y. 10010

GULF COAST FISH CHEER
Box 1583
Pensacola, Fla. 32502

HARRY
30 E. Lanvale St.
Baltimore, Md. 21202

HENDERSON STATION
Box 136
State College, Pa. 16801

HIGH GAUGE
Box 4491
University, Ala. 35486

HOME NEWS
Box 5263
Grand Central Sta.
New York, N.Y. 10017

HOOKA
4404½ Scurry
Dallas, Tex. 75204

HUNDRED FLOWERS
Box 7271
Powderhorn Sta.
Minneapolis, Minn. 55407

ICONOCLAST
Box 7013
Dallas, Texas, 75209

ISSUES
9 N. 10th St.
Columbia, Mo. 65201

JOURNAL
Box 1802
Rochester, N.Y. 14603

KALEIDOSCOPE
Box 90526
Milwaukee, Wisc. 53211

KING STREET TROLLEY
Box 881
Madison, Wisc. 53701

THE KUDZU
Box 22502
Jackson, Miss. 39205

LAS VEGAS FREE PRESS
Box 14096
Las Vegas, Nev. 89114

LEFT FACE
Box 1595
Anniston, Ala. 36201

LIBERATED GUARDIAN
14 Cooper Sq.
New York, N.Y. 10003

LIBERATION
339 Lafayette St.
New York, N.Y. 10012

LIBERATION NEWS
SERVICE (LNS)
160 Claremont Ave.
New York, N.Y. 10027

LONG ISLAND FREE
PRESS
Box 162
Westbury, N.Y. 11590

LOS ANGELES FREE
PRESS
6013 Hollywood Blvd.
Los Angeles, Cal. 90036

LOS ANGELES NEWS
ADVOCATE
15130 Ventura Blvd.
Sherman Oaks, Cal. 91403

MAGGIE'S FARM
Box 252
Dayton, Ohio 45401

METRO
906 W. Forest
Detroit, Mich. 48202

MONIEBAGUE PRESS
19 Netz Place
Riverhead, N.Y. 11901

MONTANA FREE SKWEEKER
c/o Book City
301 Central
Great Falls, Mont. 59401

MORNING STAR
2751 E. Broadway
Long Beach, Calif. 90803

MOTHER EARTH NEWS
Box 38
Madison, Ohio 44057

MOUNTAIN LIBERATOR
460½ Pine St.
Morgantown, W. Va. 26505

NEWS
766 Commonwealth Ave.
Boston, Mass. 02215

NEW YORK ACE
c/o Rex Weiner
231 Thompson St.
New York, N.Y. 10012

NOLA EXPRESS
Box 2342
New Orleans, La. 70116

NORTH CAROLINA ANVIL
Box 1148
Durham, N.C. 27702

NORTHWEST PASSAGE
Box 105
S. Bellingham Sta.
Bellingham, Wash. 98225

ORGAN
Box 4520
Berkeley, Cal. 94704

OTHER SCENES
Box 8
Village Sta.
New York, N.Y. 10014

OUTLAW
Box 9501
Cabanne Station
St. Louis, Mo. 63161

PEOPLE'S PRESS
Box 1714
Clovis, N. Mex. 88101

PROTOS
1110 N. Edgemont St.
Los Angeles, Cal. 90029

PROVIDENCE FREE PRESS
Box 1005
Annex Sta.
Providence, R.I. 02901

PROVINCIAL PRESS
Box 1276
Spokane, Wash. 99210

PURPLE BERRIES
1524 Summit St.
Columbus, Ohio 43201

QUICKSILVER TIMES
1736 R St. NW
Washington, D.C. 20009

RAG
2330 Guadalupe
Austin, Tex. 78705

RAMA PIPIEN
Box 641
Newcastle, Calif. 95658

RAT
241 E. 14th St.
New York, N.Y. 10009

REARGUARD
Box 8115
Mobile, Ala. 36608

RED EYE
30 S. 4th St. #3
San Jose, Cal. 95113

RED TIDE
Box 76, Bard College
Annandale-on-Hudson
N.Y. 12504

RISING UP ANGRY
Box 3746
Merchandise Mart
Chicago, Ill. 60654

SANTA BARBARA FREE
PRESS
Golden State Distributing Co.
21-B East Canon Perdido
Santa Barbara, Calif. 93101

SECOND CITY
1155 W. Webster
Chicago, Ill. 60614

SECOND COMING
Box 491
Ypsilanti, Mich. 48197

SEED
950 W. Wrightwood
Chicago, Ill. 60614

SPACE CITY
1217 Wichita
Houston, Tex. 77004

STAFF
6472 Santa Monica Blvd.
Los Angeles, Calif. 90038

SUN
1520 Hill
Ann Arbor, Mich. 48104

SUNDAZE
1383 Pacific Ave.
Santa Cruz, Cal. 95060

TAKE OVER
Box 706
Madison, Wisc. 53701

TORCH
c/o Roosevelt U.
430 S. Michigan Ave.
Chicago, Ill. 60605

TRASH
9426 Santa Monica Blvd.
Beverly Hills, Calif. 90216

TRIBAL MESSENGER
Box 4372
Albuquerque, N. Mex. 87106

TRUE FREE PRESS
Box 1214
Indio, Calif. 92201

UNDERCURRENT
Box 11
Norton Hall
Buffalo, N.Y. 14214

UNIVERSITY REVIEW
2929 Broadway
New York, N.Y. 10025

VENCEREMOS
1969½ University Ave.
E. Palo Alto, Calif. 94303

VOCATIONS FOR SOCIAL
CHANGE
Canyon, Cal. 94516

WEATHER REPORT
Box 1221
San Marcos, Tex. 78666

WILD RASPBERRY
Box 1541
Hartford, Conn. 06101

WIN
Box 547
Rifton, N.Y. 12471

WOODSTOCK AQUARIAN
Box 401
Woodstock, N.Y. 12498

UPS / Canada

CAMPUS
Box 1089
Bishops Univ.
Lennoxville, Quebec

CARILLON
University of Saskatchewan
Regina Campus
Regina, Saskatchewan

CHARASEE PRESS
Box 909
Hamilton, Ontario

CHEVRON
University of Waterloo
Waterloo, Ontario

GEORGIA STRAIGHT
56A Powell St.
Vancouver 4, B.C.

GUERILLA
12 St. Joseph St.
Toronto 189, Ontario

LOGOS
Box 702
Montreal 101, Quebec

MAINMISE
351 rue Emery
Montreal 129, Quebec

PARTISAN
399 5th Ave.
Vancouver, B.C.

SPIFF
7549B Centrale St.
La Salle, Quebec

TENPENNY
24 Brighton Ct.
Fredericton, N.B.

YIPPIE NEWS AND INFO.
56A Powell St.
Vancouver 4, B.C.

UPS /
Europe

UPS/EUROPE
c/o BIT
141 Westbourne Park Rd.
London W11, England

ACTUEL
60, Rue de Richelieu
Paris 2, France

ALOHA
Alexander Boersstraat 30
Amsterdam, Netherlands

BIT
141 Westbourne Park Rd.
London W11, England

BLACK BOX
Box 23
190-192 New City Rd.
Glasgow NW, Scotland

CATONSVILLE ROAD-
  RUNNER
138 Mayall Rd.
London SE24, England

CHAPTER
Box 5
1 Conference Rd.
London SE2, England

COMMUNES
12 Mill Rd.
Cambridge, England

DING
Katelijnestraat 8
Mechelen 2800, Belgium

FIRE
1 Sherwood St.
London W1, England

FORUS
8 Thormanby Rd.
Howth, Co. Dublin
Eire

FOX
Postbus 3945
Amsterdam, Netherlands

FRENDZ
305 Portobello Rd.
London W10, England

HIT
c/o ARC/DO
Via Piolti di Bianchi 29
20129 Milano, Italy

L'IDIOT LIBERTE
2 Rue de Vauvilliers
Paris 1, France

INK
73 Princedale Rd.
London W11, England

IT
11A Berwick St.
London W1, England

KABOUTERKOLONEL
Keizerstraat 2A
Amsterdam, Netherlands

KIMEN/GATE/AVISA
Hjelms Gate 3
Oslo 3, Norway

LOVE
Leibnizstraat 60
1000 Berlin 12
BRD Germany

MOLE EXPRESS
7 Summer Terrace
Manchester 14, England

THE NORTH DEVON SNAIL
The Flat
Corffe
Tawstock, Barnstaple
N. Devon, England

OEHIMSA
60 Rue de la Poudrière
1000 Bruxelles, Belgium

OEUF
6 Rue des Pavillons
1205 Geneve, Switzerland

OM
Keizerstraat 2A, II
Amsterdam, Netherlands

OPS VEDA
The Laurels
Broomgrove Crescent
Sheffield 10, England

OZ
70 Princedale Rd.
London W11, England

PANGGG
Kopernikustraat 4
8500 Nurenberg
BRD Germany

LA PARAPLUIE
105 Boulevard Malesherbes
Paris 8, France

PARIA
Box 100-CH-6960
Viganello 11, Switzerland

PEACE NEWS
5 Caledonian Rd.
Kings Cross
London N1, England

PIANETA FRESCO
14 Via Manzoni
20121 Milano, Italy

LE POP
6 Ave. Dr. Arnold Netter
Paris 12, France

PRESS-UPS
c/o GAP
190-2 New City Rd.
Glasgow C4, Scotland

REAL FREE PRESS
Runstraat 31
Amsterdam, Netherlands

RED MOLE
182 Pentonville Rd.
London N1, England

RED NOTES
298 Bethnal Green Rd.
London E2, England

RE NUDO
Via Anelli 1
Milano, Italy

ROTTEN
Husset
Raadhustraede 13
1466 Copenhagen K,
Denmark

SKELF
The Burrow
24 St. Vincent Crescent
Glasgow C3, Scotland

STYNG
12 Regent St. S.
Barnsley, Yorkshire
England

TITUS'S GROAN
c/o CWY
175 Newcastle St., Burslem
Stoke-on-Trent, England

TOUT
27 Rue du Faubourg
Montmartre
Paris 9, France

VIRGINITY
Achin Schnurrer
5000 Köln 30, Ennenstrasse
West Germany

LE VROUTSCH
7A Quai de la Bruche
67 Strasbourg, France

WHAMMLI
Postfach 31
4001 Basel, Switzerland

ZIGZAG
Yeoman Cottage
North Marston
Bucks, England

UPS / Latin America

UPS/LATIN AMERICA
c/o Contracultura
C. Correo Central 1933
Buenos Aires, Argentina

CINE & MEDIOS
San Martin 486-115
Buenos Aires, Argentina

CONTRACULTURA
C. Correo Central 1933
Buenos Aires, Argentina

EN QUESTION
c/o D. Alegre
Lavalle 406, 4A
Capital, Argentina

FOCUS
Galeria Alvear
Local 24
Av. Alvear 1761
Buenos Aires, Argentina

NADISMO
Apartado Aereo 16362
Bogotá, Colombia

O PASQUIM
Rua Clarisse
Indio do Brasil 32
Rio (GB), Brasil

PIEDRA RODANTE
Genova 70, 502/504
Zona Rosa
Mexico 6, D.F.
Mexico

UPS / Asia-Pacific

UPS/ASIA-PACIFIC
c/o The 70's Biweekly
252 Queen's Rd. East
8th floor-flat D
Hong Kong, China

ALTERNATIVE NEWS
  SERVICE
548 Drummond St.
Carlton, S. Australia 3054
Australia

COCK
Box 2538
Wellington, New Zealand

DAG
Box 633
Nelson, New Zealand

EARWIG GRAPHICS
10 Norfolk St.
Auckland 2, New Zealand

FIVE CENT JOINT
Box 100
Alexandria, N.S.W. 2015
Australia

LINK UP
23 Glencairn Ave.
Hartwell, Victoria 3124
Australia

ON DIT
University of Adelaide
Adelaide, S. Australia 5000
Australia

THE 70'S BIWEEKLY
252 Queen's Rd. East
8th floor-flat D
Hong Kong, China

Index

Thanks are due the following for the use of graphics on the pages listed below. Any inadvertent omission will be corrected in future printings upon notification to the publishers.